Spain: A guide to political and economic institutions

This book provides a comprehensive guide to the major political and economic institutions that have been established in Spain since the death of General Franco in 1975. Against the background of the dictator's institutional, political and economic legacy, the book examines the role, structure and functions of the principal institutions of post-Franco Spain, taking as a constant reference point the Constitution of 1978. Thus, following a chapter on the political and economic background, the authors describe the nature of the Spanish monarchy under Juan Carlos I, the parliament, central, regional and local government, political parties, trade unions, public sector enterprises, business and professional institutions and financial institutions. Although the purpose of the work is descriptive rather than evaluative, certain themes run through the work: the increasingly open and democratic nature of the institutions concerned, the strong trend towards decentralisation of decision-making (in particular the new regional institutions) and the impact on political and economic life of membership of the EEC. Each chapter is, to a large extent, free-standing; however, to enable the reader to appreciate the common threads that unite many of the institutions, a detailed system of cross-referencing has been adopted. In order to give additional help to the reader, a detailed index of institutions and terms used, both in English and Spanish, has been included. For those wishing to carry out a more in-depth study of the institutions concerned, for which this work provides a useful starting point, a select bibliography relating to each chapter has been incorporated.

It is hoped that this publication, believed to be the first of its kind in English, will be of interest and value to all those who wish to be informed about the new institutional framework of contemporary Spain. On the one hand, it is likely that an increasing number of businessmen, bankers and investors will see the potential of Spain within an EEC context and will need a reference guide to current institutions. On the other hand, this work should provide essential basic reading for students of Spanish on the increasing number of A-level, polytechnic and university degree-level courses which are oriented towards contemporary Spanish affairs.

Spain: A guide to political and economic institutions

PETER J. DONAGHY
and
MICHAEL T. NEWTON
Newcastle upon Tyne Polytechnic

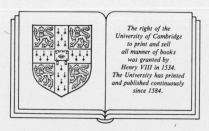

The right of the
University of Cambridge
to print and sell
all manner of books
was granted by
Henry VIII in 1534.
The University has printed
and published continuously
since 1584.

CAMBRIDGE UNIVERSITY PRESS
Cambridge
London   New York   New Rochelle
Melbourne   Sydney

Published by the Press Syndicate of the University of Cambridge
The Pitt Building, Trumpington Street, Cambridge, CB2 1RP
32 East 57th Street, New York, NY 10022, USA
10 Stamford Road, Oakleigh, Melbourne 3166, Australia

First published 1987

Printed in Great Britain at
the University Press, Cambridge

British Library cataloguing in publication data
Donaghy, P. J.
Spain: A guide to political and economic
institutions.
1. Spain – Politics and government – 1975–
I. Title II. Newton, Michael T.
306'.2'0946 JN8209

Library of Congress cataloguing in publication data
Donaghy, P. J.
Spain: A guide to political and economic institutions.
Bibliography.
Includes index.
1. Spain – Politics and government – 1975– .
2. Decentralization in government – Spain.
3. Regionalism – Spain. 4. Local government – Spain.
5. Government business enterprises – Spain.
6. Political parties – Spain. 7. Trade and professional
associations – Spain. 8. Financial institutions – Spain.
I. Newton, Michael T. II. Title.
JN8210.D66 1987 320.946   87–9384

ISBN 0 521 30032 0 hard covers
ISBN 0 521 31734 7 paperback

WD

Contents

viii   *Contents*

Figures

Preface

Since the death of Franco, on 20 November 1975, Spain has undergone substantial transformation. This is reflected in the way in which many of the political and economic institutions which characterised nearly forty years of Francoism have been either swept away or modified along democratic lines.

Largely as a result of these changes, the world in general, and Europe in particular, has focused increasing attention on Spanish affairs. Spain is once more regarded as 'respectable'. Former barriers to international relations have been gradually removed as the country, for several years now a member of the Council of Europe and NATO, establishes herself as a member of the EEC. While post-Franco Spain saw intrinsic value in democratising her many outdated institutions, the determination to secure integration with Europe injected an extra dimension of urgency into the task of modernising the country's political and economic structures.

Thus, it appears an appropriate time to publish a reference work which describes and examines the political and economic institutions of post-Franco Spain, something which, we believe, has not been attempted before, at least in English. We expect that this publication will be of value and interest to all those who need to be informed about the new institutional framework of contemporary Spain. On the one hand, it is hoped that the book will appeal to the increasing number of industrialists, bankers and investors who see the potential of the country within its new EEC context and who require a reference guide to current institutions and official bodies. On the other hand, it should provide essential background reading for students on the increasing number of A-level, polytechnic and university courses which are oriented towards Spanish contemporary affairs.

We would like to stress that in two senses this work should be regarded as only an introduction to the subject of Spain's political and economic institutions. In the first place, only the major institutions figure here since clearly a work of this nature could not hope to encompass the thousands of bodies and organisations which function at various levels of public life. Second, given that a minimum number of these institutions must be examined if anything like an authentic and representative picture of official Spain is to emerge, it has not been possible to provide more than an introductory and basically descriptive study. However, we trust that we have provided the groundwork for the further study and analysis of the major institutions of post-Franco Spain. Nevertheless, through our examination of these institutions some opinion is bound to emerge, if only incidentally, in spite of the fact that our basic aim is not to evaluate the success or otherwise of Spain's new institutional arrangements.

Although each chapter contains some reference to the historical evolution of the institutions studied therein, we have felt it appropriate to provide an overall context and background against which the institutions can be viewed. Hence Chapter 1 is devoted to a brief outline of political and economic developments since 1939. Chapter 2 examines the 1978 Constitution which provides both the theoretical framework for the new state and the principles that should govern its institutions in the post-Franco era. Chapters 3, 4 and 5 look at the major political institutions at national level, while Chapter 6 is concerned with both political and economic aspects of public administration. Chapters 7 and 8 are devoted to regional and local institutions respectively and Chapters 9 and 10 outline national and regional level organisations of political and trade union participation. Finally, Chapters 11, 12 and 13 introduce a wide range of important public and private enterprises as well as financial institutions.

Each of the above chapters is, to a certain extent, free-standing. However, it will be seen that a number of common threads unite many of the institutions concerned; for example, the consequences of reform in one area are often felt in others. To aid the reader in making these connections, a number of cross-references have been supplied wherever possible. Inevitably, because of the interlocking nature of many institutions, a certain amount of overlapping and repetition has occurred; it is hoped that this will help rather than hinder the reader by reinforcing his perception of their interdependence.

Since institutions, like the society that gives birth to them, are never static, it is possible that some (it is to be hoped, minor) changes will have occurred between the writing of these pages and their publication. Any work that attempts to reflect contemporary realities is bound to run this risk. Nevertheless, unless the country experiences a major political catastrophe, it is likely that, notwithstanding minor modifications that changes of government may well bring, the basic institutional structures described in these chapters are likely to remain largely unchanged for some time to come.

In order to facilitate the maximum accessibility to the institutions, an index has been provided. This index includes not only the names in Spanish of the institutions referred to in the text, but in many cases the Spanish acronyms, since many of these organisations are better known by these than by their full titles. As far as the text is concerned, readers need to recognise the names of institutions in their original Spanish form; however, where appropriate and when it is felt that it is not misleading to do so, English translations have been supplied.

In view of the range of areas and topics considered in this volume, it would be a daunting task to provide a fully comprehensive bibliography. Thus, we have included only a select bibliography which in our opinion contains some of the key works necessary both to provide more detailed historical background and to go beyond this introduction to a critical assessment of the institutions and their role in public life.

We would like to make it clear that in all references to office holders, the use of the masculine form is not meant to imply any favouritism towards the male sex, any more than it is intended, at least in theory, in the Spanish Constitution and other documents which, following an age-old convention, use the masculine form in a neutral sense and do not thereby imply any discrimination.

To thank individually all those who have helped us over a long period of time would be an impossible task. We are indebted to several Hispanist colleagues in the UK as well as a number of most helpful experts in Spain working both inside and outside the institutions which we have studied. We are extremely grateful to all concerned. We would like to stress that the viewpoints which we have expressed here are, in the final analysis, our responsibility alone.

Finally, we would like to thank our colleagues at Newcastle Polytechnic for their valuable suggestions, our students on the BA (Honours) course in modern languages and economic/political studies, whose questions prompted the need for such a publication and, most of all, our wives and families without whose support, patience and understanding its completion would have been impossible.

Peter J. Donaghy
Michael T. Newton

Newcastle upon Tyne

1 Introduction: political and economic background

Franco's death in 1975 marked a watershed in contemporary Spanish history. Since then Spain has witnessed the dismantling of his dictatorial regime and the gradual establishment of a genuine, if somewhat fragile, democracy. The first free elections since 1936 were held on 15 June 1977 and on 28 December 1978 a new Constitution came into effect, paving the way for the creation of a whole new political structure as well as different political and economic institutions.

1.1 Democratic tradition in Spain

It is sometimes forgotten that, in spite of her propensity for authoritarian regimes, Spain has a long, albeit turbulent, constitutional history stretching back to 1812. Although weak in comparison with the forces of reaction, a democratic tradition, founded by the Liberal politicians of the early nineteenth century, survived the vicissitudes of authoritarian rule and, prior to the post-Franco period, expressed itself most recently in the Second Republic of 1931–6. In fact, the Republican Constitution of 1931, far more progressive than anything that had preceded it in Spain, presented an important landmark in the development of the Spanish democratic tradition. It was the first Spanish constitution, for example, to grant universal suffrage to the whole adult population; it was the first to consider that the regions of Spain, traditionally a source of friction, might constitute self-governing entities within the Spanish state; it was the first to tackle seriously the problem of agrarian reform; and it was the first to embark on an ambitious programme of state education. However, it was also the first constitution not to accept the special position of the Catholic Church *vis-à-vis* the state; and indeed in attempting to separate the Church and the state, the republican government succeeded in alienating large sectors of the population which subsequently gave their support to Franco's attempted *coup d'état*. Both in its positive and negative features, the 1931 Constitution proved to be an example and a starting point for the constitution drafters of 1978 who, after a forty-year interruption, embarked on the task of providing Spain with a new framework for democracy.

1.2   Spain 1939–59

Following his victory in the Civil War of 1936–9, General Franco set about
demolishing the whole progressive political structure and the institutions
established under the ill-fated Second Republic, replacing them with structures that reflected his own authoritarian instincts. The dictator's so-called
constitution, the seven Fundamental Laws (*Leyes Fundamentales*) represented a complete rejection of the ideals that lay behind the 1931 Constitution. In particular, Franco turned the clock back regarding the crucial
issue of the relations between the executive and the legislature, ensuring
that the *Cortes* was to be no more than a rubber-stamp Parliament to
which the executive was not accountable. Moreover, Republican legislation on the Church, education, the regional problem and land distribution was annulled. The Church regained its privileged relationship with
the state, including its traditionally dominant role in education. The
regions were once more subjected to a repressive centralism. Property
expropriated by the state during the Republic, both land and industrial
enterprises, was restored to former owners, who were henceforth to
benefit from state paternalism. It is significant that whereas the 1931
Constitution stressed liberty, Franco's basic laws laid emphasis on unity.
In the case of unity, the traditional separation of powers was rejected, all
political organisations apart from Franco's all-embracing National Movement (*Movimiento Nacional*) were outlawed, all trade union groupings,
with the exception of the state-run *sindicatos*, were abolished, and many
basic civil rights were denied. For a period of nearly forty years rigid
centralist control of both the political structure and the economy was
imposed. The effects of this regime are, to some extent, still plaguing the
Spain of the 1980s.

Once the basic political apparatus of Francoism was established, the
regime could concentrate on the resuscitation of the war-ravaged
economy. Partly inspired by Fascist ideology and partly imposed by sheer
economic necessity as a result of being ostracised by the victorious allied
powers, Spain embarked on a course of economic autarky or self-
sufficiency. This policy was most obvious during the 1940s and 50s, a
period characterised by protectionism, economic nationalism and state
intervention. Responding to the needs of a war-torn economy that was
short of raw materials and energy, in 1941 Franco created the National
Institute for Industry (*Instituto Nacional de Industria*/INI), a state holding
company the original objectives of which were to strengthen defence
industries and promote economic viability in sectors where private
interests could not or were not willing to do so.

INI in turn spawned a whole series of public sector enterprises where,
for a long time, senior posts were the prerogative of political appointees or
retired military personnel. In addition, numerous semi-autonomous

bodies were established to administer particular services at the behest of the regime.

While the fragile economy of the nineteenth century had been boosted by foreign investment, this was not the case for a long time in the post-Civil War period. US-backed Marshall Aid programmes, which did so much to restore other war-damaged economies, were not forthcoming for Spain, which furthermore had to suffer an economic boycott by nations distrustful of this former ally of Hitler and Mussolini. The government had to increase the national debt at the expense of its own citizens and companies had to mortgage their boardrooms to the banking sector.

Labour was in no position to resist the inflationary pressures which suppressed workers' livelihoods. From its inception the Franco regime was determined to bring the whole apparatus of labour organisation under state control. The free trade unions of the Republican era were outlawed and replaced by a single vertical system encompassing both management and labour. Strikes were made illegal and wages were strictly regulated by the Ministry of Labour.

By the late 1950s it had become plain that autarky had failed and that Spain was on the verge of bankruptcy. The new 'technocratic' and outward-looking cabinet, which had strong links with the influential Catholic organisation, the Opus Dei, realised that the only solution lay in a break away from the economic policies of the past. This was facilitated by the fact that gradually during the 1950s Spain had gained admittance to a number of international organisations ranging from the United Nations to the International Monetary Fund (IMF). It was, in fact, with the help of IMF officials that an austerity programme was drawn up to bring the economy more on to an even keel and to enable Spain to embark upon normal multilateral trade. The subsequent Stabilisation Plan of 1959 was accompanied by measures to liberalise foreign investment.

1.3   Spain 1959–75

During the second half of the Franco era, only minor steps were taken to modify the monolithic political edifice that had been erected in 1939. Such steps responded to the regime's new-found interest of the early 1960s in integration with Europe, a concept unthinkable in the xenophobic days of the 1940s and 50s. In its clumsy and unconvincing attempts to present a more respectable image to its European neighbours, the regime introduced a small 'democratically' elected element into the *Cortes*, accepted the need for religious toleration, approved a new press law which substantially reduced the use of prior censorship, introduced a limited form of collective bargaining into industrial relations and made minor cultural concessions to the regions. However, none of this tampering with the façade impressed either Europe or the opposition groups which, in spite of the continuing

4   *Spain*

Figure 1.1. *Distribution of working population*

	1950	1960	1970	1980	1985
Agriculture and fishing	48.8	41.7	29.0	19.6	16.7
Industry and construction	26.1	30.0	34.8	35.9	32.2
Services	25.1	28.3	36.2	44.5	51.1
Total	100.0	100.0	100.0	100.0	100.0

Source: Banco de Bilbao/INE.

repression, were growing more vocal and confident in their demands for change.

The economy, meanwhile, began to take off; the economic boom enjoyed by Spain's EEC neighbours and other Western economies exerted a considerable influence. Foreign investment, under the terms of very liberal legislation, flowed into Spain at ever-increasing rates, bringing with it much-needed technology and know-how. The surplus labour created by the shakeout resulting from the Stabilisation Plan was able to find an outlet in the prosperous industrial areas of Northern Europe. Workers, officially encouraged by the Spanish Emigration Institute (*Instituto Español de Emigración*), sent back remittances which made a further contribution to Spain's balance-of-payments surplus. Other workers migrated from the land only as far as the larger cities of Spain itself and came to constitute the new industrial proletariat as the country's own industries began to prosper.

One industry that made spectacular progress was tourism. Again Spain's more affluent neighbours sought areas where they could enjoy their increased leisure possibilities. Between 1960 and 1980 the number of tourists rose from six million to forty million. This brought enormous benefits to the balance of payments and to allied industries, such as construction. However, the consequent misallocation of resources, the infrastructural pressures and environmental problems which resulted are still in evidence today.

The rapid economic growth of the 1960s and early 1970s was such as to merit the classification 'economic miracle' and to place Spain in second position behind Japan in terms of growth in gross national product (GNP). This period saw the final transformation of Spain into an industrialised, as opposed to an agricultural, economy and this was reflected, for example, in the movement of labour from agriculture to industry and services (see Figure 1.1).

There is no doubt that, in global terms, the performance of the Spanish economy between 1960 and 1973 was impressive, and in overall terms Spain moved into the league of the top ten industrial nations of the West.

However, the price for this progress was high in several respects: first, Spaniards in the 1970s were still often deprived of basic civil and political rights; second, the migrations of the 1960s involved untold personal hardship for thousands of families and the pressures on the services of the rapidly expanding urban sprawls were enormous; third, the benefits of economic growth were not shared equally among the regions and great disparities in *per capita* income levels remain prevalent even today; and, fourth, industry, cushioned by high protective tariffs, concealed considerable inefficiency and in many sectors suffered from an excessive proliferation of small firms. In addition to all these problems, due to the oil crises and consequent economic recession of the mid-1970s, even before Franco's death the economy had begun to flag. Emigrants returning from a Western Europe which was also forced to lay off much of its workforce only fuelled the growing unemployment and added to the accumulation of social and infrastructural problems. Thus, economically, the circumstances in which Spain made her second attempt in the twentieth century to implant a democratic regime were not very auspicious.

1.4   Spain since 1975

Since the death of General Franco in 1975 and the restoration of the Spanish monarchy in the person of King Juan Carlos, a remarkable transformation has taken place. Between 1976 and 1978, against a background of potential political instability and economic crisis, Spain made considerable progress towards the establishment of new democratic institutions based on the twin principles of modernisation and decentralisation. Some tentative steps were taken between December 1975 and July 1976 to liberalise the political structures during the premiership of Carlos Arias Navarro, Franco's last prime minister, reluctantly re-appointed by King Juan Carlos; however, these pseudo-reforms did not satisfy the accelerating pressures for substantial change. Nevertheless, the pace of change quickened under his successor, Adolfo Suárez, whose Political Reform Law (*Ley para la Reforma Política*) paved the way for a genuine restoration of democracy, promising Spain's first genuine elections for forty years on 15 June 1977. In these historic elections Suárez, with his newly formed Union of the Democratic Centre (*Unión de Centro Democrático/* UCD) won a clear victory over his nearest rivals, the Spanish Socialist Workers' Party (*Partido Socialista Obrero Español*/PSOE), led by Felipe González. However, the elections represented only the first step on the long road to a complete restoration of democratic processes and institutions, to achieve which a new constitutional framework was required. Thus the newly elected Parliament (*Cortes*) saw its main task as the drafting of Spain's first democratic constitution since 1931. Significantly, all the major parties represented in Parliament, including the UCD, the PSOE, the conservative Popular Alliance (*Alianza Popular*/AP), the Communist Party of Spain (*Partido Comunista de España*/PCE) and Basque and Catalan Nationalists, participated in this historic process, which culminated in December 1978 with the publication of the new Constitution. The general elections of 1979, again won by the UCD, thus constituted the first to be held under this Constitution.

During the period 1976–8 so much was the emphasis on political change that economic reform tended to be neglected, although it has to be recognised that the priority given to tax legislation in 1977 was an important first step in economic reform. Moreover, the Moncloa Pacts (*Pactos de la Moncloa*) of that year represented an encouraging willingness to co-operate in economic affairs on the part of the major political parties who were all signatories to that document. However, the deterioration of the economic situation between 1976 and 1981, by which time both inflation and unemployment had soared over 20 per cent, plus the escalation of Basque-inspired terrorism, soon drowned the euphoria that had accompanied the restoration of democracy and provided ammunition for frustrated reactionary generals to indulge in sabre-rattling and in the more serious attempted *coup* of 23 February 1981. Nevertheless, the measure of *desencanto* or disillusion which had characterised the years 1978–81 was suddenly dissipated by this *coup*, which galvanised wide sectors of the population into demonstrating in favour of democracy and the new Constitution. A further healthy sign was the level of moderation and willingness to compromise shown by the major political parties and the trade unions, the members of which showed considerable restraint in sacrificing personal and sectorial advancement in the interests of the consolidation of democracy.

The reaction of the outside world, and of Western Europe in particular, to the process of reform in Spain has been generally very positive. The first sign that Europe recognised the new direction the country was taking came in October 1977 when Spain was admitted to the Council of Europe. Three months earlier the Spanish foreign minister, following the elections of June 1977, had formally presented Spain's application for full membership of the EEC, to which previously she had only been linked by a very modest commercial agreement known as the Preferential Trade Agreement (PTA) signed in 1970. Both Western Europe and the United States, which had established military bases on Spanish soil in 1953, were now anxious to integrate Spain more closely into the defence programmes of the Atlantic Alliance. This process culminated, in May 1982, with the UCD government of Leopoldo Calvo-Sotelo (who became leader of the party following Suárez's resignation in January 1981), securing the approval of the Spanish Parliament for Spain's entry into NATO. At that time the move was strongly opposed by Felipe González and the PSOE, who argued that the government had a moral obligation to consult the people in a referendum before taking such a momentous decision, promising that, once elected, they would hold such a referendum and abide by its result.

Moderation would seem to have been the key-note of the Socialist government first elected in October 1982 and re-elected in June 1986. Rather than radically alter things, the Socialists under Felipe González have tended to build on the reforms of their predecessors. Working equally harmoniously with the constitutional monarchy of Juan Carlos, the government has striven to consolidate the country's new system of decentralised administration based on autonomous regional institutions; it has accepted the realities of its role within the Western Alliance, eventually urging the electorate to vote for continued membership of NATO in the long-delayed referendum held in March 1986; and it has grasped the nettle of industrial restructuring as a prerequisite for efficient operation within the framework of the EEC. Politically there have been major successes, not the least of which has been the ability to convince the armed forces to agree to structural change and accept their more professional role within the new democratic Spain. On the negative side, however, in spite of some limited successes, the government has still not been able to resolve the continuing problem of terrorism committed by the Basque separatist organisation, ETA. Economically some progress has been made, notably in the gradual reduction of inflation to tolerable levels and in the improvement of the balance-of-payments situation; however, unemployment has continued to rise and the overall figure of 22 per cent disguises rates of almost double that level in some of the poorer rural parts of central and southern Spain.

Spain's path to membership of the EEC was long and arduous. The negotiations which began in 1979 faltered on many occasions and it took until January 1986 to convert Spain's long-cherished aspiration into a reality. However, ultimately this wait probably benefited the country since it permitted some measure of harmonisation to take place in advance of entry and a number of important institutional reforms to be carried out in the economic sphere, in addition to the major shift that occurred in the political system. Nevertheless, EEC membership, seen by all the major parties and the majority of the population as politically desirable, involves considerable economic risks, as well as long-term opportunities, for a country the economy of which has for decades been protected by the state. However, Spain has political and cultural as well as economic reasons for wanting to 'come in from the wilderness' and sees integration with Europe as a way of consolidating its new democracy and protecting its still-fragile political and economic institutions.

2 The Constitution of 1978

2.1 Approval

With its 169 articles the 1978 Constitution represents one of the longest in Spanish constitutional history, taking longer to draw up than any previous constitution. It was drafted and approved by both Houses of Parliament (*Cortes Generales*), the Lower House or Congress of Deputies (*Congreso de los Diputados*) and the Upper House or Senate (*Senado*). During the sixteen months of its gestation it passed through an unprecedented number of committees and, in the course of its approval, over one thousand amendments were tabled; no previous constitution had been subjected to such searching scrutiny.

The 1978 Constitution started life in the Committee of Constitutional Affairs and Public Liberties (*Comisión de Asuntos Constitucionales y Libertades Públicas*) consisting of thirty-six members of the Congress drawn from the major parties represented in Parliament in proportion to their strength in the Lower House. The Committee appointed a seven-man working party with a similar composition, whose task was to draw up the original draft of the Constitution. The draft was passed to the Constitutional Committee of the Congress (*Comisión Constitucional del Congreso*) before being submitted for approval to the full Congress. Subsequently it was considered by the Constitutional Committee of the Senate (*Comisión Constitucional del Senado*) prior to being approved by the full Senate. In the final stage of the process, the draft was scrutinised by a joint committee of both Houses of Parliament before being approved in a full joint session of both Houses on 31 October 1978. Finally, on 6 December of the same year the final text was submitted to the direct vote of the Spanish people in a referendum. Following ratification by the people, the new Constitution was signed and promulgated by King Juan Carlos in an historic gathering of both Houses of Parliament held in the Congress building on 28 December 1978. The following day the Constitution was published in the Official State Gazette (*Boletín Oficial del Estado*/BOE).

At each stage of its approval the new Constitution was supported by

Figure 2.1. *Approval of Constitution in Parliament (October 1978)*

	'Yes' votes	'No' votes	Abstentions
Congress	326	6	14
Senate	226	5	8
Both Houses	551	11	22

Figure 2.2. *Approval of Constitution in national referendum*
(December 1978)

	'Yes' votes	'No' votes	Blanks	Void
Number of votes	15,782,639	1,423,184	636,095	135,193
Percentage of votes	87.79	7.9	3.53	0.75
Percentage of total electorate	59.40	5.3	2.39	0.50

large majorities, thus lending conviction to the commonly expressed belief
that it was a Constitution 'of all the people for all the people'. As shown in
Figure 2.1, the Congress approved the document by 326 votes to 6 with 14
abstentions (mainly Basque Nationalists), while the Senate did so by 226
for, 5 against and only 8 abstentions. In total therefore, 551 members of
Parliament out of a possible 598, approximately 90 per cent, gave their
support to the document which, it was hoped, would formally end the
transition from dictatorship to democracy. In the referendum campaign
which followed, of the parliamentary parties, only the Basque Nationalist
Party (*Partido Nacionalista Vasco*/PNV) urged voters to abstain or
register a negative vote, although several small, generally extremist, non-
parliamentary parties like the extreme right *Fuerza Nueva* and the Catalan
Republican Party, the *Esquerra*, also recommended rejection. In the event,
when Spaniards went to the polls on 6 December 1978, the Constitution
was approved by 87.8 per cent of those who voted. Whilst the percentage
of abstentions, 32 per cent in Spain as a whole and 56 per cent in parts of
the Basque Country, gave the government and the major opposition
parties some cause for concern, none the less the Spanish people seemed to
have voted convincingly, if not overwhelmingly, to open a new democratic
chapter in the country's history (see Figure 2.2).

In political circles and the press, the Constitution was hailed as a
triumph for common sense and compromise, the tangible result of months
of consensus politics. The need for consensus in fact derived from three
main causes: first, no single party was in a strong enough position to
achieve a satisfactory solution by itself; Franco's heirs and the opposition
needed each other to overcome the impasse created by the dictator's death.

Second, the victors in the 1977 elections, the UCD led by Adolfo Suárez, did not have an overall majority in Parliament. Third, there was a tendency among all parties to gravitate towards the centre of the political spectrum, either to disguise their past associations with *franquismo* or to demonstrate a commitment towards the vote-catching concept of moderation.

Consensus certainly produced positive results and the document can be regarded as a symbolic reconciliation of the two Spains divided first by the Civil War and then by the policies of the Franco regime. However, it has to be recognised that, to a large extent, this consensus was not an agreement among equals: not only did the government negotiate from a position of strength, making full use of the bureaucratic machinery of the previous regime, but certain issues like the role of the monarchy, the Church and the armed forces were not open to serious negotiation and simply had to be accepted by the parties of the Left, in particular the PSOE. Other negative features of the process were the fact that certain sections of the Constitution are contradictory, reflecting the conflicting attitudes of Left and Right towards such issues as the role of the state within the economy; and some are ambiguous, like parts of the protracted section on regional autonomy. Most objective commentators agree that, while the end might have justified the means, many cracks were papered over during the functioning of consensus and many agreements were reached not in the committee rooms of the *Cortes* but behind closed doors in party offices or Madrid restaurants.

2.2   Structure

The 1978 Constitution is divided into eleven major sections (*títulos*) including the Introductory Section (*Título Preliminar*) which lays down the guiding principles which regulate the functioning of the new Spanish state and Spanish society. Section I enumerates a whole range of civil, political and socio-economic rights. The remaining nine Sections deal with the division of the powers of the state, the nature and functions of the different institutions of the state and the territorial organisation of the country. Section II examines the role of the monarchy, laying particular stress on its role *vis-à-vis* the Constitution and the question of the succession. Section III outlines the composition, functions and powers of both Houses of Parliament. Section IV deals with the organisation of the government and public administration, while Sections V and VI respectively refer to the relationship between the government, the legislature and the judicial authorities. Section VII breaks new ground in Spanish constitutional history by laying down the basic principles by which the economy shall be run. Section VIII concerns the territorial organisation of the state and thus the whole question of the relationship between central government and the regions and peoples of Spain. Section IX outlines the composition and competences of the constitutional court and Section X the processes by which the Constitution may be reformed. It is worthy of note that, compared to its predecessors, the 1978 Constitution devotes much more attention to such key aspects as rights (forty-six Articles), the legislature, which embodies popular sovereignty (thirty-one Articles) and the rights of the regions of Spain *vis-à-vis* the state (twenty-three Articles).

2.3   Basic principles and provisions

The more idealistic clauses of the Constitution are contained in the Introductory Section. Article 1, for instance, proclaims that Spain is a 'social and democratic state based on the rule of law' and that 'national sovereignty resides in the people from whom all powers derive'. Article 2, while referring to the 'indissoluble unity of the Spanish nation' recognises and guarantees the 'right of the nationalities and regions of Spain to autonomy' (see Chapter 7). Article 3 recognises regional languages as co-official in the regions concerned alongside Castilian, the official language of the Spanish state. It is interesting to note that on two occasions the Constitution refers to the concept of 'political pluralism' (Articles 1 and 2) and in this context both political parties and trade unions, the internal structures and functioning of which are to adhere to democratic practices, are expressly recognised (see Chapters 10 and 11). Article 9.1 affirms that both citizens and the authorities are subject to the Constitution and to the law in general. Clause 2 of this Article puts an obligation on the public authorities to create the conditions in which the freedom and equality of the individual and groups can be genuine and effective, and to remove obstacles to the full participation of all citizens in the political, economic, social and cultural life of the country. Though not inserted in this outline of general principles, there is no doubt that the concept of decentralisation enshrined in Article 103, referring to the government and civil service, was also a major guiding principle.

Two major provisions refer to Spain's major socio-political institutions, the armed forces and the Catholic Church, often referred to by contemporary politicians and commentators as the *de facto* powers (*poderes fácticos*). These institutions, as is well known, have played such a dominant role in the political and constitutional history of Spain that their interests have always, to some extent at least, had to be accommodated and their role clearly defined. Even the Constitution of 1978 has had to take them into account and indeed has tried to ensure that, unlike the case in 1931, they are not alienated to the point where they become forces of dissension and opposition.

2.3.1   The armed forces (fuerzas armadas/FFAA)

Article 8 of the Constitution states that the role of the armed forces is 'to safeguard the sovereignty and independence of Spain, defend its territorial integrity and the constitutional order'. On the face of it this wording does not seem to differ significantly from that of Franco's 1967 Organic Law of the State. Traditionally suspicious of all moves towards a weakening of central control, the armed forces have once again been granted the role of safeguarding 'the territorial integrity' of the country, a direct allusion to the possible attempt of any region of Spain to secede. Moreover, Article 2 of the new Organic Law on National Defence and Military Organisation (*Ley Orgánica de Defensa Nacional y Organización Militar*) of 1980, makes it clear that one of the aspects of national defence, in which the armed forces are obviously involved, is guaranteeing 'the unity of Spain'. The opening sentence of this Article reads: 'National defence is the deployment, integration and coordination of all the moral and material energies of the nation in the face of any form of aggression, and all Spaniards must participate in the achievement of this objective'.

The same Article stresses that the ultimate responsibility for national defence lies not with the armed forces but with the popularly elected government. Furthermore, since the new arrangements for territorial organisation are enshrined in the Constitution (Section VIII) the armed forces' obligation to safeguard 'the constitutional order' must extend to the protection of this new status quo. While no written document could prevent army intervention in the last resort, and the proclivity of at least certain sections of the military to contemplate intervention was clearly demonstrated in February 1981, there is growing evidence that in the 1980s the Spanish military is prepared to work with the politicians to protect the country's new democracy.

2.3.2   The Church (Iglesia)

Unlike the armed forces, the Church would seem to play only a minor role within the new Constitution, especially when we consider the importance Franco attached to it in his fundamental laws (see 1.2 above). However, unlike the 1931 Constitution, which effectively paved the way for the establishment of a completely secular state and thus provoked the conservative elements of Spanish society, the 1978 document merely states in Article 16 that there will be complete religious freedom and that there will be no state religion. However, Clause 3 goes on to say that 'the public authorities shall take into account the religious beliefs of Spanish society and shall maintain consequent links of co-operation with the Catholic Church and other faiths'. While in theory this prepared the way for a gradual move towards the separation of Church and state – involving, for example, the eventual financial independence of the former – the Church, which has basically accepted the new order, has in practice retained much of its influence, not least within the education system. Moreover, both under UCD and PSOE governments, the Church has not been averse to lending both moral and material support to groups protesting against government policies on education, divorce and abortion. Statistics show, however, that society is becoming increasingly secularised and it is highly unlikely that the Church will again be the predominant factor that it has been in the past.

2.4   Fundamental rights within the Constitution

By far the longest section of the Constitution deals with fundamental rights and the obligation of the state to uphold and guarantee these rights, except in the most exceptional circumstances. It is worthy of note that Article 10 declares that such rights shall conform to those listed in the Universal Declaration of Human Rights. Following a now classical categorisation, three types of rights can be identified: basic human or civil rights; political rights; and socio-economic rights. The latter involve some positive action on the part of the state to benefit the public.

2.4.1   Civil rights

The most basic rights enumerated are:

2.4.1.1 Right to life (derecho a la vida) and right to personal physical integrity (derecho a la integridad física)
For the first time in Spanish constitutional history the death penalty is expressly abolished 'except for those offences covered by military law in times of war' (Article 15).

2.4.1.2 Right to equality (derecho a la igualdad)
This refers above all to equality before the law irrespective of differences of birth, race, sex, religion or belief (Article 14). This general affirmation is reinforced by more specific references in later provisions of the Constitution: for example, Article 32.1 insists on the equality of partners in a marriage and Article 35.1 upholds the ideal of equal opportunities in the workplace for both sexes.

2.4.1.3 Right to freedom (derecho a la libertad) and right to security (derecho a la seguridad)
This includes the protection of habeus corpus under which no person can be detained by the authorities for longer than seventy-two hours without being set free or handed over to the judicial authorities. Similarly any

detainee has the right to be informed of his rights and the reasons for detention as well as the right not to make a statement without the presence of a lawyer (Article 17).

2.4.1.4 *Right of effective access to the Courts* (derecho al efectivo acceso a los Tribunales)

This is guaranteed in Article 24, which, among other safeguards, includes the right of the accused to be defended in court and to have access to a solicitor while in detention. An accused person is not obliged to plead guilty; indeed innocence is assumed until guilt is proved. Article 9.3, significantly situated in the Introductory Section of the Constitution, expressly forbids the application of retroactive legislation. Another 'progressive' clause in the Constitution (Article 25.2) states that convicted offenders should not be obliged to undergo hard labour and that prison regimes should be geared towards rehabilitation and re-education.

2.4.1.5 *Right to private property* (derecho a la propiedad privada)

This right, plus the associated right of inheritance, is enshrined in Article 33 which affirms that a citizen can only be deprived of property 'for a justified cause of public utility or social interest' and then only with appropriate compensation.

2.4.1.6 *Right to free enterprise* (derecho a la libertad de empresa)

Article 38 recognises this within the framework of the market economy and, where appropriate, of national planning.

2.4.1.7 *Right to religious liberty* (derecho a la libertad religiosa)

This right is enshrined in Article 16, which links this freedom with that of ideological freedom and guarantees to protect the religious activities of either individuals or groups. No one shall be obliged to reveal his or her religion or ideology. Moreover, as already stated above, no particular religion shall enjoy state protection. Closely linked to this freedom is that of the right to conscientious objection (*derecho a la objeción de conciencia*) (Article 30). Objectors are now given the option of undertaking social work deemed equivalent to military service.

2.4.1.8 *Right to honour* (derecho al honor) *and right to privacy* (derecho a la intimidad)

Article 18 recognises a series of rights linked to the theme of personal and family privacy: for example, Clause 2 recognises a limitation of entry to property except where, in very exceptional circumstances, a judicial warrant is granted to the police; Clause 3 guarantees secrecy of correspondence and, indeed, of all communications, including the telephone, with the same exceptions.

2.4.1.9 Right to freedom of abode (derecho a la libre elección de domicilio) and right to free movement (derecho a la libre circulación)

Entry to and exit from the country cannot be denied for political or ideological reasons, except when a state of exception or siege has been declared (see 4.6.3.2).

2.4.2 Political rights

The major political rights to be protected are:

2.4.2.1 Right to freedom of expression (derecho a la libre expresión de ideas)

The Constitution recognises and protects the right 'to express and disseminate freely thoughts, ideas and opinions by word, in writing or any other means of reproduction' (Article 20.1). The same Article also recognises rights to production and creation in the fields of literature, art, science and technology. Clause 2 of the same Article expressly forbids any form of prior censorship, something that was widely practised during the greater part of the Franco regime. Clause 3, in a highly significant statement, ensures that the means of communication belonging to the state or other public entities shall be subject to parliamentary control and that access to the same shall be guaranteed to all social and political groups, 'respecting the pluralism of society and the various languages of Spain'.

2.4.2.2 Right of assembly (derecho de reunión) and right to demonstrate (derecho de manifestación)

Article 21.1 recognises the right of assembly provided it is peaceful and does not involve the use of firearms. Assemblies in public places or demonstrations require the permission of the authorities but can only be forbidden when there is a serious risk to public order or to the safety of people or property (clause 2).

2.4.2.3 Right of association (derecho de asociación)

This has particular relevance to political parties and workers' organisations and trade unions, which, over the last century in Spain, as well as in other European countries, have waged an often one-sided battle to have these rights recognised. Following forty years of illegality for any organisation that did not conform in its aims and ideology to the narrow concepts enshrined in Franco's National Movement (see 1.2), Article 22 recognises the right of association for all organisations except those whose objectives include activities declared to be of a criminal nature. Secret or paramilitary organisations are banned.

2.4.2.4 Right of participation (derecho de participación)

Article 23 recognises two ways in which the citizen has a right to participate in public affairs: first, he has a right to vote (*derecho de sufragio universal*); second, all citizens have the right to compete on equal terms for access to public office.

2.4.2.5 Right to initiate legislation (derecho de iniciativa legislativa)

Article 87 recognises the possibility that legislation can emanate directly from the will of the citizenry, provided that at least half a million signatures are obtained and that the proposal does not refer to taxation, international affairs or the prerogative of pardon (see 4.7.2).

2.4.2.6 Right of petition (derecho de petición)

Article 29.1 recognises the right of citizens to make an individual or collective petition in writing to the government, although, in the case of the armed forces and police forces subject to military discipline, this can only be done on an individual basis.

2.4.2.7 Right of union association (derecho de asociación sindical)

In spite of the existence of the all-embracing right of association granted in Article 22, the constitution drafters, perhaps not surprisingly after forty years' suppression of union activity, deemed it essential to provide specific protection for the trade unions (see 11.2.1). Article 28 includes the right to found a trade union, the right to join the union of one's choice, the right of unions to form confederations and found international organisations. At the same time no citizen is bound to join a trade union.

2.4.2.8 Right to strike (derecho de huelga)

This right is expressly recognised in Article 28; the only limit to its use is the need to protect the essential services of the community (see 11.2.1).

2.4.3 Socio-economic rights

Since the Constitution defines Spain as a social as well as democratic state governed by the rule of law, it is not surprising that it should recognise a series of social and economic rights of the type found in the most advanced European constitutions. It is precisely in this area that the constitution makers have projected the most progressive image of the new Spain. To a large extent the rights that are here recognised, many of which did not appear in previous constitutions, are an extension of the civil rights already listed. The majority of them require positive, often financial, action on the part of the state. The major rights in this category are:

2.4.3.1 *Right to work* (derecho al trabajo)

Article 35 links the right to work with the duty of work, the right to the free selection of one's profession or job, the right to promotion through work, the right to a remuneration that is sufficient to cover one's needs and those of one's family, and the right of women to equal treatment to men in all the above respects.

2.4.3.2 *Right to collective bargaining* (derecho a la negociación colectiva laboral)

Article 37 recognises the right of representatives of labour and management to negotiate collective agreements, and ensures the binding nature of such agreements.

2.4.3.3 *Right to education* (derecho a la educación)

This right is recognised in Article 27, which also upholds the freedom to choose the type of education and school one wishes. The authorities guarantee the rights of parents to acquire for their children the religious and moral education that accords with their own convictions (clause 3). The authorities also undertake to provide a general programme of education for all citizens, with the participation of all those affected in decision-making, and to create new centres of learning. Significantly, however, clause 6 recognises the right of individuals and groups to found centres of learning. This is of particular interest to the Catholic Church the religious orders of which control most of the private schools in Spain, the private sector providing education for 40 per cent of the 6–14 age group.

Also of interest to the Church is the fact that, albeit couched in vague terms, the Constitution endorses the obligation of the state to continue giving grants to private schools. Between 1983 and 1984 the Socialist minister of education came under frequent attack from the Church for demanding more control over private institutions in exchange for continuing financial support from the state. Changes in this sphere were contained in the Law on the Right to Education (*Ley del Derecho a la Educación*/LODE) approved by Parliament in 1984.

2.4.4 *Principles guiding economic and social policy*

Closely linked to the rights referred to in 2.4.3 above are a series of socio-economic commitments on the part of the state, which in practice amount to an extension of these rights. These include:

2.4.4.1 *Protection of the family* (protección a la familia)

In particular both the state and parents have obligations to protect children, whether or not born in wedlock (Article 39).

2.4.4.2 Protection of health (protección a la salud)
Article 45 ascribes a fundamental role to the state in relation to the organisation and protection of health care and welfare. The same article refers to the authorities' role in promoting physical education, sport and the adequate use of leisure time.

2.4.4.3 Protection of the elderly (protección a la tercera edad)
Article 50 guarantees that all senior citizens shall enjoy economic self-sufficiency, with adequate pensions that are periodically updated in line with the cost of living. The social services are to pay particular attention to their needs in housing, health, culture and leisure.

*2.4.4.4 Protection of the right to decent housing (protección del derecho
         a una vivienda digna)*
The authorities are stated to be under an obligation to provide all citizens with adequate housing and to provide necessary conditions, backed up by the appropriate legislation, to make this possible. Land use will be controlled to avoid speculation (Article 47.)

*2.4.4.5 Protection of the right to work and satisfactory working
         conditions (protección del derecho al trabajo y de unas
         condiciones laborales satisfactorias)*
In this regard the state undertakes to pursue policies that ensure economic stability and full employment, as well as professional training and re-training. The same Article obliges the state to protect the safety and health of the citizen at the place of work, to place a limit on the working day and to provide adequate holidays. The social security system will be maintained to protect citizens' financial position and this will include unemployment benefit (*seguro de desempleo*) (Article 41). Article 42 offers to safeguard the social and economic rights of emigrant workers abroad and to facilitate their reintegration at work on their return to Spain.

2.4.4.6 Protection of the handicapped (protección a la minusválidos)
Article 49 obliges the state to provide for the adequate treatment, care and rehabilitation of all types of handicapped people, ensuring that they are not deprived of the basic rights which apply to all citizens.

2.4.4.7 Protection of the environment (protección del medio ambiente)
According to Article 45 all Spaniards have the right to enjoy an adequate environment and they are also under an obligation to conserve it. Severe penalties are envisaged for those who damage the environment. It is worth noting that this Article is the result of growing pressure from environ-

mental and ecological groups that, in parallel with counterparts in the rest of Europe, are gaining in strength in Spain.

2.4.5   Theory and practice

Needless to say even in the most advanced and developed democratic system difficulties are often expressed in translating constitutional ideals into everyday realities. In the case of Spain, which has only recently emerged from a dictatorial regime where civil and political liberties were constantly denied, this task will be all the harder, especially in view of the fact that not all sections of society accept the desirability of constitutional rule. As far as the socio-economic rights are concerned, whatever obligations theoretically bind the authorities, in the final analysis their protection and consolidation will depend on the success of the economic policies pursued by successive governments. In the short term at least such goals may be considered utopian. A court ruling may be sufficient to ensure that a woman has the right to equal treatment to a man either in marriage or in terms of job opportunities, but only an increase in the overall economic prosperity of the country, coupled with the will of central and regional governments to distribute fairly their resources, will ensure improvement in such vital areas of education, health and housing that have, even in years of relative prosperity, been severely neglected.

2.5   Constitutional court (*tribunal constitucional*)

The constitutional court, envisaged in Section IX of the Constitution, is the supreme interpreter of the Constitution and a theoretically impartial body which has the final say in the settling of appeals arising from legislation that emanates from the Constitution. There is no appeal against the decisions of this court.

2.5.1   Composition

The constitutional court consists of twelve members formally appointed by the king: of these, four are elected by the Congress by a majority of three-fifths of its members, four by the Senate by a similar majority, two by the government and two by the general council of the judiciary (*consejo General del Poder Judicial*). The members of the court must be lawyers of recognised competence with more than fifteen years' experience in the legal profession. They are appointed for a period of nine years; a third of their number will be replaced every three years. No member of the court can simultaneously be a public representative, i.e. as national or regional deputy, a member of the government or any branch of public administration, an office holder in a political party or trade union; neither can he practise privately in the legal profession. All members are expected to be independent and permanent in the exercise of their duties (Article 159). The court elects a president, appointed for three years, from among its members by secret ballot prior to formal appointment by the king.

2.5.2   Powers

According to Article 161 the court has jurisdiction throughout the national territory. Its judgements (*sentencias*) may be sought in the following cases:

2.5.2.1   Appeals against unconstitutional laws and regulations
            (recursos de anticonstitucionalidad)
These can be made in the case of statutes of autonomy, organic laws, ordinary laws of the national or regional parliaments and international treaties.

2.5.2.2   Appeals for protection (recursos de amparo)
These can be lodged when a citizen's fundamental rights or freedoms have been allegedly violated by the state, the autonomous communities or other official bodies or authorities.

2.5.2.3   Official appeals concerning the autonomous communities
Such appeals can be submitted in cases of dispute between the state and the autonomous communities over areas of competence (see 7.8.1). The government, for example, can appeal to the court if it feels that certain legislation adopted by the autonomous communities is unconstitutional; in such cases the legislation is suspended for a maximum of five months while the court decides whether to ratify or lift the suspension.

In recent times one of the most publicised appeals to the constitutional court was initiated by the autonomous communities of the Basque Country and Catalonia who claimed that certain Articles of the controversial Law on the Harmonisation of the Autonomy Process (*Ley Orgánica de Armonización del Proceso Autonómico*/LOAPA) contravened the Constitution (see 7.4 and 7.7.5). In fact the court, to the great embarrassment of the government, found in favour of the autonomous communities, thus leaving a dangerous constitutional void in August 1983. Other appeals, presented under both the *recurso de anticonstitucionalidad* and under the *recurso de amparo* were filed by the right-wing AP party during the first period of Socialist government between 1982 and 1986, when the latter was trying to push through legislation relating to education and abortion. In all cases the appeals were rejected. None the less, in the absence of an effective Upper House of

Parliament (see 4.7.3.1), the court is likely to retain its semi-political, as well as its judicial, role for the foreseeable future and its rulings are likely to provide a substantial corpus of case-law related to constitutional issues.

2.6   Ombudsman (*defensor del pueblo*)

The ombudsman (or defender of the people) is a post envisaged in Article 54 of the Constitution. This figure is designated by both Houses of Parliament and his role is to defend the rights enshrined in Section I of the Constitution, monitoring the activities of all branches of public adminis-tration and reporting to both Houses of Parliament.

The role of the ombudsman was explicated in an organic law of April 1981 (see 4.7.1.1). This law permits him to watch over the activities of ministers, administrative authorities, civil servants and persons working for any branch of public administration. All public authorities are obliged to assist him in his investigations, giving him preference over other claim-ants on their time. In practice this post was left unfilled throughout the period when the Centre–Right (UCD) was in power; after the 1982 elec-tions, when the Socialists (PSOE) came to power, Parliament voted to appoint to this prestigious office a jurist of international repute and former Christian Democrat leader, Joaquín Ruiz-Giménez.

2.7   Constitutional reform

The initiative for reform of the Constitution may come from the govern-ment, the Congress, the Senate or the autonomous communities (Article 166). Proposals for constitutional reform must be approved by a three-fifths majority in each House of Parliament. If there is a disagreement between the Houses a joint committee, composed of an equal number of deputies and senators, will draft a text which will again be put to the vote of the Congress and the Senate. If this procedure fails, the text can be approved by a two-thirds majority of the Congress provided that an absolute majority of the Senate has already approved it. Following approval in the *Cortes* the reform may be put to a national referendum to be ratified, provided that fifteen deputies or senators request it within fifteen days of the reform being approved in the *Cortes* (Article 167).

According to Article 168, if the proposed reform refers to a total revision of the Constitution or to a partial reform that affects the Introductory Sec-tion or the first part of Section I or the whole of Section II, the proposal has to be approved by two-thirds of each House. This is followed by the dissol-ution of Parliament. Following elections, the newly elected Parliament must ratify the original decision by a two-thirds majority in each House. Subsequently the reform must be put to a national referendum for final ratification.

No initiative for constitutional reform can be taken while the country is at war or when a state of alarm, exception or siege is in force (Article 116).

It need hardly be emphasised that, in the face of such stringent requirements, it is very unlikely that the country will witness a plethora of proposals for constitutional reform; indeed the constitution drafters and numerous parliamentary committees, having spent a considerable amount of time agreeing on the final text of the Constitution, have clearly set out to discourage all but the most determined reformers. In recent years, since 1978, the only time it was seriously posed as a possibility was in 1983, when the right-wing opposition party, the AP, considered constitutional reform as the only way of escape from the apparent impasse reached over the question of the relationship between the government and the autonomous communities. Since this party had barely half the number of deputies of the ruling Socialist party in the Congress, almost inevitably the proposal was defeated.

2.8   Conclusion

The 1978 Constitution undoubtedly paved the way for a radical transformation of the nature of the Spanish state which it attempted simultaneously to democratise and decentralise. The many ways in which these changes have affected Spain's political and economic life and institutions are examined in the chapters that follow. Suffice it to say at this point that not only have Spain's constitution drafters reinstated the concept of a democratic state based on the rule of law (*estado democrático de derecho*), the corner-stone of which is the new parliamentary monarchy, but they have laid the foundations for a complete restructuring of the state in which regional parliaments, executives and judiciaries share responsibilities with their counterparts in Madrid. The Constitution, of course, represents only the first step in this long and complex process of creating a whole new political structure and a new set of institutions. Onto this basic framework politicians have had to graft a web of detailed legislation which, over time, will enable administrators to translate the theory of this new democratic state into practical reality.

3 The monarchy

3.1 Monarchy prior to 1975

Prior to the restoration of the Bourbon monarchy in 1975, the last King of Spain was Alfonso XIII who effectively ruled from 1902 to 1931. Following a period of political unrest during which the monarchy fell into increasing disrepute and the political tide turned strongly in favour of republicanism, Alfonso fled the country in April 1931 'to save the country from civil war'. Until after the Civil War of 1936–9, the Spanish royal family was to remain in exile in Italy. Shortly before his death in 1941, Alfonso abdicated in favour of his son Don Juan, Count of Barcelona, who was to live in exile in Portugal up to and beyond the end of the Franco era (see genealogical table in Figure 3.1).

3.2 Monarchical restoration

On 22 November 1975, two days after the death of General Franco, Juan Carlos de Borbón, son of Don Juan and grandson of Alfonso XIII, was proclaimed King of Spain. In a simple ceremony the new monarch was sworn in by the president of the *Cortes*; on this occasion, as in 1969, Juan Carlos pledged to uphold Franco's fundamental laws, which include the Succession Law and the Organic Law of the State (see 3.2.1).

Since Juan Carlos had been appointed successor to the headship of state by a widely hated dictator and since in November 1975 his father, Don Juan, had not renounced his dynastic rights, it is worth asking what legitimate authority, if any, did the new monarch have for ascending the long-vacant throne of Spain. This question is very pertinent when we consider that not only had Juan Carlos' acceptance of the succession led to a certain friction between father and son, but the majority of Spaniards at that time were at best indifferent and at worst hostile to the idea of a monarchy, particularly if it meant, as Franco no doubt intended, a continuation of Francoism in a more respectable guise.

Thus, prior to examining its nature, role and functions, it would seem appropriate to examine the process by which the monarchy was restored in the person of Juan Carlos and, in so doing, attempt to examine its possible sources, if any, of legitimacy.

Figure 3.1 *Genealogical table of the Spanish monarchy*

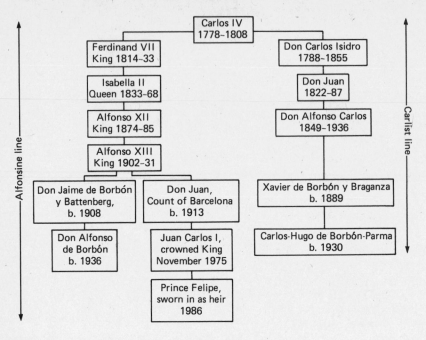

3.2.1   Constitutional legitimacy

3.2.1.1 Succession Law *(Ley de Sucesión)*

Between 1939 and 1947 the form of the new Spanish state that emerged from the Civil War was left an open question. However, in 1947, whether to appease monarchist opinion in Spain or to convey a more democratic image abroad, Franco issued the Succession Law which, while conferring on himself for life the powers of regent, envisaged the eventual restoration of the monarchy. No particular pretender was nominated at that time; it was not even clear whether Franco intended to select his successor from the Alfonsine or the Carlist line of Bourbons (see Figure 3.1) since followers of both were represented in his cabinets and other institutions of government. The only conditions laid down for the future monarch were that he should be male, Spanish, Catholic and over thirty years of age (Article 9). It is interesting to note that Article 11 refers to an *instauración*, not a *restauración* of the monarchy, stressing, as Franco did in speeches of the time, that this was not to be a continuation of the traditional, that is, constitutional monarchy, but a new monarchy rooted in the uprising of 18 July 1936 – the day when Franco launched his so-called crusade against the Second Republic. This concept was reiterated in 1969 when Franco presented Juan Carlos to the *Cortes* as his successor.

3.2.1.2 *Organic Law of the State* (Ley Orgánica del Estado)

The monarchical form of the state was confirmed in two later fundamental laws, namely the Law of Principles of the National Movement (*Ley de Principios del Movimiento Nacional*) issued by Franco in 1958 and the Organic Law of the State, promulgated in 1967. The latter, which like the Succession Law was submitted to a carefully controlled national referendum, outlined the function and powers of the Head of State and other national institutions. In theory the limitations placed on the powers of the former were to apply to Franco as well as to his successor, still at that time unknown, but in practice the dictator retained reserve powers dating back to 1938 and 1939 which allowed him, whenever he deemed fit, to rule in a dictatorial way without consulting his cabinet. The powers conferred on the future head of state were still considerable, however, extending to the realms of the executive, legislature, judiciary and the armed forces. There were to be no concessions to liberal concepts such as accountability and the separation of powers. In reality, the Organic Law envisaged a kind of executive monarchy, very different from the constitutional monarchies of Western Europe or pre-republican Spain. Thus, any successor to Franco would enjoy very considerable constitutional powers.

3.2.1.3 *Nomination of Juan Carlos*

Preferring to keep his options open and to play off competing groups against each other, Franco delayed the nomination of his successor for as long as possible. For many years the odds had been in favour of Juan Carlos who, following a meeting between Franco and Don Juan, had been educated in Spain since the age of ten and had served in all three armed services and several ministries. Moreover, especially after his marriage to Princess Sofía of Greece in 1962, he had appeared increasingly with Franco in public and it appeared that he was being groomed for the succession in spite of the Dictator's known antagonism towards Don Juan. However, other claimants did exist in the form of Juan Carlos' cousin, Alfonso Borbón y Dampierre, married to Franco's own grand-daughter, and Carlos-Hugo de Borbón-Parma, the Carlist pretender, by this stage a less favoured claimant. At all events, in line with predictions, on 22 July 1969 Franco proposed Juan Carlos to the *Cortes* as his intended successor; the proposal was approved by 491 votes to 19 with 9 abstentions. Subsequently Juan Carlos was to be known as Prince of Spain (not Prince of Asturias, the traditional title of the heir to the throne) and his wife as Princess. Thereafter, *los Príncipes* appeared more frequently in public with Franco and assumed the role of ambassadors-extraordinary to several foreign countries.

It should be stressed, however, that even after this nomination Franco could have implemented Article 13 of the Succession Law, which allowed him to revoke this decision and to nominate an alternative successor; the possible justifications for such a revocation were either a demonstrated incapacity to govern or 'blatant deviation from the fundamental principles of the state'. No doubt, if at this time Juan Carlos had expressed the sort of democratic sentiments that he was later to embrace, Franco would have had no hesitation in invoking this provision.

3.2.2 · Dynastic legitimacy

With his nomination of Juan Carlos in preference to his father Don Juan, Franco had appeared deliberately to sever all connections between his monarchy and that of pre-republican days, which in numerous speeches he had associated with allegedly decadent liberal democracy and the party system. This was sufficient reason for many monarchist supporters to rally to the cause of Don Juan whose liberal and democratic leanings were well-known. Indeed, while he was living in exile in Portugal, Don Juan's Privy Council was composed of a wide range of democratic liberal opinion from conservatives and ex-Francoists like José-María de Areilza to socialists like Raúl Morodo. Though the Pretender remained in close contact with his son, the latter's apparently passive acceptance of all the dictator's instructions met with a certain amount of paternal disapproval, not least his acceptance of the succession in 1969. It was only in May 1977, a month before the first democratic elections were held, that Don Juan publicly renounced his claim to the throne.

However, it has to be recognised that during the Franco era Don Juan's supporters were few in number. Opponents of Franco tended to identify democracy not with the restoration of the monarchy but, if anything, with republicanism. Hence Juan Carlos' link with the traditional monarchy, as far as the general public was concerned, offered little more source of legitimacy than his adoption by the Franco regime. One might indeed argue that his acceptance of the succession, apparently against his father's wish, effectively debarred him morally, if not legally, from claiming to be the legitimate heir of the traditional monarchy.

3.2.3   Earned legitimacy

On Franco's death a crisis of legitimacy occurred for the Spanish monarchy, caught as it was between three rival groups: those who wished to use it as a means to perpetuate Francoism; the reformists (*reformistas*) who wanted to employ it as a protective umbrella for the operation of a smooth transition from dictatorship to democracy; and those (the *rupturistas*) who were at the outset totally opposed to the monarchy, considering that not only was it discredited for historical reasons, but that Juan Carlos' apparently close identification with the Franco regime disqualified him from holding office. The fact that the monarchy has now survived over a decade would seem to bear testimony to the ability of Juan Carlos to tread a carefully chosen path among these conflicting groups. His manner of doing so has in fact conferred on him a third and much more durable form of legitimacy – one that he has earned by his commitment to democracy.

An examination of the king's role in the transition properly belongs to works of political history, hence reference here will be made to his role only in so much as his actions implied changes to the institutions of the new state. In this context Juan Carlos' outstanding contribution, apart from his unequivocal support, if not inspiration, for the fundamental reform process initiated by Adolfo Suárez (1976–81) has been his determination to divest himself of the substantial powers conferred upon him by Franco and to rule as a constitutional monarch within the framework of the new democratic order. Although at the time of the attempted military *coup* of February 1981 Juan Carlos exercised a kind of political power, this could surely be justified in terms of his evident concern for the survival of democracy; in any case, the king subsequently made it clear to both the military and the politicians that he never again wanted to have to intervene so directly in the political arena.

3.3   Monarchical form of the state

According to Article 1.3 of the 1978 Constitution 'the political form of the state is the parliamentary monarchy'. The significance of this is that under the new order the king is not sovereign; sovereignty is exercised by the people, whose will is expressed through their democratically elected representatives in Parliament. It is very significant that the above clause follows Article 1.2, which states that 'national sovereignty resides in the Spanish people from whom all the powers of the state derive'. Thus, since the king is not sovereign, it is not correct to talk of a monarchical state; the overriding characteristic of the Spanish state, as described in Article 1.1, is that it is 'a social and democratic state based on the rule of law'. This is a vitally important consideration because it embodies the concept that parliamentary democracy emanates from the will of the people and not from that of the monarch. Neither would it be correct to refer to the monarchy as Spain's form of government for, in constitutional law and historically, this would imply that the king was the titular head of the executive or government, which, as we shall see, is far from the case. Basically the nature of the Spanish state is a parliamentary democracy organised in such a way that currently its head of state is a hereditary and constitutional monarch.

3.4   Role and functions of the monarch

These are outlined in Article 56 of the Constitution where it is possible to distinguish three types of function. In the first place, as head of state (*jefe del estado*), he is its supreme representative and this is most obviously manifested in the area of international relations; moreover, he is the symbol of its unity, acknowledged as head of state by all the autonomous communities; furthermore, he is the symbol of continuity, enhanced by the hereditary principle of succession (see 3.7). Second, the king has the responsibility of ensuring that the institutions of the state run smoothly; where necessary he is required to exercise an arbitrating or restraining influence in pursuit of this goal. Third, the Constitution confers on him a limited number of specific functions which enable him to carry out effectively the above roles. It cannot be over-emphasised, however, that the monarch has no powers outside the Constitution. These different functions will now be examined separately.

3.4.1   Symbolic functions

The first of these concerns international relations. Although the monarch has no power constitutionally to direct foreign affairs, which are the responsibility of the government, he nevertheless plays a vital role as chief representative of the state both at home and abroad. In a sense his most important function is that of communication with other countries and their leaders; through his numerous journeys abroad and his contacts with visiting foreign leaders, Juan Carlos has often served a valuable purpose in preparing the ground for later links, both commercial and political, forged by the Spanish government.

The extent of the king's involvement in this sphere is reflected by the fact that in 1984 alone Juan Carlos made six official and four private visits to various countries and received visits from no less than eighteen heads of state. It is interesting to note that, while all official royal business is conducted in the Royal Palace (*Palacio Real* or *Palacio del Oriente*), the traditional home of Spanish monarchs, Juan Carlos and his family live in relatively modest surroundings in the mansion of *La Zarzuela*, just outside Madrid.

The king's responsibilities in the international field also include: accrediting Spanish ambassadors and other diplomatic representatives of the country and receiving the credentials of resident ambassadors and diplomats (Article 63.1); indicating the consent of the state to international treaties and agreements in accordance with the Constitution (Article 63.2); and declaring war and peace, following approval by the *Cortes* (Article 63.2).

With regard to the judiciary, Article 117 of the Constitution lays down that the judges administer justice in the name of the king; clearly this is a purely formal and symbolic attribute. The same Article makes it clear that justice emanates from the people and that the judges are independent and subject only to the law. None the less, the association of the crown with the judiciary helps to stress its impartiality and imbue it with an aura of traditional dignity.

One of the king's major functions as head of state is to make various civil and military appointments, as well as to award special honours and distinctions (Article 62f). It should be stressed, however, that the government has the right to control both the civil and military administration (see 5.5.2) and that the king's role is limited to the act of ratifying appointments already made by the government. The only exception to this is outlined in Article 65.2, referring to the king's right freely to select the staff for his civil and military households (see 3.6).

The king is normally invited to act as honorary patron of such august societies as the eight Royal Academies the members of which all belong automatically to the Institute of Spain (*Instituto de España*). This is, of course, only a symbolic function, yet it has its importance in demonstrating the support of the crown and therefore the state for the highest level of cultural and scientific endeavour (Article 62j).

Finally, but by no means least in importance, Article 62h confers on the monarch the title of Commander-in-Chief of the Armed Forces (*Mando Supremo de las Fuerzas Armadas*). This title is commonly assumed by heads of state and certainly in the Spanish case does not imply any special constitutional relationship between the head of state and the armed forces; the monarch can make no decisions with regard to the latter, which are in any case ultimately under the control of the government. On the other hand, as we have already seen, in practice this particular monarch has clearly exercised considerable influence over the military in his determination to consolidate democracy. Juan Carlos has always remained in regular contact with the armed forces and uses the annual military celebration of the *Pascua Militar* on 6 January both to reiterate his approval of their endeavours and, on occasion, to remind them of their duty to uphold the Constitution.

3.4.2   Moderating functions

This function involves the collaboration of the monarch with the organs of the state to ensure that extremist or arbitrary tendencies are avoided which might threaten the proper functioning of the system. To a large extent, these functions are carried out in relation both to the legislative and the executive power, and, as with most of the other functions of the king, they are subject to limitations and controls which reduce their practical significance to a minimum.

With regard to the legislature, the king requires the backing of either the government or the head of government in order to perform the following functions:

3.4.2.1 To call elections to Parliament

Article 62b grants this 'power' to the king 'in the terms envisaged in the Constitution' meaning, in practice, that when Parliament has run its normal course or when the government decides to call an election (see 4.5.1). At all events he must, on the advice of the prime minister, call elections between thirty and sixty days following the dissolution of Parliament.

3.4.2.2 To summon and dissolve Parliament

The same article refers to the king's responsibility to summon and dissolve Parliament again 'in the terms envisaged in the Constitution'. Article 68.6 lays down that he must summon the Congress within twenty-five days following elections. With regard to the dissolution the Constitution distinguishes four possible scenarios: (i) when the maximum four-year mandate has expired; (ii) when the Congress, within the two-month period following elections, fails to give its support in a vote of confidence to the candidate for the premiership (see 4.6.3.4); (iii) when the *Cortes*, by a two-thirds majority in each House approves a proposal for a total or partial revision of the Constitution; and (iv) when the prime minister proposes a dissolution of Parliament for whatever reason.

It should be stressed that in none of the above cases are we dealing with a power of discretion granted to the monarch; at no time can the king prevent the dissolution of the *Cortes*. The only person to exercise this prerogative is the prime minister of the day.

3.4.2.3 To sanction and promulgate laws

Article 62a grants the monarch the right to sanction and promulgate laws that have already been approved either by Parliament or the council of ministers. With his signature the king is confirming that all the formal requirements for approval of any given law have been met and he can only withhold his signature, something which in practice is barely conceivable, if such requirements have not been fulfilled. In a sense this function bears comparison with others which we have included in the section on symbolic functions. It need hardly be said that the king has no legislative power; as we shall see in 4.6 this belongs almost exclusively to the *Cortes*.

With regard to the executive, the 'powers' of the monarch are similarly limited. These include the following:

3.4.2.4 To terminate a premiership

The monarch has the right to terminate the functions of the prime minister according to Article 62d, which in practice means the acceptance, for whatever reason, of the resignation of the latter. In no circumstances does he have the authority under the Constitution to dismiss him or oblige him to resign (see 5.2.2).

3.4.2.5 To appoint and dismiss ministers
Clause f of the same Article grants the king responsibility with regard to government ministers; here his role is essentially that of a rubber-stamp since the basic decisions are taken by the prime minister (see 5.4.1).

3.4.2.6 To issue cabinet decrees
According to clause f the monarch must issue and make arrangements for the publication of decrees agreed in the council of ministers (see 4.7.1.6/7).

3.4.2.7 To attend meetings of the council of ministers
Clause g of the same Article, as well as allowing the king to be informed about matters of state, also grants him the right to attend sessions of the council of ministers when he should consider it appropriate, but only on the request of the prime minister.

3.4.3 Arbitrating functions

The only area where the king may possibly exercise some residual discretionary powers concerns the proposal of a candidate to head the government either following elections or following the resignation of an existing premier. In normal circumstances this 'power' is very restricted: following consultations with party leaders, the monarch automatically calls on the leader of the majority party in the Congress to head the next government, and provided that the latter obtains the required vote of confidence from that House, the king appoints him and swears him in. If, following an indecisive election, no obvious candidate emerges, the arbitrating role of the king might well assume more importance. However, it must be stressed that the king has no executive power as such, only a certain moral authority and influence, which, of course, has no constitutional basis.

3.5 Limitations to role

As has already been shown, none of the functions of the monarch outlined above grant him any independent decision-making powers within the judicial, executive or legislative institutions of the state. Juan Carlos is a constitutional monarch in the full sense of the word, having no reserve powers outside the Constitution.

One of the major constitutional devices for limiting the monarchy is the use of the endorsement (*refrendo*). By means of this device no official document is issued solely with the signature of the king but must be countersigned either by the prime minister or one of his ministers. In the case of the recommendation and appointment of the premier or the dissolution of the *Cortes*, such documents must be endorsed by the president of the Congress (Article 64a). In a sense it is the king who is countersigning or endorsing the document and the others referred to who exercise the real power.

3.6   Privileges

In fact the *refrendo* is a kind of monarchical privilege as well as a limitation on his power. Since the Constitution states that 'those who endorse the acts of the king are responsible for them' the king is absolved of all responsibility for them. In this way the monarchy is spared the risk of becoming politically involved and associated with unpopular legislation.

This basic constitutional concept is repeated in Article 56.3, which also states that the monarch is inviolable. This does not mean, however, that he stands outside the criminal law, for if he were to commit a criminal offence, Article 59 would come into force; this envisages the possibility of the king, for whatever reason, being found unfit to rule by the Joint Houses of Parliament. It should be stressed that only the *Cortes* can act as a court in the case of any offences allegedly committed by the king.

Two further privileges which the monarch enjoys refer to the royal family and household. Article 65.1 enables the king to receive a global sum from the state budget for the maintenance of his family and household, a sum which he has the right to distribute as he wishes. He enjoys a similar and rare freedom to appoint and dismiss the members of his civil and military households (see Figure 3.2).

As can be seen in Figure 3.2, the royal household (*casa real*) consists of four major departments, three of which are military, all under the control of the head of the royal household (*jefe de la casa real*). It should be noted that it is through the head of the security service (*jefe de seguridad*) that the king exercises his symbolic command of the armed forces.

3.7   Succession and regency (see Figure 3.3)

In the constitutional, if not the political, sense Juan Carlos' position as head of state and monarch, rooted in Franco's fundamental laws, has been ratified and legitimised in the 1978 Constitution which, by converting the king's role into a constitutional one, is able to designate him as 'the legitimate heir of the historic dynasty' (Article 57.1). At the same time the succession is attached to his heirs in a traditional and hereditary monarchy.

As far as the order of succession is concerned, the above Article states that a male heir is always preferred to a female of the same generation, even

Figure 3.2 *Royal household*

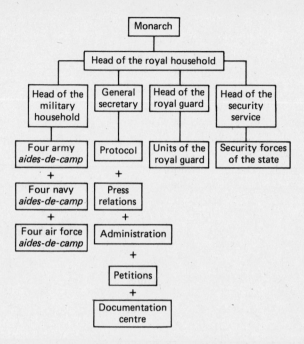

Figure 3.3 *Line of succession to the Spanish throne*

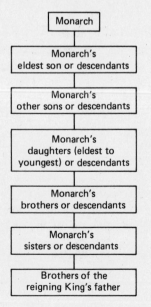

if the female is older. If the heir to the throne dies prematurely, his eldest child, first males then females, inherits the throne. Only if the heir dies childless does the throne pass to his younger brother(s) or sister(s). This is the theory of representation whereby the son or daughter of an heir who dies prematurely is considered to represent the rights of that heir. In the case of the present royal family for example, although the current heir, Prince Felipe, has two elder sisters, Elena and Cristina, he is the first in line to the throne; one of them could succeed to the throne only if Felipe died childless. Under this system, therefore, unlike that obtaining under Franco's Fundamental Laws, which forbade a female monarch, females can accede to the throne. It is clear, however, that males enjoy a privileged position with regard to the succession. The main reason for its adoption in 1978 is that it is in line with a Spanish tradition dating back to the fourteenth century.

The heir to the throne from birth enjoys the traditional title of Prince of Asturias (Article 57.2). On attaining the age of majority (eighteen), which Prince Felipe did in January 1986, he must take the same oath as taken by a monarch on ascending the throne, that is, faithfully to carry out his functions, to observe and ensure the observance of the laws and respect the rights of citizens and of the autonomous communities. He must also take the oath of loyalty to the king. These oaths also apply to a regent or regents on taking office (Article 61.2).

If all legal lines of succession are extinguished, the Joint Houses of Parliament, according to Article 57.3, 'will provide for the succession to the throne in the form most suitable for the interests of Spain'. It is interesting to note that no particular type of majority is referred to in this vitally important constitutional matter (see 4.6.1).

One important principle and advantage of the traditional monarchy is the provision of continuity even at the time of a monarch's death. Constitutionally the state can never be without a head of state because at the moment of such a death the heir automatically becomes king; it is not required that he should previously be sworn in before he assumes office. Nor is there a problem even if the heir is still below the age of majority: although it may take some time for the regency to take effect, the heir is still recognised as the monarch and titular head of state. Thus, unless the last heir to the throne dies childless, a highly unlikely circumstance, there can never be a vacuum in the headship of state.

There are two possible scenarios for the establishment of a regency in Spain and these are spelt out in Article 59. First, as indicated above, if the heir to the throne should not have attained the age of majority; and, second, if the king should be declared unfit to rule by the joint *Cortes*. In the first case the regency would be assumed by the father, mother or the next adult in line of succession. In the second case the heir himself would automatically assume the regency; if he were still not of age, the order outlined above would be followed until the heir became of age. If no clear candidate for the regency were available, the joint *Cortes* would have the right to appoint a regent. The latter would have to be Spanish and have attained the age of majority; in this case the regency could consist of one, two or more persons. It should be stressed that a regency is always provisional and all its functions and acts are carried out in the name of the king. Normally, too, any regency would have a fixed time-span, for example, until the heir had attained the age of majority.

3.8   Conclusion

It is ironic that prior to the 1978 Constitution Juan Carlos used the wide powers bequeathed to him by Franco to steer the country away from dictatorship and towards democracy. He used these powers partly to encourage the new political establishment to draw up a Constitution under which he himself would be divested of his executive authority and would become a constitutional monarch with very few powers. In doing so Juan Carlos earned for himself the kind of moral authority which, it is probable, no successor could hope to obtain. At the same time, for the foreseeable future, unless his heirs prove to be extremely incompetent, it would seem that the monarchy as an institution is likely to benefit from this authority and from the popular legitimacy which the actions of Juan Carlos have conferred upon it.

4   Parliament

4.1   Franco legislature

From 1939 to 1977 Spain was endowed with a one-chamber legislature known as the *Cortes*. Franco, profoundly hostile to the legislative systems of liberal democracies, swept away the democratically elected single-chamber Parliament of the Second Republic and imposed what amounted to a rubber-stamp chamber packed with his own supporters. In this chamber Franco included representatives from various sectors of society, the municipalities, the syndical organisations, professional bodies, academic institutions and so on, claiming in this way to be establishing what he considered to be a more representative system, based on the principles of 'organic democracy'. In reality, however, since the members were either indirectly elected or directly appointed by Franco or his immediate subordinates and since Parliament functioned more as an arm of the executive than as a body to which the latter was accountable, the *Cortes* was much closer in conception to the corporativist models of Fascist states of the 1930s than to those of liberal democracies.

Although a modest attempt was made in the Organic Law of 1967 to introduce a more democratic element, offering the voter an opportunity to elect 108 so-called 'family MPs', the result meant little change to the existing system. On the one hand, these comprised no more than a fifth of the membership of the House and, in any case, candidates were carefully screened by the officials of the regime to ensure that only approved figures were allowed to stand. On the other hand, in terms of its mode of functioning, the *Cortes* was subjected to constant interference from the executive; debates were rarely held, ministers were not obliged to appear on request before the House, and certain issues such as foreign policy and public order were not deemed to be part of its remit.

4.2   Post-Franco legislature

The above situation, however, changed dramatically in October 1976 when, in an historic decision, the Franco *Cortes* signed what amounted to its own death-warrant by approving Adolfo Suárez's Political Reform Law (see 1.4). This paved the way for fully democratic elections and envisaged, pending the drafting of a new constitution, the establishment of a bi-cameral Parliament with a Congress of Deputies and a Senate. These far-reaching reforms were later to be enshrined in the Constitution of 1978.

In accordance with the principles of liberal democracy, post-Franco Spain has implicitly, if not explicitly, recognised in the Constitution a separation of powers between the legislature, the executive and the judiciary. Following the guidelines of the Political Reform Law, the Constitution (Sections III and V) outlines the nature, composition and functions of the new legislature as well as its relationship to the executive and other institutions of the state. Article 2 makes it clear that 'national sovereignty resides with the Spanish people, from whom all the powers of the state derive'. This sovereignty is expressed through the *Cortes* the elected members of which are the trustees and representatives of the will of the people. Parliament is the supreme institution of the state and, as we have already seen, even the monarchy, quite deliberately defined as a 'parliamentary monarchy', is, in the last resort, subject to its will (see 3.3).

4.3 Basic structure of Parliament

The term *Cortes* has come to refer to the national Parliament, whether expressed through one or two Houses or chambers (*cámaras*). In the course of this chapter it will be seen that, while certain functions are carried out separately by each chamber, a number of important functions, mainly related to the monarchy, are exercised by both Houses, in which capacity they are known as the *Cortes Generales* or Joint Houses of Parliament.

Like many European democracies, Spain has established a bi-cameral Parliament consisting of a Lower House (*Cámara Baja*) or Congress and an Upper House (*Cámara Alta*) or Senate. As in the UK, for example, the Lower House has precedence in most matters, including legislative affairs, and this is represented symbolically by the fact that the president of the Congress (see 4.3.1) presides over sessions of the *Cortes Generales*. The individuality of the two chambers, however, is emphasised by the fact that they occupy separate premises in Madrid: the Congress assembles in the *Palacio del Congreso* (still known by many by its former name, the *Palacio de las Cortes*), while the Senate meets in the *Palacio del Senado*.

4.3.1 Congress of Deputies (Congreso de los Diputados)

According to Article 68 of the Constitution, the Congress consists of a minimum of 300 and a maximum of 400 deputies (*diputados*). In fact both the Electoral Law of March 1977 and that of June 1985 (which updates the

Figure 4.1 Electoral constituencies: the provinces of Spain

former), have established that 350 should be the norm. As in the case of the Senate (see 4.3.2), elections are held through universal, free, direct, equal and secret suffrage, and both males and females over the age of eighteen are eligible to vote. Votes are cast not for individual candidates but for a party list in which candidates appear in a ranking order fixed in advance by the parties concerned. The constituency for elections to the Congress is the province (see Figure 4.1). Article 68.3 establishes a system of proportional representation for allocating seats to the fifty-two provinces and the details of this are spelt out in Article 162 of the 1985 Election Law. Article 163 of the same law specifies the details of the method by which votes are distributed among candidates in each province: this is the D'Hondt system, which is also used in regional and local elections. This system is commonly accepted to favour large parties and less populated, often more conservative, rural areas. The life-span of the Congress is a maximum of four years, after which elections must be called. In any event, the term of office of a deputy ends when Parliament is dissolved by the head of state.

4.3.2   Senate (Senado)

Basically the Senate is what Article 69 of the Constitution calls 'the chamber of territorial representation', which claims to represent the interests of the country's newly formed autonomous communities (see Chapter 7); in fact this is only partly the case. A number of senators (*senadores*) are indeed elected from among the members of the regional assemblies through a system which reflects both the population size of the regions and the political composition of their assemblies. However, the vast majority of senators, 208 out of a total in 1986 of 253, are elected from the provinces which, as with the Congress, provides the normal electoral constituency. Each province elects four senators, with each elector casting only three votes, in a first-past-the-post or majority system, which makes no allowance for the enormous variations in population between sparsely populated areas like Soria and Teruel and enormous urban conurbations like Madrid and Barcelona. Generally speaking, this system favours the conservative rural areas and for that reason was vigorously defended by the Right in the constitutional debates. However, in 1982 and 1986 this bias did not prevent the Socialists from winning twice as many seats in the Senate as their main rivals, the Popular Alliance.

4.3.3   Members of Parliament (Parlamentarios)

Parlamentarios is the umbrella term used in Spanish to refer to both deputies and senators, whose rights and duties are laid down in both the Constitution and the standing orders (*reglamentos*) of the Congress and Senate. These important documents, which in fact detail all matters relating to the internal organisation of each House, are dated respectively 10 February 1982 and 26 May 1982. Although the statutes of the deputies and senators are spelt out separately in these documents, their rights and obligations are substantially the same, as suggested in Articles 70 and 71 of the Constitution.

4.3.3.1 Prerogatives and rights

Both deputies and senators, during their term of office and even after it has expired are not liable in respect of verbal opinions expressed in the performance of their parliamentary duties.

During their term of office they can only be arrested if caught in the act of committing a crime and, in any case, they cannot be indicted or prosecuted without the previous authorisation of the *Cortes*. To obtain the latter the court concerned must seek an injunction (*suplicatorio*) from the House concerned within a fixed period of time before proceedings can commence.

Parliamentarians are not bound by any compulsory mandate; their votes are personal and they are not obliged to vote in accordance with previous instructions emanating from individuals or groups.

They have the right to attend and vote at all plenary sittings of Parliament and all committees of which they are members. Deputies are allowed to attend any committee without the right to vote, although this is not stated in the case of senators. The latter would appear not to enjoy the right which deputies have to be members of as many committees as they wish.

All have a right not only to a fixed salary, annually reviewed, but allowances for all expenses incurred in the exercise of their duty. Senators may travel free on agreed systems of public transport. Each House agrees to adopt the social security payments made by former employers in order to safeguard their health, pension and other rights while members of Parliament.

Deputies have the right to demand from any branch of public administration data or information that might be useful to them in the exercise of their duties. Interestingly, this right does not seem to be accorded to senators, although the latter may request the minutes and documents emanating from any body within the House.

4.3.3.2 Restrictions and duties

Parliamentarians are not allowed to be members of both Houses of Parliament at the same time, neither is it lawful to occupy a seat simultaneously in the Congress and a regional assembly. Presumably senators are allowed to sit in the latter, however, since nothing is stated to the contrary.

According to Article 70, the following are not allowed to stand for Parliament: members of the constitutional court, high-ranking civil servants, the ombudsman, practising judges and public prosecutors, professional soldiers and other military personnel, active members of the police and security forces, and members of electoral boards.

All parliamentarians not only have the right but the obligation to attend plenary sittings of the appropriate House and the committees of which they are members. Senators may incur a financial penalty following consistent failure to attend.

All parliamentarians are required to make a public statement before a notary (*notario*) of their assets and of any activities which provide them with an income. Deputies and senators have two months and four months respectively to make such statements following their election to the House.

Parliamentarians must respect Article 79.3 of the Constitution which states that votes are personal and cannot be delegated.

4.4   Internal organisation

According to Article 72 of the Constitution each House is free to draw up standing orders governing its own internal organisation and mode of functioning, including its own budget and the establishment of offices to administer such affairs.

4.4.1   President

The president of the Congress (*presidente del Congreso*) and the president of the Senate (*presidente del Senado*) have several functions in common. Basically, their main task is to supervise the everyday running of the House both inside and outside the debating chamber. Within the chamber they and their presiding councils (see 4.4.2) are responsible for drawing up the legislative agenda in consultation with the board of party spokesmen (see 4.4.6) and for exercising discipline within the House. As we shall see later, there are rigorous regulations controlling procedures in each House and the president is empowered to take strong disciplinary action against members who contravene the regulations and practices of the House.

In addition the president of the Congress performs several special constitutional functions. For example, Article 99 of the Constitution implies that he must be consulted or at least informed before elections are called and the decree convening elections must have his countersignature. According to the same Article, it is through the president of the Congress that the king proposes a candidate for the premiership.

4.4.2   Presiding council (mesa)

The presiding council is elected at the constituent meeting of the Congress and Senate following elections. It includes the president, vice-presidents and secretaries of each House. The secretaries, like the vice-presidents, are drawn from the major political groupings represented in each chamber. In each case the council is responsible for the overall management and organisation of the work of the House; in this context one of its main functions is to establish conventions of procedure within the House, draw up the order of business of the plenary sittings and committees and co-ordinate the activities of the various bodies established within the House. Other tasks are: to prepare a draft budget; to supervise and control its administration; and to present an annual report on its implementation to the full House. The council is also entrusted with the task of evaluating all parliamentary papers and documents in accordance with the standing orders and to rule on their admissibility.

To assist it in the above functions, each presiding council can call on a team of special legal advisers or *letrados*. These non-political figures are lawyers trained in every aspect of parliamentary procedure, who play a vital technical role in the day-to-day running of each chamber. Their main function is to supervise and authorise, with the approval of the president of the House, the minutes of plenary meetings of the Congress or Senate and their respective presiding councils and boards of party spokesmen (see 4.4.6). During full meetings of each House they assist the president in ensuring the smooth running of debates and voting. In their work they are advised and guided by the chief legal adviser (*letrado mayor*) in the case of the Senate, and the general secretarial adviser (*letrado secretario general*) in the case of the Congress.

4.4.3 Secretariat (secretaría)

These bodies, established under the standing orders of each House, basically represent the bureaucracies of the Congress and the Senate. The secretariat is composed of secretaries (not to be confused with those on the presiding council), who, like the *letrados*, are non-political experts. The major functions of the secretariat are to provide all the bodies operating within the House, particularly the committees, with legal, technical and administrative assistance. Each of the two secretariats is headed by a general secretary (*secretario general*) who, in addition to the above functions, is specifically responsible for the registration and distribution of documents, protocol, the diffusion of information and relations with the media. The make-up of the Congress secretariat is shown in Figure 4.2.

4.4.4 Standing committee (diputación permanente)

The other major body within each House is the standing committee which consists of the president of the House and at least twenty-one members. These are elected at the constituent meeting of the House in proportion to the membership of the parliamentary groups (see 4.4.5) from among the

Figure 4.2. *Composition of general secretariat of the Congress*

Technical and parliamentary assistance	Asistencia técnico-parlamentaria
Parliamentary committees	Comisiones
Economic affairs	Asuntos económicos
Research and documentation	Estudios y documentación
Interparliamentary relations	Relaciones interparlamentarias
Internal organisation	Gobierno interior
Audit department	Intervención

members of the latter. Apart from the president, the council consists of two vice-presidents and two secretaries, elected from among the members of the committee and not to be confused with their counterparts in the presiding council. The main purpose of the committee is to provide continuity between sessions of Parliament, including the period after Parliament has been dissolved and before a new Parliament has been elected and convened. Each council has the right to request an extraordinary sitting of Parliament. One of the major functions of the standing committee of the Congress is to approve or reject decree-laws which are submitted to it by the council of ministers and to act in the name of the House as a whole.

4.4.5   *Parliamentary groups* (grupos parlamentarios)

From the political point of view, these are the most important bodies within each House. They are the organs through which the bulk of parliamentary business, and certainly the work of full sittings of the House and committees, is conducted. In general each group consists of the deputies or senators within the House belonging to one political party or coalition. The Popular Alliance, being a coalition at the time of writing, consists of the parliamentarians belonging to its various constituent parties (see 10.3.3). In the case of the Congress each group must contain a minimum of fifteen deputies, although provision is made for a smaller group of no less than five deputies representing one or more parties provided that together they represent fifteen per cent of the votes in the constituencies in which they have put up a candidate. All remaining deputies must join the mixed group (*grupo mixto*). In the case of the Senate, each group must contain at least ten senators; if the membership falls below six, the group must be dissolved until the end of that session of Parliament. Following the 1986 elections the configuration of parliamentary groups in each House is as shown in Figure 4.3.

From several points of view the composition of the above groups has various important implications: (i) members of Parliament are elected to serve on parliamentary committees, composed in strict proportion to the political structure of each House (see 4.5.4); (ii) the size of the parliamen-

Figure 4.3. *Political division of Parliament: parliamentary groups (1986)*

Congress		Senate	
Name of group	No. of members	Name of group	No. of members
Socialist group (*grupo socialista*)	184	Socialist group	134
Popular group (*grupo popular*)	105	Popular group	54
Democratic and Social Centre Group (*grupo* CDS)	19	Centrist group	4
Catalan Minority (*minoría catalana*)	18	Catalan group (*grupo de Cataluña*)	7
Basque Nationalist Party (*Partido Nacionalista Vasco*)	6	Basque Nationalist Party	7
Mixed group[a] (*grupo mixto*)	18	Territorial representation[a] (*representación territorial*)	42

[a] Since the 1986 elections the ranks of this group, which originally consisted mainly of United Left (including PCE) deputies and an assortment of regionalists, have swollen to over 50 with the defection of the two partners in the Popular Coalition, PDP and PL, and the split in the PNV.

[b] These are the senators elected from the Regional Assemblies mentioned in 4.3.2; they do not constitute a parliamentary group, but may form groups representing the Autonomous Communities along with elected senators in the provinces.

tary groups also governs the length of time granted for speeches, questions, and so on as well as the order in which they are called to speak; and (iii) in both the Senate and the Congress the members are seated according to the group to which they belong.

Figure 4.4 shows how, in 1986, the debating chamber of the Congress, often referred to as the *hemiciclo* because of its semi-circular shape, is divided to accommodate the various parliamentary groups.

4.4.6 Board of party spokesmen (junta de portavoces)

Each parliamentary group elects a spokesman (*portavoz*) to represent its interests in its dealings with the president and the administration of the House. The various spokesmen, together with the president of the House, who chairs their meetings, constitute the board of party spokesmen. The meetings of the Congress board must be attended by at least one vice-president, one of the secretaries of the House and the general secretary. Recently it has also been customary for the minister for parliamentary liaison/cabinet secretary (see 5.5.1 and Figure 6.2) to attend. The composition of the Senate board is similar; in addition its meetings may be attended by a representative of the government.

The main functions of the board in each House, in collaboration with the presiding council, are: to fix the dates for the start and end of par-

Figure 4.4 *Debating chamber of the Congress*

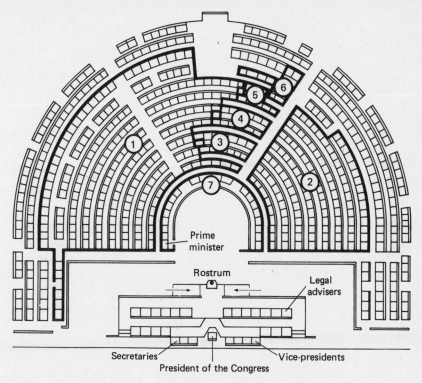

Key:

1. Socialist group 184[a]
2. Popular group (105)
3. CDS group (19)
4. Catalan group (18)

5. Basque Nationalist Party (6)
6. Mixed group (18)
7. Government benches[b]

[a] The numbers in brackets represent the number of members of the group in July 1986.
[b] The government benches are known as the *banco azul*, blue seats, clearly distinguishable from the red ones occupied by other deputies and officers of the Congress.

liamentary sessions; to agree on the agendas for plenary and committee meetings of the Houses; and to suggest means of ensuring the smooth operation of debates and other aspects of parliamentary activity. The boards normally meet on Tuesdays prior to full sittings of the *Cortes* (see 4.5.3).

4.5 Procedures

In addition to the internal organisation of the Houses of Parliament, the standing orders lay down detailed procedures regarding the way in which each House operates from day to day in the fulfilment of its various tasks.

Although there are slight differences here between the Congress and the Senate, they are not great enough to warrant separate treatment for each.

4.5.1   Summoning and dissolution

As we have already seen (3.4.2.2) one of the king's prerogatives is to summon and dissolve Parliament. In reality, of course, as will be seen in Chapter 5.2.4, it is the prime minister who decides to dissolve Parliament and call elections; the monarch's role is merely symbolic. A point worth noting at this juncture is that the Houses must be dissolved and convened simultaneously, although it may well be a government defeat, for example, in a confidence vote in the Congress, that leads directly to a dissolution.

4.5.2   Parliamentary sessions

Article 73 states that the Houses of Parliament convene in ordinary session twice a year, between September and December and between February and June. In between these sessions, however, as we have seen, a parliamentary presence is maintained through the standing committee (4.4.4) and, of course, the two respective bureaucracies continue to function. The same Article goes on to admit the possibility of calling an extraordinary session of both Houses of Parliament at the request of the government, the standing committee or an overall majority of the members of either House. Such extraordinary sessions must address themselves to a specific agenda and Parliament must be adjourned once this has been completed.

4.5.3   Plenary sittings (plenos)

Article 75.1 of the Constitution makes it clear that Parliament operates in both plenary sittings and committees. In recent years plenary sittings of both Houses have tended to take place on Tuesday and Wednesday afternoons and all day Thursday during three weeks of any month, although this pattern can vary depending on the amount of business to be transacted. Plenary sittings are convened by the president of each House either on his own initiative or at the request of at least two parliamentary groups or a fifth of the members of the House concerned. Sittings of the Senate are not supposed to last more than five hours, though no maximum is laid down for the Congress, where in practice sittings tend to be much longer.

As we have seen, agendas for plenary sittings are fixed by the president in consultation with the board of party spokesmen. However, at least in the case of the Congress, the government has the right to insert in the agenda a matter which it considers deserves priority treatment. Likewise, on the initiative of the government or a parliamentary group, the board of spokesmen can have an urgent matter included at any time, even without the normal statutory criteria having been met. Moreover, a full sitting of the House can agree to change the order of the agenda either on the recommendation of the president or on the request of two parliamentary groups or a fifth of the total membership of the House concerned.

With respect to debates, all reports, information and documents relating to the topic to be debated must be circulated to all members of the House at least forty-eight hours before the debate, unless the presiding council has agreed a different arrangement. In the course of the debate no member is allowed to speak without having first requested and obtained the permission of the president. However, a speaker, who may intervene from his seat or from the rostrum, has the right to speak without interruption. Without prejudice to the overall rights of the president to control procedure, the members of the government present in the Congress may request the right to speak at any time.

As stated earlier, the procedure of these sittings is rigidly controlled by the president who, with the aid of sophisticated electronic equipment, can determine the length of time allotted to each speaker, which will depend on the parliamentary group to which he belongs. This applies whether the task in hand is the questioning of the premier or a debate on a parliamentary bill. Speakers who abuse these limitations and ignore two warnings will have their microphones disconnected and may be subject to disciplinary action by the president and his presiding council.

4.5.4 *Parliamentary committees (*comisiones parlamentarias*)*

The bulk of parliamentary work is done through various types of committee, most of which consist exclusively of the members of each House, although some, the joint committees (*comisiones mixtas*), include both deputies and senators. Committees are either permanent or *ad hoc*. The majority of the committees in both Houses are in fact legislative permanent committees (*comisiones permanentes legislativas*). In addition, each House has created several non-legislative permanent committees (*comisiones permanentes no-legislativas*), known in the Senate as general committees (*comisiones generales*), which, as the name implies, deal with non-legislative affairs. In addition each House has exercised its right, under Article 76 of the Constitution, to set up *ad hoc* committees; in the case of the Congress these are known as committees of investigation or enquiry (*comisiones de investigación o encuesta*) and in the case of the Senate as special committees (*comisiones especiales*).

The permanent committees created by the Standing Orders of 1982 are shown in Figure 4.5.

According to the standing orders of each House, the number and composition of each committee is decided by the presiding council concerned following consultations with the board of spokesmen. Each parliamentary

Figure 4.5. *Permanent committees*

	Congress	Senate
General committees		Internal organisation Ineligibilities Petitions Injunctions
Legislative committees	Constitutional affairs Foreign affairs Justice and home affairs Defence Education and culture Economy, commerce and finance Budgets Agriculture, cattle-rearing and fishing Industry, public works and services Social and employment policy Public administration	Constitutional affairs Foreign affairs Justice Defence Education, universities, research and culture Economy and finance Budgets Agriculture and fishing Industry, energy, commerce and tourism Health and social security Presidency and home affairs Autonomous regions and territorial organisation Public works, the environment, town planning, transport and communications Labour
Non-legislative committees	Internal administration The Statute of the Deputies Petitions	Latin American affairs Liaison with the Ombudsman and human rights

group is represented in proportion to its numerical strength in the chamber. For example, following the 1982 elections it was agreed that the Congress committees should have thirty-eight members and that each parliamentary group should be allocated one member for every ten deputies: this produced the composition shown in Figure 4.6.

The Senate committees, most of which have a maximum of twenty-five members, have a similar composition calculated according to the relative strength of each party. The size of certain committees, usually the non-legislative committees, is laid down in the appropriate standing orders. Members of the government are allowed to attend and speak at all committees but are not allowed to vote unless they happen to be members. At its first meeting every committee must elect a presiding council composed of a chairman, two vice-chairmen and two secretaries. Meetings are called by the chairman, on the request of two parliamentary groups or a fifth of the members of the committee concerned.

The major function of the legislative committees is to examine, amend

Figure 4.6. *Composition of Congress committees (1982–6)* *

Parliamentary group	No. of members
Socialist group	21
Popular group	11
Centrist group	2
Catalan minority	2
Basque Nationalist Party	1
Mixed group	1

*Modified after the elections in June 1986.

and approve legislation, most of which emanates from the council of ministers or the ministries. As can be seen in Figure 4.5, the purpose of the non-legislative committees is quite distinct and relates to either the internal affairs of the House concerned or liaison with outside bodies and organisations. Over and above all these committees, which are of a permanent nature, each House can create *ad hoc* committees to deal with specific problems as and when they arise. These must be disbanded once their work is completed and in any case at the end of the legislative period in question. These may be Congress, Senate or joint committees. In the early 1980s some of the most notable joint committees were set up, mostly on an *ad hoc* basis, to examine such matters as: liaison with the audit tribunal (see 9.7.3); the financing of political parties (following allegations that the PSOE had received large sums of money for its 1982 election campaign from the German Company Flick; the RUMASA affair (following the collapse and government expropriation of this one-time giant company); test-tube fertilisation; and the contaminated cooking-oil scandal of 1981.

4.5.5 Voting procedures

In order for plenary sittings and committees to adopt valid agreements, there must be a quorum of members present, that is, half the total membership plus one. Agreements must normally be approved by a simple majority of those present.

Both Houses of Parliament have agreed on a more or less common pattern of voting procedures. These are as follows:

4.5.5.1 Normal voting procedure
The commonest form of this occurs when, following a debate, members are called upon to stand up in a certain order; first those who approve the motion, then those who disapprove and finally those who abstain. Votes are counted by the secretaries. Alternatively, voting can be done by an electronic system which allows individual as well as totals to be displayed.

4.5.5.2 Roll-call voting

Under this system, members' names are read out in alphabetical order beginning with one name drawn at random by a secretary and they must answer 'yes' or 'no' or 'abstain'. Voting on the investiture of the prime minister, motions of censure and votes of confidence are always conducted by this method. It can at any time be requested by two parliamentary groups or one-fifth of the deputies or committee members.

4.5.5.3 Secret voting

This can be carried out by one of two methods: either by an electronic system which displays only the final results of the voting or by the use of ballot papers (*papeletas*).

4.5.6   Public, media and publicity

Plenary sittings of both Houses of Parliament are open to the public and the media. In the case of the former, entry to the public galleries can be secured either by invitation or by queueing. Committee meetings of the Congress and Senate are not, however, open to the public but, unless a secret session has been decreed by the presiding council concerned, the media may have access to them.

Transcriptions of the proceedings of both Houses are published in a document known as the *Diario de sesiones*: in the case of the Congress this includes the proceedings of both plenary sessions and committees, while in the case of the Senate only those of the plenary sessions are transcribed. Draft laws at different stages of approval are published in the *Official Cortes Gazette (Boletín Oficial de las Cortes)*, while only fully approved Acts of Parliament, along with other decrees and ministerial orders and so on, are published in the *Official State Gazette (Boletín Oficial de Estado/ BOE)*.

All plenary sittings of both Houses are recorded on tape for the parliamentary archives, but only certain important sessions of the Congress, such as investitures and censure motions, are broadcast or televised.

4.6   Functions and powers

In Article 66 of the Constitution it is stated that the major functions of the *Cortes* are: 'to exercise the legislative power of the state, to approve the state budgets, to control the actions of the government and to exercise the other powers vested in them by the Constitution'. The latter refer, among other things, to three non-legislative areas mentioned in Article 74.2 of the Constitution: (i) the approval of certain international agreements and treaties; (ii) agreements of co-operation between autonomous communities; and (iii) the allocation of resources to the latter through the

Inter-regional Compensation Fund (see 7.5.3.1). Each House shares in these responsibilities in the parallel but separate exercise of its powers. Prior to examining these, however, some consideration needs to be given to the specific functions of the *Cortes Generales* when, on only rare occasions, they meet in joint session.

4.6.1   Joint sessions

The two Houses of the Spanish Parliament meet in joint session in accordance with certain requirements laid down in Section II of the Constitution which refers to the monarchy. Some of its functions in this context are merely ceremonial: for instance, the *Cortes* must assemble jointly on the occasion of the inauguration of the king, and heir to the throne or the regent. In December 1978 King Juan Carlos I made what was possibly a unique appearance for such a purpose before the Joint Houses of Parliament (*Cortes Generales*) when he signed the new Constitution.

Joint sessions are also held for the following, non-legislative purposes: (i) to approve the appointment of a regent (Article 59.3) following agreement that all the legal lines of royal succession have been extinguished (Article 57.3); (ii) to agree on the monarch's incapacity to rule and thereby set the succession procedure in motion (Article 59.3); (iii) to authorise the king to declare a state of war or peace (Article 63.3).

As we have already observed, such joint sessions are chaired by the president of the Congress and indeed it is in the *Palacio del Congreso* that such sessions take place.

4.6.2   Shared functions

Apart from the major legislative function, both Houses of Parliament share responsibility for exercising parallel power in the following areas:

4.6.2.1 Constitutional matters
They can require the constitutional court to decide whether a treaty contains elements contrary to the Constitution (Article 95).

Having obtained the signatures of fifty deputies or senators, the *Cortes Generales* can present an appeal against unconstitutional laws (Article 162) (see 2.5.2.1); they must approve by a three-fifths majority in each House all constitutional reform bills (Article 167). A tenth of the members of either House can request that a constitutional reform bill be submitted to a national referendum (Article 167.3).

4.6.2.2 Regional matters
As already indicated above (see 4.6), both Houses of Parliament must approve agreements of co-operation (*acuerdos de cooperación*) between

autonomous communities (Article 145.2). They must also decide on the criteria for and the allocation of grants to the autonomous communities through the Inter-regional Compensation Fund (Article 158.2).

In both the above cases, if agreement between the two Houses cannot be reached, a joint committee with equal Congress–Senate membership is set up to find a formula for resolving the issue; if the amended text is not approved in both Houses by a simple majority, the Congress then has the right to decide the issue by an overall majority.

Both Houses may decide, by an overall majority in each case, that there is a need to draw up legislation to harmonise laws affecting the autonomous communities. This power was first used in 1981 when the UCD and the PSOE agreed the approval of four laws to harmonise the autonomy process (see, for example, 7.8.4.2).

4.6.3 Specific powers of the Congress

These refer to the relationship of the Congress to the government and constitute part of the Lower House's powers of control over the government, thus conferring on it important political authority.

4.6.3.1 Ratification of decree-laws
Either through the full House or the standing committee, the Congress must ratify or reject decree-laws adopted by the government within a period of thirty days (Article 86).

4.6.3.2 States of alarm, exception and siege
The Congress is obliged to authorise the extension of a state of alarm and the declaration of a state of exception. By an overall majority it can authorise a state of siege (Article 116).

4.6.3.3 Treasonable offences
The Congress carries the heavy responsibility, should circumstances demand it, of having to accuse the prime minister, or his ministers, of treason or any other offence against the security of the state, obliging them to face criminal proceedings (Article 102).

4.6.3.4 Prime minister
The Congress also enjoys a unique and vitally important role related to the appointment and dismissal of the premier (see 5.2.1 and 5.2.2). As laid down in Article 99.2, the latter must submit himself to a vote of investiture (*voto de investidura*) in the Congress before he can be formally sworn in by the king as prime minister. As we shall see in Chapter 5.2.1, in the first vote an overall majority is required, although in succeeding rounds of voting, a simple majority will suffice.

At any time, a premier can seek from the House a vote of confidence (*voto de confianza*) in his leadership and programme, in which case a simple majority is required; failure to achieve this will normally result in the dissolution of both Houses of Parliament and the calling of elections (Article 112).

In accordance with Article 113, the Congress is also the protagonist of a censure motion (*moción de censura*). In order to succeed, the motion must be approved by an overall majority of the House and its text has to contain the name of the opposition's candidate for the premiership; if the motion is carried, that candidate automatically becomes prime minister without elections having to be called.

4.6.4 Specific powers of the Senate

The only power which the Constitution grants exclusively to the Senate, without any involvement on the part of the Congress, concerns the autonomous communities. Article 155.1 states categorically that if a community fails to fulfil the obligations placed on it by the Constitution or other laws, the government, following the approval by an overall majority of the Senate, is empowered to force such a community to comply with its obligations and to take steps to protect the general interest.

4.7   Legislative function

Quite clearly this is by far the most important function of any democratic Parliament and is no less the case with the Spanish *Cortes*.

4.7.1 Hierarchy of laws

A simplified resume of the hierarchy of laws and regulations at present operating in Spain is presented in diagrammatic form in Figure 4.7. Naturally, at the apex of this structure, we find the Constitution which, as we saw in Chapter 2, provides the basic principles which must inspire and inform all subsequent legislation and regulations. The major laws will now be considered in descending order of importance. At the outset it should be stressed that at the level of the autonomous community ordinary laws of a community are of the same hierarchical level as those of the state, just as directives issuing from a department of regional government have the same force at regional level as those emanating from a ministry in Madrid.

4.7.1.1 Organic laws (leyes orgánicas)
Modelled on the French Constitution of 1958, these highest ranking laws enjoy a status midway between the Constitution and ordinary laws. They can only be approved by the *Cortes*. The approval, modification or repeal

Figure 4.7. *Hierarchy of state laws and regulations*

Constitution

Laws

Organic laws of the state (including Statutes of Autonomy)

Ordinary laws of the state Basic laws Framework laws Basic legislation

Royal decree laws

Legislative decrees

Regulations

Royal decrees

Orders of the delegated committees of the government

Ministerial orders

Circulars and regulations of the central administration

of these laws requires an overall majority of the Congress in a final vote on the complete text of a bill (Article 81.2), although no type of majority is specified for the Senate, from which one assumes that a simple majority will suffice. Clause 1 of this Article makes it clear that organic laws are required in the following fields of legislation: the development of fundamental rights and public liberties; electoral arrangements; statutes of autonomy; and 'others envisaged in the Constitution'.

In fact the latter cover a wide range of areas, including: the royal succession (Article 57); international treaties (Article 93); the council of state (Article 107); states of alarm, exception and siege (Article 116); the creation of regional police forces (Article 149); the transfer and delegation of powers to the autonomous communities (Article 150); and the constitutional court (Article 165). Between October 1979 and April 1983, forty-five organic laws were approved, including the seventeen required to approve the statutes of autonomy of the new autonomous regions (see 7.5.1).

A point to stress about the organic laws is that in no circumstances are they to be delegated to other authorities, since the areas which they encompass are considered to be of special national interest.

4.7.1.2 *Ordinary laws (*leyes ordinarias*)*
These constitute the bulk of laws passed by ordinary procedure either at the national or regional level. At the national level they must be approved by both Houses of Parliament before they can be put on the statute book. At both levels, bills of ordinary laws must normally be examined in both plenary session and committee; in the final vote, a simple majority of both Houses of Parliament is required before such bills become law.

Since these are the most common type of law, it is these that will be used in 4.7.3 below to examine some of the details of the legislative process.

4.7.1.3 *Basic laws (*leyes de base*)*
These are of the same rank as ordinary laws. By means of such laws the *Cortes* can delegate legislative power to the government in specific fields. According to Article 82 of the Constitution, such laws must spell out in broad terms the purpose and scope of the legislation to be delegated as well as the principles and criteria which must govern them. Such delegation must be granted to the government in an express manner, identifying concrete items and specifying the time-scale of the process; in fact once the government has published its legislation on the subject, its jurisdiction expires. The government is not permitted to subdelegate this power to any other bodies.

4.7.1.4 *Framework laws (*leyes marco*)*
These laws are of similar rank to ordinary laws. As a kind of basic law they outline the objectives and principles underlining legislation on matters which the state is willing to delegate or transfer to the autonomous communities (see 7.7.3.1).

4.7.1.5 *Basic legislation (*legislación básica*)*
Basic legislation is comparable to the framework laws and refers to areas of competence shared between the state and the autonomous communities (see 7.7.2).

4.7.1.6 *Royal decree-laws (*reales decretos-leyes*)*
According to Article 86 of the Constitution, as we have already seen in 4.6.3.1, the government is empowered, 'in situations of extraordinary and urgent necessity', to issue temporary legislative provisions (*disposiciones legislativas provisionales*) which take the form of royal decree-laws sometimes known simply as decree-laws. These must not refer to the basic institutions of the state, the rights, duties and liberties of citizens referred to in Section I of the Constitution (see 2.4), the political system of the

autonomous communities or the provisions of electoral law. Such decrees, which are applicable across the whole nation, must be submitted to the Congress for ratification within thirty days. The full House or the standing committee must debate the decree and decide whether to process it as a law using the emergency procedure referred to in 4.5.3. Between 1979 and 1982 the total number of decree-laws issued was seventy, of which only one was repealed and of which thirty-three were processed as ordinary laws.

4.7.1.7 *Legislative decrees* (decretos legislativos)
This is legislation issued by the government when exercising delegated law-making authority following authorisation in the basic laws referred to in 4.7.1.3. Such decrees have the force of law and they are known as *normas con rango de ley*.

4.7.1.8 *Royal decrees* (reales decretos)
Within the hierarchy of regulations emanating from national or regional government departments, these are of the highest rank. Because of the importance attaching to them they must be signed by the minister of the presidency and countersigned by the king. Such royal decrees, not to be confused with royal decree-laws, were used frequently in the early 1980s to transfer or delegate very specific powers to the autonomous communities following the previous approval of framework laws.

4.7.1.9 *Other regulations*
As can be seen in Figure 4.6, after the royal decrees the highest-ranking regulations are the orders (*órdenes*) emanating from the delegated committees of the government (see 5.6). These are followed by the ministerial orders (*órdenes ministeriales*) issued by the ministries in Madrid, which are of equal rank to the resolutions (*resoluciones*) of regional ministries. At the lower end of the hierarchy are the circulars (*circulares*) and instructions (*instrucciones*), issued by either national or regional ministries.

4.7.2   *Legislative initiative*
Several bodies have the authority to initiate legislation: the government, the Congress, the Senate and the assemblies of the autonomous communities. If the government takes the initiative or if a regional assembly proposes that the former should adopt a particular bill, the draft law is known as a *proyecto de ley*. If the initiative, however, comes from either of the Houses of Parliament or if the regional assembly submits a draft law direct to the Congress, it is known as a *proposición de ley*. In the case of *proyectos de ley* submitted to the Congress by the government, they must previously have been approved by the council of ministers (see 5.5.3.1) and

must be accompanied by a rationale (*exposición de motivos*) and all background material relating to the subject in question. With respect to *proposiciones de ley* emanating from a regional assembly, the latter may designate a maximum of three of its members to defend the bill in Parliament. In the case of *proyectos de ley* it is considered to have delegated this task to the government, which has 'adopted' the bill.

In addition to these sources of legislation, Article 87 of the Constitution permits recourse to a direct popular initiative, providing that it is backed up by 500,000 signatures and an appropriate rationale. However, such draft laws, known as *proposiciones de ley*, cannot refer to tax affairs, international affairs, the prerogative of pardon or indeed any matters that would normally be dealt with by an organic law (see 4.7.1.1).

4.7.3 Legislative process

4.7.3.1 Draft laws (proyectos de ley)
As can be seen in Figure 4.8, the first political decision to enact legislation of this kind is taken in the council of ministers. A preliminary draft law (*anteproyecto de ley*) is then prepared by the relevant minister or ministers concerned with technical help from the appropriate departments before being submitted for approval by the council of ministers. The bill is then submitted to the presiding council of the Congress and is simultaneously published in the *Boletín Oficial de las Cortes, Sección del Congreso*. Deputies are allowed fifteen days from publication to present amendments either to the whole bill or to particular clauses. The committee concerned elects a working party (*ponencia*) which on the basis of any amendments draws up a report (*dictamen*) containing recommendations for improving the text. This modified text is then debated in the committee, article by article. If rejected, the bill is normally sent back to the government for reconsideration and the whole process must then be repeated. If approved, it is passed on to the full Congress for a parliamentary debate in which the bill is first defended by a member of the government. At this stage a text that is considered obscure or inconsistent may be sent back to the committee for further study.

If approved by the full Congress, the president passes the text on to his counterpart in the Senate where a similar process of scrutiny, amendment and approval is carried out by the appropriate committee and plenary sitting of the Upper House. At the time of receipt, the modified text is published again in the *Boletín Oficial de las Cortes, Sección del Senado*. In the case of the Senate, however, only ten days are allowed for the presentation of amendments and a limitation of two months is imposed for the whole process of approving the bill submitted by the Congress. Once a bill has been approved in the Senate, it is returned to the Congress and its president submits it to the king for final ratification. This must be carried out within fifteen days of its final approval in Parliament. The bill is then promulgated and prepared for publication in the *Boletín Oficial del Estado*.

According to Article 90 of the Constitution, the Senate has the right to apply a veto on the whole law provided that a statement of reasons is submitted with it or it can simply table amendments to it. A veto must be approved by an overall majority of the Senate. The Congress is empowered to overturn the veto by approving its initial text by an overall majority or, after a period of two months has expired, by a simple majority. Amendments can be accepted or rejected straight away by a simple majority. The two-month period required for Senate approval of bills is reduced to twenty days for legislation which has been declared urgent by either the government or the Congress.

From the foregoing it can be clearly seen that the Lower House of the Spanish Parliament takes precedence over the Senate. Using its veto the latter can delay a bill for twenty days but, providing that there has been no change in the voting intentions of the deputies since their approval of the original text, there is little chance that the bill will not become law. Apart from its limited capacity to delay the approval of legislation, the most that the Senate can hope for is that the Congress will accept some of its amendments. In these circumstances, it is not surprising that between 1982 and 1986 a frustrated opposition preferred to obstruct government legislation by referring laws or clauses of laws to the constitutional court (see 2.5). In practice the latter became an alternative and, in some ways, more effective Upper Chamber.

4.7.3.2 *Draft laws* (proposiciones de ley)

In the case of *proposiciones de ley*, the nearest equivalent to UK private members' bills, only the initial stages of this process are different. In the case of a bill proposed by the Congress, the initiative can be taken by one deputy with the signatures of fourteen other members of the House, or by a parliamentary group with the signature of their spokesman alone (*Reglamento*, Article 126). Following publication the government has a right to decide (i) whether or not to 'take it into consideration', and/or (ii) whether its approval would imply an increase in borrowing or a reduction in budgetary income. If, within thirty days, the government presents no objections to the bill, it is submitted to the full Congress for a special debate to decide whether or not to accept it for parliamentary processing. If the outcome is positive, the bill is passed on to the appropriate committee and processed in the same way as a *proyecto de ley*. The procedure for initiating a bill in the Senate is similar to that of the Congress, except that the initiative must come from a parliamentary group or from twenty-five senators and the detailed text must be accompanied by a rationale. *Proposiciones de ley* issuing from a regional assembly or a popular initiative must first be examined by the presiding council of the Congress

Figure 4.8 *Legislative process for draft laws*

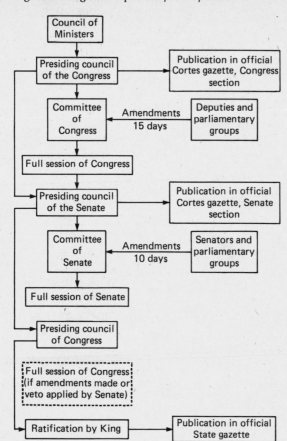

to ensure that all legal requirements have been fulfilled, after which they are submitted for special debate as outlined above.

Although the vast majority of laws start life as *proyectos de ley*, in the first legislature of 1979–82 as many as 206 bills were tabled in the Congress; these included a Basic Law on Employment, the Ombudsman Law, the creation of the University of Castilla–La Mancha and the Modification of the Referendum Law. It should be remembered, however, that *proyectos de ley* have priority over *proposiciones de ley*, which can never be declared priority or emergency bills.

4.8   Parliamentary control

This is examined in Section V of the Constitution and refers basically to the accountability of the government to Parliament. Article 108 of the Constitution makes it clear that the goverment is accountable to the Congress for its actions. The government is obliged to give account of itself or subject itself to parliamentary control in a number of ways including: (i) measures of political control, such as the votes of confidence and censure motions (see 4.6.3.4); and (ii) budgetary and fiscal control, which is ensured by parliamentary scrutiny and approval of the annual state budgets, as well as the activities of the Audit Tribunal (see 9.7.3).

Legislative control is also exercised through Congress's right to approve or reject decree-laws, including those referring to states of alarm, exception and siege (see 4.6.3). To a large extent these can be regarded as means of extraordinary control since they are only used on rare occasions. Day-to-day control over the government is exercised through a series of parliamentary rights and conventions, which are itemised in Articles 109 to 111 of the Constitution.

4.8.1   Right to information

Both Houses of Parliament and their Committees have the right to demand, through their presidents, that the government, its departments or any authorities of the state or autonomous communities provide them with any help or information that they may require for the exercise of their duties (Article 109).

4.8.2   Right to governmental presence

Both Houses and their committees can demand that members of the government should appear before them. In theory the prime minister is absolved from this obligation, although in practice recent premiers have appeared quite regularly in the Congress. As a counterweight to this right, the government has the right to attend all sessions of the Houses and their committees, including the right to be heard in them; they may also request that officials from their departments report to them (Article 110).

4.8.3   Right to question

Article 111 of the Constitution grants the Houses of Parliament the right to submit two kinds of question to the government or to any of its individual members, and requires that the standing orders of both Houses shall devote a minimum amount of weekly parliamentary time to them. These are known as *preguntas* and *interpelaciones*. Question time is normally Wednesday afternoons.

4.8.3.1 *Questions* (preguntas)

These must be presented to the presiding council of the House concerned in written form; members must specify if they wish to receive an oral reply, in default of which they will receive a written reply from the member of the government concerned. If an oral reply is specified and if the question is accepted as valid by the appropriate presiding council, it will be included on the agenda of the corresponding plenary session. A maximum period of five minutes is allowed for the defence of and reply to the question. A similar formula applies to questions requiring an oral answer in committee. At the end of any legislative session outstanding questions are dealt with by written answer. In any case, these must always be answered within a period of twenty days unless agreed otherwise by the government or the presiding council.

4.8.3.2 *Questions* (interpelaciones)

These are similar to *preguntas* but may be formulated by parliamentary groups as well as individual members of Parliament. These too must be presented in written form to the appropriate presiding council and in this case they must refer to the reasons for or intentions underlying the conduct of either the council of ministers or any ministerial departments in matters of general policy. *Interpelaciones* are often presented in the form of a motion which is then debated in the full House concerned. At the end of any legislative period, any outstanding questions are dealt with as if they were questions requiring a written answer. These are a device commonly used by parliamentarians to attract publicity either to themselves or to a particular cause.

4.9   Conclusion

After a lapse of four decades parliamentary life in Spain has, over the last ten years or so, been steadily revitalised. Following the first democratic elections for forty years in 1977, the reformed *Cortes*, with some old but many more new faces, slowly began to acquire the long-lost habits of parliamentary democracy. By the end of 1978 they had completed the mammoth task of drawing up Spain's first democratic Constitution for nearly half a century. Subsequently, they undertook the even more daunting task of fleshing out the skeletal provisions of the Constitution, enacting hundreds of organic, ordinary and other laws with the objective of imbuing all the political, economic and other institutions of public life with the spirit and practices of democracy. Not the least arduous of these tasks has been the ongoing challenge of transforming the very nature of this once strongly centralised state into one composed of self-governing regions, each endowed with its own legislature.

To the average Spanish citizen Parliament may still seem a very remote institution, far removed from his everyday concerns. However, every four years at least, he now knows that he has the power to change the composition of that Parliament; for example, he was able to see a peaceful handover of power from Right to Left in 1982 that must have gone some way to dispelling some of the traditional Spanish scepticism towards official institutions.

5   Central government

Since it is not easy to draw a line between 'government' and 'administration', logically these should be dealt with in one chapter. However, for reasons of presentation and balance, it has been thought preferable to make a break, however artificial, between the two. Thus, Chapter 5 will deal with the executive or decision-making tier, including the prime minister, the ministers and the council of ministers, while Chapter 6 will examine the administrative levels, including the ministerial departments and the various autonomous bodies dependent on them. It is accepted, however, that there are risks in any neat form of categorisation and that, particularly in Spain where the term 'central administration of the state' is commonly used to embrace all the above institutions, there will inevitably be some measure of overlap between the two. This is especially so in the case of the ministers who belong to the executive but head large departments of public administration. Thus Chapters 5 and 6 should be regarded as a continuum.

In the course of Chapters 5 to 8 it will also become apparent that in present-day Spain government and administration operate at four levels. These four tiers of authority are: (i) central; (ii) regional (relating to the autonomous communities); (iii) provincial; and (iv) municipal (see Figure 5.1). It should be stressed that, while the central and regional authorities enjoy basic legislative and decision-making power, the provincial and municipal institutions, although exercising authority over minor matters, in general tend simply to administer policies agreed at higher levels.

5.1   Government under Franco

The separation of powers was acknowledged theoretically in the more progressive constitutions of nineteenth-century Spain and clearly accepted in the Republican Constitution of 1931. Franco, however, made no pretence of following this tradition, affirming that his preference was not for the separation of powers but their unity. In practice, of course, this meant that the legislature and the judiciary played subordinate roles, becoming in effect simply instruments of an all-powerful executive which was accountable to no body outside itself – in reality the executive was a tool in the hands of one man.

The approval of the 1967 Organic Law of the State (see 3.2.1.2) appeared to be diffusing to some extent this massive concentration of power, but in fact at any time he wished Franco was able to fall back on reserve powers, dating back to 1938, which allowed him to govern by decree without reference to the council of ministers. Even if the institutions had been granted more freedom of action under this Organic Law, the executive remained dominant. Moreover, power remained rigidly centralised in Madrid. Only with the promulgation of the Constitution of 1978 was the traditional division of powers between the three main branches of central authority restored, as Spain became, as we have seen, a 'social and democratic state based on the rule of law' (Article 2).

5.2   Prime minister (*presidente del gobierno*)

5.2.1   Method of appointment

According to Article 99 of the Constitution, after elections to the Congress of deputies, the king, following consultations with representatives of the main political groups in Parliament, will propose a candidate for the premiership, indicating his choice to Parliament through the president of the Congress. The candidate must then present his programme to the Congress and attempt to secure the support of the House by means of a vote of investiture (*voto de investidura*).

If this support is granted by the required overall majority, the king will then name the candidate prime minister; if this is not achieved, there will be a second ballot, forty-eight hours later, when a simple majority will suffice.

If this procedure fails to produce a premier, the king must propose other candidates until one eventually gains the confidence of the House. If no candidate has succeeded within two months of the first vote, the king is obliged to dissolve both Houses of Parliament and convene new elections with the backing of the President of the Congress. Naturally, all efforts would normally be made to avoid the necessity of having recourse to a second round of elections and, at least up to 1986, there had been no need for this procedure to be enacted.

5.2.2   Method of dismissal

A prime minister will normally leave office in one of the following three circumstances: (i) if the Congress denies him its support in a vote of confidence (Article 114.1, and see 4.6.3.4); (ii) if the Congress approves a motion of censure against him (Article 114.2, and see 4.6.3.4); and (iii) a

Figure 5.1 *Tiers of government and administration*

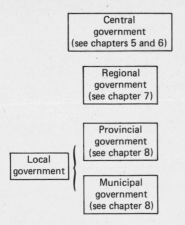

prime minister must resign if he and his party or coalition is defeated in the general elections, in these circumstances he will stay in office until the new premier-designate has been sworn in as prime minister. Clearly a head of government may resign of his own accord for reasons of his own choosing – such was the case of Adolfo Suárez in January 1981. This eventuality, and indeed the possible death of a premier while in office, is provided for in Article 101. The latter states that in both cases the king, after consultations with the various political groups represented in Parliament, must propose another candidate who, as stated in Article 99.2, is required to present his programme to the Congress and seek a vote of investiture. In the case of death, a deputy prime minister or senior minister will automatically assume the premiership until the above procedure has been followed. It should be stressed that resignation or death does not automatically need to involve new elections, although a new premier may feel that, as well as the confidence of Parliament, he requires a popular mandate.

It is interesting to note that it was during the investiture of Calvo Sotelo, following the resignation of Suárez, that the attempted *coup* of 23 February 1981 took place. At the time it was doubtful whether the new premier-designate would secure an overall majority because of defections from the ruling UCD party; after the *coup* he was given quite a convincing overall majority, no doubt because Parliament was determined to stabilise the severely threatened democratic system.

It should also be stressed that if a prime minister leaves office for whatever reason, his government, i.e. his council of ministers, must also resign with him. However, to ensure continuity, the government stays on in a caretaker capacity until a new government has been installed. Politically a vacuum may exist but constitutionally it may not.

5.2.3   Role

Just as the king is the symbol and highest representative of the state, so the prime minister, according to the 1957 Law on the Organisation of the Administration (*Ley de Régimen Jurídico de la Administración*/LJRA) is the symbol and highest representative of the government. Unlike the king, he is responsible for his actions, as well as those of the whole government. According to Article 98 of the Constitution 'the head of government directs the activities of the government and coordinates the functions of the other members of the government . . . '. This means that he plays the major political role in the preparation, promotion and execution of the government's programme. He also performs the key administrative role, in the co-ordination of the work of the various ministries.

5.2.4   Powers

Expressed in more concrete terms, the most important powers and functions of the Spanish premier are as follows:

(i)   He can propose the appointment and dismissal of his ministers (Article 100). He also has a similar right to recommend appointment to hundreds of junior government and civil service posts, as well as the civil governors in each province and the government delegates to the autonomous communities. Moreover, in practice, as the leader of the dominant party in Parliament, he has the right to select the persons to be elected presidents of the Congress and the Senate. In addition, he proposes the nomination of the heads of important state institutions like the council of state (see 5.7) and the National Institute for Industry (see 9.2).

It should be stressed that technically it is the king in all these cases who appoints and the prime minister who nominates candidates for appointment. In reality, of course, the real decision-making power rests with the premier, not the king.

(ii)   He can propose the dissolution of the Congress, Senate or the Joint *Cortes* (Article 115.1).

(iii)   He can endorse the acts of the king, for which he, the premier, is ultimately responsible (Article 64.1).

(iv)   He can request that the king should preside over the council of ministers (Article 62g). It should be noted that the king does not have the right to do so whenever he thinks fit.

(v)   He can propose the convening of a referendum on an issue of overriding national importance (Article 92.2).

(vi)   He can request a vote of confidence from the Congress (Article 112).

5.2.5   *Prime minister's office* (presidencia del gobierno)

In addition to all his other functions, the premier is in nominal charge of the prime minister's office which over the years grew from a small department with limited and specific responsibilities into a large ministry embracing a wide range of affairs. This office is divided into two sections, one headed by the deputy prime minister and the other by the minister of the presidency (see 5.3). This office is not to be confused with the group of personal advisers and assistants who constitute the *gabinete del presidente*.

5.2.6 Limitations to powers

The powers of the prime minister are limited either by the need to consult with the council of ministers or the need to seek the authorisation of the Congress. Indeed, Article 98 makes it clear that the prime minister directs the government's actions and co-ordinates the functions of his ministers 'without prejudice to the powers and direct responsibility of the latter in the running of their own departments . . . '

5.2.7 Accountability

When we examine the accountability of the premier, it is hard to escape the conclusion that he becomes almost synonymous with the government. One example of this is that he himself, rather than the government, is the object of a motion of censure and in this motion an alternative head of government must be named (see 4.6.3.4). Like his ministers, he is politically accountable to the Congress and criminally responsible to the courts. With regard to the latter, if the crime involves treason or any offence against the security of the state, he is answerable to Congress, four-fifths of which must propose an accusation, which must in turn be approved by an overall majority. This, of course, is another way in which the prime minister may leave office, i.e. as a result of being dismissed or being persuaded to resign. In this case the Constitution does not actually state that the premier would be forced to leave office, but one can safely assume that this would be the case. It would also presumably be the consequence of any successful court case against the head of government involving criminal proceedings.

5.3 Deputy prime minister (*vicepresidente del gobierno*)

Article 98.2 envisages the possible existence of one or more deputy prime ministers. Although neither the Constitution nor other legislation says so, one can assume that he is appointed and dismissed in the same way as other ministers (see 5.4). Again, there are no constitutional guidelines with respect to specific duties and powers, and it would seem that this depends very much on the premier of the day. In fact, in order to fill this constitutional and legal vacuum, the government drafted the Law on the Organisation of the Central Administration of the State (*Ley de Organización de la Administración Central del Estado*/LOAE) which the *Cortes* approved in August 1983. This law spells out what are to be the ministries and their major divisions; of relevance here is Article 3 which outlines the role of the deputy premier. This states that he will assume the functions of the head of government if the latter should die, be ill or absent abroad, and in practice this has already been applied in the case of presidential visits abroad, when the prime minister is never accompanied by his deputy.

Apart from such anticipated functions, the role of the vice-president is still very much a matter for the discretion of the incumbent premier. Under the governments of the UCD (1977–82) the prime minister appointed more than one vice-president, each in charge of a particularly important department, such as defence or economic affairs. Under the PSOE, however, only one deputy has been appointed and he is not responsible for any of the traditional ministries. Rather he has tended to play a co-ordinating role working closely with the prime minister, the minister for parliamentary liaison/cabinet secretary (see 5.5.1 and Figure 6.2), senior ministers and high-ranking members of the party. Prior to the departmental reorganisation of July 1986, the deputy premier was additionally directly in charge of various departments within the former ministry of the presidency (*ministerio de la presidencia*), most of which are now the direct responsibility of the cabinet secretary's office.

5.4   Ministers (*ministros*)

5.4.1   Method of appointment and dismissal

Ministers are appointed and dismissed by the king on the recommendation of the prime minister, who in reality exercises the power to 'hire and fire'. On appointment, like the premier, they must swear loyalty to the Constitution before the king. Government ministers must resign, as we have seen, following the departure of the premier, but will continue in a caretaker capacity until a new government is formed (Article 101.2).

5.4.2   Role

As heads of the large ministries (*ministerios*) the ministers carry immense responsibilities and, within certain limitations, enjoy a good deal of discretion and autonomy. They are ultimately responsible to the prime minister for the efficient running of their departments. They exercise initiatives of both a legislative and executive nature and they manage and inspect all the services within their departments. They are nominally in charge of the departmental inspectorate. They are also responsible for the autonomous bodies (see 6.3) linked to their ministries.

5.4.3 Powers

These can usefully be divided into three categories: those concerned with legislative, executive and judicial matters.

5.4.3.1 Legislative responsibilities

Each minister is ultimately responsible for presenting to the council of ministers the draft laws or draft decree-laws (see 4.7.1) which have been prepared within his department. He is also responsible for exercising rule-making powers (*potestad reglamentaria*) where these are required to implement government policy as reflected in higher laws approved in Parliament. Specifically he may issue ministerial orders (*órdenes ministeriales*) without the approval of the council of ministers.

5.4.3.2 Executive responsibilities

Where the responsibility has not been expressly granted to either the council of ministers or the delegated committees of the government (see 5.6), the ministers have the right to appoint and dismiss other high-ranking civil servants within their departments; they are also responsible for the management of the civil servants and all disciplinary matters relating to staff within their departments. Moreover, they are empowered to sign state contracts related to matters concerning their ministries. In addition they are required to draw up a draft budget for their departments as well as to allocate expenditure for departmental matters outside the competence of the council of ministers, making arrangements with the Ministry of Economy and Finance for payment of such amounts.

5.4.3.3 Judicial responsibilities

In the last resort, each minister can be called upon to resolve administrative disputes concerning the work of his department or its dependencies, provided that neither a lower nor higher authority is competent to deal with them. He is also empowered to resolve conflicts within his department related to the distribution of responsibilities between its different branches.

5.4.4 Limitations to powers

All ministers with departmental responsibilities can be called to account for or to explain their policies or actions before one or both of the Houses of Parliament or before one of the parliamentary committees linked to either House. In a general sense, of course, the ministers are always individually responsible for their actions to the council of ministers, even for those which require the signature of the king (Article 98.2). At meetings of the council of ministers, of course, it usually soon becomes clear if an individual minister is failing to implement the policies agreed at cabinet level, in which case he may be subject, without appeal, to dismissal.

5.4.5   Accountability

Like the prime minister, the ministers may be held responsible for actions committed against the criminal code, in which case they will be brought before the Criminal Division of the High Court (*Sala de lo Penal del Tribunal Supremo*). If the crime concerns treasonable offences or any other offence against the security of the state, Parliament must take the initiative to prosecute. Such an initiative must have the backing of a quarter of the members of the Congress and the vote to prosecute must receive an overall majority in the House. Although the Constitution and other laws are silent on the subject, it can be safely assumed that in this way they would be dismissed from office. It is interesting to note that, according to Article 102.3 of the Constitution, neither the premier nor his ministers can hope to benefit from a royal pardon (*prerogativa real de gracia*) for such offences.

5.4.6   Incompatibility

Article 98.3 of the Constitution requires that government ministers, shall not be able to hold representative posts other than those in Parliament nor will they be permitted to occupy any public post that is not directly related to their governmental office. They are also debarred from indulging in any professional or commercial activity. The aim of such measures is clearly to prevent a re-occurrence of the kind of corruption that was common in the Franco era with senior government ministers occupying important positions in the financial and business world, as well as, on many occasions, more than one post within the system of public administration. The theory of this provision was fleshed out in the December 1983 Law on the Incompatibility of Offices among Senior Civil Servants (*Ley de Incompatibilidades de Altos Cargos*) the preamble of which stresses the need for the law to respect the principle of the separation of functions. In practical terms, the law makes it impossible for a whole range of high ranking personnel, from junior ministers down to the assistant directors of state enterprises, to hold either two paid posts within the civil service or one within the administration and one in certain areas of private enterprise (Articles 2 and 7).

5.5   Council of ministers (*consejo de ministros*)

This is the highest political and executive body in the land, corresponding to the British cabinet. Normally it consists of the prime minister, the deputy prime minister, where appointed, and the ministers, including the cabinet secretary, the *ministro secretario del consejo de ministros* (see Figure 6.2). On rare occasions a secretary of state (see 6.2.3) may be invited to attend. Meetings of the council of ministers are normally chaired by the prime minister, unless the king is present or unless the premier is ill or absent abroad, in which case, as we have seen, his place is taken by his deputy.

5.5.1 Procedure

The council of ministers normally meets once a week in ordinary sessions on Fridays, even during the vacation periods, although extraordinary sessions can be held at any time should the political situation or some emergency require it. Decision-making meetings (*consejos decisorios*) alternate with discussion meetings (*consejos deliberantes*); the former are more technical and specific in character, while the latter tend to have a more political flavour and may cover a wider range of issues. Although no norms are laid down in this respect, it is assumed that votes are taken at the *consejos decisorios*, but not at the *consejos deliberantes* for which it is not even usual to draw up an agenda.

Preparation of the cabinet meetings is in the hands of the committee of under-secretaries (*comisión de subsecretarios*) chaired by the cabinet secretary. This vitally important committee consists not only of under-secretaries but secretaries of state and general secretaries (see 6.2). It meets on Thursdays and prepares the agenda for the fortnightly *consejos decisorios*. Nothing is allowed through to the council of ministers without passing first through this committee. The latter, in fact, has the power to approve certain minor matters without reference to the cabinet, matters which are then 'nodded through' the council of ministers; such items appear under what is known as the green index (*índice verde*). More important items, including draft laws and decree-laws are classified as red index (*índice rojo*) and must be referred to the council of ministers for discussion. The committee of under-secretaries may also refer proposals back to their source, usually the directorate general of some ministry (see 6.2.6), for further study before it is re-submitted for its approval.

In Franco's time, certain matters like foreign affairs and delicate matters of state security were excluded from the agenda. However, because of the highly centralised nature of the state, agendas were still long, since many detailed matters, for example, the appointment of local political and administrative figures and the approval of certain educational programmes, were dealt with in-cabinet. To some extent this overloading has persisted in the post-Franco era. However, as powers are progressively devolved to the new regional authorities, this burden should be gradually lightened.

5.5.2   General responsibilities

The general responsibilities of the council of ministers are those outlined in Article 97, which refers to the role of the government. This article states that 'the government directs internal and foreigy policy, the civil and military administration and the defence of the state. It exercises the executive function and rule-making powers . . . '. Like the prime minister, it has both a political, i.e. policy-making, and an administrative role. In the latter capacity it controls the activity of the various branches of public administration and ensures that it is following agreed guidelines. It should also be stressed that, in addition to its control over the civil administration, it has ultimate control over military affairs and is responsible for national security and defence.

A further point worth making is that, since the government must endorse the acts of the king, it exercises the rights, or at least participates in the rights, granted to the king in the Constitution (Articles 56.64 and 65, for example). However, the government has no powers relative to the dismissal of the prime minister nor to the dissolution of the *Cortes*. Above all it should be emphasised that it is ultimately accountable, in all its decisions and actions, to Parliament.

5.5.3   Specific responsibilities

These fall into the following four categories: legislative, executive, judicial and defence. Each will now be examined separately.

5.5.3.1   Legislative
It may seem a paradox that a basically executive body may exercise some legislative power under a constitutional system that recognises the separation of powers. However, in most liberal democracies it is common for Parliament to grant the Executive the opportunity to share in the legislative process. The areas in which the cabinet participates in the legislative process, i.e. through draft laws, decree-laws and legislative decrees, have already been examined (see 4.7.2).

5.5.3.2   Executive
The council's major function is to formulate and approve national policy over the whole area represented by the various ministries; it takes the initiative in preparing draft laws which are normally drawn up in particular departments or joint departmental committees prior to being approved by the cabinet and then being submitted to the *Cortes*.

Under its rule-making power (*potestad reglamentaria*) the council of ministers proposes to the head of state a series of regulations or minor laws designed to implement laws already approved by Parliament.

The cabinet, prior to submission to the king, considers the proposals of the head of government for the appointment and dismissal of high-ranking civil and other public servants; these include ambassadors, under-secretaries of state, director generals, civil governors, government delegates to the autonomous communities, captain-generals of the army and so on.

It is required to establish and disband the delegated committees of the government (see 5.6) which are permanently constituted as well as certain other inter-ministerial committees set up on an *ad hoc* basis.

The council must ensure the smooth running of all public services, inter-vening with emergency measures where necessary.

It also has the right to call elections at regional and local although not at national level.

The cabinet enjoys certain executive rights related to the autonomous communities:

(i)   It names and dismisses the government delegates who direct state administration within their respective regions (see 6.5.2).
(ii)   It has the right to oblige the autonomous communities to carry out their responsibilities according to the Constitution.
(iii)   It also has the right to bring a regional authority before the constitutional court if the latter adopts regulations which contravene the Constitution, and has the power to suspend such regulations.

5.5.3.3 *Judicial*
The council of ministers can nominate a candidate to be appointed attorney-general of the state (*fiscal general del estado*) as well as two members of the constitutional court (see 2.5).

The council is also expected to resolve certain appeals that are brought before it involving disputes between ministries where these cannot be solved by other competent authorities.

5.5.3.4 *Defence and security*
Article 97 of the Constitution makes it clear that the government, through the council of ministers, is responsible for the control of military affairs and for the defence of the state. This is clearly a role which it shares with the head of state who, as we have seen, is the Commander-in-Chief of the Armed Forces (see 3.4.1). Article 104 also assigns to the council of ministers responsibility for the security and police forces of the country, whose role is 'to protect the free exercise of rights and liberties and to guarantee public security'.

5.6   Delegated committees of the government (*comisiones delegadas del gobierno*)

These are inter-departmental committees composed of the ministers con-cerned and established with the approval of the council of ministers. They are the equivalent of UK cabinet committees. The Royal Decree of December 1981 reduced their number to five and specified the ministries to be represented on each one.

5.6.1   Foreign affairs committee (comisión de asuntos exteriores)

Members: The minister and secretary of state for foreign affairs plus members who may be co-opted depending on the area of policy under discussion.

5.6.2   State security committee (comisión para la seguridad del estado)

Members: The ministers of foreign affairs, justice, defence, interior and the director general of state security.

5.6.3   Economic affairs committee (comisión de asuntos económicos)

Members: The ministers of economy and finance, public works, labour, industry, agriculture, transport and tourism and the under-secretary of state for the economy.

5.6.4   Autonomy policy committes (comisión de política autonómica)

Members: The ministers of justice, economy and finance, public administration (and his deputy) and the secretary of state for the autonomous communities.

5.6.5   Committee for educational, cultural and scientific policy (comisión para política educativa, cultural y científica)

Members: The ministers of education and science, culture, the secretary of state for the universities and research, and any other ministers who may be co-opted, depending on the policy area under discussion.

These committees, which meet when required (normally on Wednesday mornings) are chaired either by the prime minister or by the deputy premier who is automatically a member of all these committees. The premier may invite other members of the government to meetings of the committees, as well as secretaries of state and other high-ranking civil servants. The cabinet secretary (see 5.5) acts as secretary for all meetings of these committees, for which minutes must be kept.

The main function of these delegated committees, outlined in the Law on the Organisation of State Administration, is to provide a forum for specialists within the government to come together to discuss problems relating to areas of interdepartmental interest and enable co-ordination between ministries to take place. In fact these specialised bodies may exercise decision-making powers in matters which do not need to be approved at the level of the council of ministers. Thus, although they often act in an advisory capacity, they are technically important components of the executive authority.

5.7   Council of state (*consejo de estado*)

Since it is referred to in the Constitution (Article 107), this advisory body has constitutional status. Indeed, it constitutes the highest consultative organ of the government. It has no executive functions. Its president is appointed by the council of ministers, although he is not expected to be a political appointment; he is usually a jurist of recognised experience and prestige. Apart from the president and a general secretary, the council of state includes various categories of members (*consejeros*):

5.7.1   Permanent members

This group includes high-ranking representatives of the autonomous communities, the royal academies, the legal, economic and social disciplines of university faculties, the armed forces and the civil service. Such members are appointed by decree for an indefinite period and usually head a department of the council.

5.7.2   Ex-officio members

This group includes such high-ranking national figures as the director of the Spanish Royal Academy, the presidents of the Royal Academies of Moral and Political Sciences and of Jurisprudence and Legislation, the attorney-general of the state, the president of the Joint Chiefs of Staff and the director of the Centre for Constitutional Studies.

5.7.3   Elected members

The ten elected members are appointed by decree for a period of four years among persons who have held various specific offices; these offices include parliamentary deputies or senators, members of the constitutional court, the ombudsman, the presidents or ministers of autonomous communities, ambassadors, mayors of provincial capitals and presidents of provincial councils.

The council functions either in plenary session (*pleno*) or through its standing committee (*comisión permanente*). This consists of the permanent members, plus the president and the general secretary of the council. The council also functions through sections headed by the permanent members and specialising in specific areas of concern. These departments prepare material for deliberation by both the standing committee and the full council.

The basic function of the council is to advise the government and the autonomous communities on a wide range of administrative and legal matters where doubts, queries or potential conflicts between organisations may exist in order to pre-empt litigation at a later stage. The full list of areas in which the council has competence is given in the Law on the Council of State (*Ley del Consejo de Estado*) of 22 April 1980.

5.8   Other advisory bodies

While the council of state is the highest government advisory body, other important institutions exist to provide an advisory service for the administration:

5.8.1   *Directorate general for litigation* (dirección general de lo contencioso)

This is the highest consultative body for the central administration, that is, for ministerial departments (see 9.7.2).

5.8.2   *Legal consultancy departments* (asesorías jurídicas)

The ministries, in addition to being able to seek advice from the above directorate, each have at their disposal the services of a legal consultancy service within the ministry concerned.

5.8.3   *State lawyers' offices* (abogacías del estado)

In addition there is a state lawyers' office in each province of the country. Such offices are composed of state lawyers whose duty is to provide advice verbally or in written form for the heads of the provincial offices of the Ministry of Economy and Finance, civil governors and other officers working for the delegated branches of public administration (see 6.5).

5.9   Conclusion

In Franco's time not only was there no separation of powers between the legislature, the executive and the judiciary, but until June 1973, when Admiral Luis Carrero Blanco was appointed prime minister, there was no separation between the functions of head of state and head of government, which were both exercised by the dictator. Between June 1973 and Franco's death in November 1975, the role of head of state was clearly predominant over that of head of government. Now, however, as we have seen in the previous chapters, the roles are reversed: the titular head of state is a symbolic figure with no real power, while authentic political authority lies in the hands of the head of government or prime minister. However, because of the restoration of the concept of the separation of powers, neither the prime minister himself nor the government has complete freedom of action, but are subject to both parliamentary and judicial control and are accountable for their actions. Moreover, of course, in their manner of coming to office the prime minister and his ministers differ considerably from their predecessors of the dictatorship: instead of simply being appointed by the head of state, they must first belong to a political grouping that has won a popular mandate in general elections and the premier must have secured the confidence of the Congress of Deputies in a vote of investiture (see 4.6.3.4). It is possible, in fact, for a prime minister to appoint his ministers from outside the *Cortes*, but in practice since 1977 the vast majority of them have been previously elected deputies to the Congress. The regular presence of the prime minister and his ministers in Parliament symbolises their ultimate dependence on the legislature to which they are continually accountable.

In recent years the much more open nature of government in Spain has been reflected in the creation of special parliamentary committees such as the Flick Committee and the Toxic Syndrome Committee set up to investigate the scandal surrounding contaminated cooking oil in May 1981 (see 4.5.4). In another important way too the government is much more open than ever it was under Franco: its accessibility to the media which have escaped from the shackles imposed by the dictator and which play a vital role in the formation of an informed and critical public opinion. In terms of freedom of action, the government may have lost in the transition from an authoritarian to a democratic regime, but in terms of moral authority it has gained enormously.

6 Public administration

The term 'public administration' (*administraciones públicas*) in Spain is used to cover a variety of institutions and services operating at central, regional and local level, as can be seen in Figure 6.1. Since the departmental reorganisation of July 1986, the co-ordination and overall control of this vast bureaucracy has been the responsibility of the Ministry of Public Administration (*Ministerio para las Administraciones Públicas*).

This particular chapter is organically linked, as we have seen, to the previous chapter on central government and is primarily concerned with examining central public administration. The regional and local authorities are dealt with respectively in Chapters 7 and 8. This chapter examines the structure and functions of the ministerial departments and the numerous autonomous administrative bodies which are dependent on these ministries. However, autonomous commercial bodies, which are linked to certain departments, are seen as forming part of 'public sector enterprises' and they are thus dealt with in Chapter 9. The social security institutions which constitute a large operation run by the state are an important part of public administration and they are therefore considered in this chapter. Finally, although recent years have seen the transfer of many powers and functions from central administration to the autonomous communities, reference is made to the institutional structure through which central government is administered at a local level through the system of delegated administration (*administración periférica*).

6.1 Background

Spain has a long tradition of strong control from the centre dating back to the beginning of the nineteenth century when the foundations of the modern system of administration were laid. Even under the Second Republic, which granted autonomy to Catalonia and, belatedly, to the Basque Country, the basic structure was barely modified. Indeed, while Franco's system of government differed radically from that of the republicans, the system of administration had many features in common. One of these features was the delegation of central administration to provincial

Figure 6.1. *Public administration in Spain*

Central administration, including delegated administration
Regional and local authorities
Autonomous administrative bodies
Social security institutions

outposts which, as we shall see in 6.5, has even now survived in some form. The traditional tendency towards centralism was also reflected in the establishment of autonomous administrative bodies based in Madrid. These, together with the various social security institutions, have until relatively recently been run as part of central public administration.

However, two tensions have emerged since 1975. On the one hand there is clearly a need to rationalise the structure in order to improve control and co-ordination; on the other, the regions have claimed a greater say in the running of their own affairs (see Chapter 7), hence the transfer of the functions of some of these bodies to the domain of the autonomous communities. Clearly the position is no longer static but nevertheless it is important to appreciate the existing role and functions of these different institutions.

6.2   Ministries (*ministerios*)

The selection and denomination of the ministries are clearly important in that they reflect the priorities and emphases attached by a particular government, and indeed by a given society, to areas of economic, social, political and cultural concern. The list that follows in Figure 6.2 refers to ministerial departments established by the government of Felipe González in 1986.

6.2.1   Internal structure

The basic structure of the ministries, at least up to very recent years, and the system of public administration were established at the beginning of the nineteenth century when the Napoleonic model of the state was imported into Spain. Though certain modifications were made towards the end of the century, basically the system remained unchanged until the 1980s, when the governments of Adolfo Suárez and Felipe González (particularly the latter), set about reforming government administration. Apart from the rearrangement of ministries and indeed the reduction of their number, the most important change introduced by the first government of Felipe González, at least as far as the top echelons of power were concerned, was to introduce in certain departments secretaries of state and general secretaries.

Figure 6.2. *Ministerial departments in Spain (1986)*

Ministry of	Ministerio de
Foreign Affairs	*Asuntos Exteriores*
Justice	*Justicia*
Defence	*Defensa*
Economy and Finance	*Economía y Hacienda*
Home Affairs	*Interior*
Public Works and Town Planning	*Obras Públicas y Urbanismo* (MOPU)
Education and Science	*Educación y Ciencia*
Labour and Social Security	*Trabajo y Seguridad Social*
Industry and Energy	*Industria y Energía*
Agriculture, Fisheries and Food	*Agricultura, Pesca y Alimentación*
Public Administration[a]	*Administraciones públicas*
Transport, Tourism and Communications	*Transporte, Turismo y Comunicaciones*
Culture	*Cultura*
Health and Consumer Affairs	*Sanidad y Consumo*
Parliamentary Liaison/Government Secretariat[b]	*Relaciones con las Cortes y Secretaría del Gobierno*

[a] This 'superministry', responsible for the co-ordination of all levels of public administration, was created as recently as July 1986 following Felipe González's second electoral victory. It incorporates the former Ministry of Territorial Administration (*Ministerio de Administración Territorial*) which was responsible for overall co-ordination of regional affairs and the prime minister's office (*presidencia del gobierno*) (see 5.3).
[b] This Ministry was only created in July 1986, having been previously a department of the prime minister's office. In addition to his role as Minister for Parliamentary Liaison, the incumbent also holds the office of Cabinet Secretary in which capacity he is known as *Ministro Secretario del Consejo de Ministros*.

6.2.2   Hierarchy within ministries

Figure 6.3 illustrates the hierarchy that obtains at the apex of each ministry.

As we saw in 5.4, the minister is the head of the department concerned and is responsible to the prime minister and the council of ministers and ultimately to Parliament, for the efficient running of that department. In his task he is aided by a team whose size will vary according to the size of the ministry in question. Only the largest ministries, for example, include a secretary of state (such as Foreign Affairs, Defence and Economy and Finance), while some small departments, such as Justice, have only three director generals and no secretary of state or general secretary. Not all departments by any means are staffed by general secretaries who, like the secretaries of state, are a relatively recent creation (1981). All, however, contain the all-important offices of under-secretary of state and the technical general secretary both of whom can in many ways be regarded as the pivots of the activity of every ministry.

With the exception of the assistant director general, all the above offices

Figure 6.3 *Typical ministerial hierarchy*

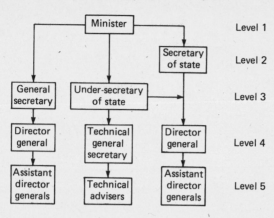

are within the appointment of the council of ministers, though recommendations for appointment or promotion are usually made by officials at one level higher than the one concerned. Thus the under-secretary will often recommend the appointment of staff at the level of director general. Strictly speaking, no official below the rank of minister is expected to resign when the prime minister leaves office, not even the secretary of state; in practice, however, government changes since 1977 have often led to wide-scale reshuffles at all these levels, with the exception of the technical general secretary.

6.2.3 Secretary of state (secretario de estado)

This new ministerial rank, equivalent to a British minister of state or junior minister, was created by the Royal Decree of July 1977. At the time of writing (1986) within eight of the fifteen ministries there are nine secretaries of state, whose permanent nature, title and location has been enshrined in the LOAE. Three of these secretariats are situated within the Ministry of Economy and Finance, in charge respectively of financial affairs, economic planning and commerce. The secretary of state enjoys fewer powers than a minister; unlike the minister of the department, he has no power with regard to the legislative function, he cannot resolve demarcation disputes and he is not involved in the drawing up of the draft budget for the department. However, this figure, situated mid-way between the minister and the under-secretary, does wield a good deal of power and has responsibility for a large and clearly defined area of that ministry's activities. He is directly in charge, for example, of one or more directorates general.

6.2.4   *Under-secretary of state (*subsecretario de estado*)*

The under-secretary has played an important part in Spanish administration since the post was first established by the Royal Decree of 1834. In
a ministry without a secretary of state, and in practice in many cases where
one exists, he is the most powerful figure after the minister. The under-
secretary performs a dual function: on the one hand, he is directly responsible under the minister for the administration of the whole or a large part
of the ministry; on the other, he exercises an important role of communication between the different divisions of the department as well as with
other departments and any other bodies that might be related to his
ministry. Moreover, he is in charge of all the staff within the department
and, where appropriate, it is his responsibility to resolve all matters related
to staffing. In addition he has the authority to inspect all the centres and
dependencies connected to the ministries concerned, including autonomous bodies.

One of the most important functions of the under-secretary is to attend
the weekly Monday meetings of the committee of under-secretaries
(*comisión de subsecretarios*), to approve certain measures which fall
within its competence and to draw up the agenda for the meetings of the
council of ministers, in consultation with the cabinet secretary (see 5.5.1).

6.2.5   *General secretary (*secretario general*)*

As we have seen, the figure of the general secretary was only created
recently and has consequently not had much time to establish itself. In
January 1986 there were nine such posts, situated in seven ministries, three
of these being located in the Ministry of Economy and Finance. Like the
ranks already mentioned, these have been officially 'institutionalised' by
the LOAE. In theory, the general secretaries have the same rank as the
under-secretaries, but partly because of their lack of tradition and partly
due to the under-secretary's special responsibilities within the committee
of under-secretaries, they do not, in practice, enjoy the same prestige.
Apart from not attending the meetings of the under-secretaries, the general
secretaries have the same powers and responsibilities as the latter.

6.2.6   *Director general (*director general*)*

In accordance with the need of modern administration to divide and
delegate labour, departmental divisions or sections headed by director
generals have been established. Thus the director general is responsible,
under the minister and under-secretaries or general secretaries, for a
specific area of departmental work. All ministries contain several directorates general but, since their number and the internal organisation of any

one department fall within the discretion of the minister in consultation with his subordinates, there is no reference to them in the LOAE. The specific responsibilities of the director general include: directing the services and resolving any problems within his section; and monitoring the activities of all the bodies dependent on his section and providing the minister with an annual report on the progress, expenditure and revenue of his section. In addition, like the under-secretaries, they may dictate circulars and instructions concerning the internal organisation of the bodies and services dependent on their section. The director general is normally assisted in his duties by one or more assistant director generals (*subdirectores generales*). In line with the general expansion in recent years of government administration, these particular appointments have tended to proliferate.

6.2.7   *Technical general secretary* (secretario general técnico)

The office of the technical general secretary was created in 1952. Unlike the above-mentioned officials, this figure is likely to be appointed more for his professional or administrative expertise than for his political leanings and is thus more likely than many of his colleagues to survive a change of government. He is, nevertheless, still appointed, on the recommendation of the minister concerned, by the council of ministers. In spite of being technically, and certainly financially, on a lower level than the under-secretaries and the general secretaries, his particular function and the prestige attaching to his office have always enabled him to maintain a direct line to the minister in his capacity as head of an important team of technical experts, statisticians and researchers, whose task is to provide a continuous advisory service for the whole of the department concerned.

Surprisingly, perhaps, the office of the technical general secretary is not mentioned in the LOAE, but the fact is that not only is the office very well established but every single ministry is endowed with one. The office is, however, institutionalised in the Law on the Organisation of Administration (*Ley de Régimen Jurídico de la Administración*/LRJA) which states that the responsibilities of the technical general secretary include the following: drawing up draft general plans and programmes required within the department; providing technical and administrative assistance (including the compilation of statistics) for the minister when the latter judges such assistance to be vital to the co-ordination of services; recommending reforms designed to improve the services provided by the different bodies within the ministry; and suggesting organisational reforms, paying strict attention to costs and productivity.

It is interesting to note, and a reflection of the influence wielded by the technical general secretary, that, in order to carry out his responsibilities, he is able to insist that director generals and other officials within the ministry supply him with as many reports, data and documents as he may require.

6.2.8   *Minister's private office* (gabinete del ministro)

Each minister, in addition to the technical general secretariat, is assisted by a more personal team of advisers (*asesores*). The latter, unlike those in the secretariat, are appointed directly by the minister concerned and will normally be obliged to resign the moment the minister leaves office. They are nearly always members of the same party as the minister and may well be long-standing confidants. The advisers in the private office may well make proposals along certain political lines which for technical or administrative reasons are rejected because the technical secretariat argues strongly against them. On the whole, in spite of the close relationship between the minister and his personal advisers, in such situations the views of the secretariat are likely to prevail because of the latter's greater experience of the ministry as well as his greater experience in general of administration.

6.2.9   *Anatomy of a ministry: the Ministry of Education and Science*

In order to show how the above officials relate to each other within a particular ministry, in Figure 6.4 the Ministry of Education has been dissected into its component parts.

As can be seen, this Ministry is basically divided into two branches, one of which is headed by the secretary of state for the universities and research, and the other which is directed by the under-secretary; they are responsible for two and six directorates general respectively. The diagram clearly shows how the technical general secretary has a function embracing the whole department and that, unlike the director generals, who are technically equivalent to him in rank, he is directly responsible to the minister to whom he has a direct and regular line. Figure 6.4 also shows the autonomous nature of the minister's private office (*gabinete del ministro*) which is likewise directly responsible to the minister and not subject to the control of the secretary of state or the under-secretary.

6.3   Autonomous administrative bodies (*organismos autónomos administrativos*/OOAA)

These are organisations which operate under the auspices of the various ministries in order to carry out specific administrative responsibilities. They are intended to give greater flexibility in the day-to-day operation of particular functions while overall policy and budgetary control remain

Figure 6.4 *Ministry of Education and Science*

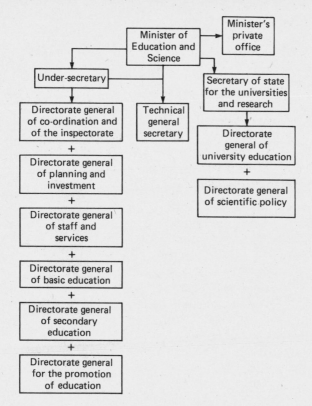

with the ministry responsible. They enjoy a separate legal status and they have their own budget allocation. Their status was regulated by the Law of Autonomous State Bodies (*Ley de Entidades Estatales Autónomas*) of 1958 which, among other things, exempts them from taxes, rates, duties and registration fees. The membership of their boards of management is composed of senior officials from the relevant ministry and people with specific expertise or interests, such as union and employers' representatives who are appointed by the relevant minister. The Budget Law (*Ley de Presupuestos Generales*) of 1977 subsequently made a distinction between autonomous administrative bodies and autonomous commercial, industrial and financial bodies (see 9.1).

The proliferation of autonomous administrative bodies, of which there were 177 in 1985, has given cause for concern. There is also considerable difference between the scale and importance of their operations. Some of them, for example, are entrusted with considerable financial resources, adding to the complexity of overall budgetary control and co-ordination. Thus the National Employment Institute (*Instituto Nacional de Empleo/*

INEM), under the auspices of the Ministry of Labour and Social Security, has the important task of supervising the whole area of unemployment, assisting unemployed workers with retraining and providing unemployment benefits (see 6.4.3 and 11.5.5). The twenty-seven universities also figure as autonomous bodies, a status which is embodied in the University Reform Law (*Ley de Reforma Universitaria*) of 1982.

Some of these bodies have major functions delegated to them by the relevant ministry but at times this appears to cause an overlap of responsibilities. The Ministry of Agriculture, Fisheries and Food, for example, has a number of bodies under its tutelage which carry out major aspects of the Ministry's work. Thus the Institute for Agricultural Reform and Development (*Instituto de Reforma y Desarrollo Agrario*/IRYDA) is involved in a wide variety of activities including the execution of legislation concerning the development and/or expropriation of large estates, the consolidation of small plots, and the modernisation of access roads and drainage schemes. In this case the situation is further complicated by the fact that more than one body may be functioning in a particular area of responsibility, as is the case in the training of agricultural workers with the involvement of the IRYDA, the *Servicio de Extensión Agraria*, the *Instituto de Relaciones Agrarias* (IRA) and the INEM.

At times, even within a single ministry, there may be several directorates general operating in the same areas of activity and similarly able to provide loans and subsidies. In the case of agriculture, for example, in addition to the autonomous bodies described above, we find the *Dirección General de la Producción Agraria* (DGPA) responsible for sectorial restructuring and increasing production; the *Dirección General de Investigación y Capacitación Agrarias* (DGICA) involved in research and training; and the *Dirección General de Industrias Agrarias y Alimentarias* (DGIAA) with responsibility for the food and agricultural industries. Sometimes there may be other ministries which have responsibilities within an area covered by one of these bodies. Thus, while irrigation comes within the ambit of the IRYDA, its plans in this respect are co-ordinated in conjunction with the *Dirección General de Obras Hidráulicas* (DGOH), which is under the Ministry of Public Works and Town Planning. There are also several important agricultural bodies which have commercial and marketing functions and which therefore come under different classifications, as will be seen in 9.1.

On the other hand, other autonomous administrative bodies are involved in more narrowly defined areas of activity. Some are concerned with research in subjects ranging from geology to constitutional studies like the *Instituto Geológico y Minero* and the *Centro de Estudios Constitucionales*. Others operate in the cultural areas, such as museums and art galleries, for which there is the *Patronato Nacional de Museos*, or sport in the case of the *Consejo Superior de Deportes*. Many ministries

Figure 6.5. *Examples of autonomous administrative bodies, 1985*

Ministry responsible	Autonomous body	Function
Ministry of Education and Science	*Instituto Nacional de Asistencia y Promoción del Estudiante* (INAPE)	Student grants
	Consejo Superior de Investigaciones Científicas	Scientific research
	Universidad Nacional de Educación a Distancia (UNED)	Open University
Ministry of Labour and Social Security	*Instituto Nacional de Empleo* (INEM)	Provision for unemployed
	Instituto Español de Emigración (IEE)	Provision for Spanish emigrants
	Fondo de Garantía Salarial	Wage fund to protect workers in firms subject to closure
Ministry of Industry and Energy	*Instituto Geológico y Minero*	Geological and mining research
Ministry of Agriculture, Fisheries and Food	*Instituto Nacional de Investigaciones Agrarias* (INIA)	Agricultural research
	Servicio de Extensión Agraria	Agricultural training
	Instituto de Relaciones Agrarias (IRA)	Improve social conditions and training
	Instituto Nacional de Reforma y Desarrollo Agrario (IRYDA)	Improvement of agricultural structures and production
Head of Government's Office	*Centro de Estudios Constitucionales*	Constitutional and political research
Ministry of Culture	*Patronato Nacional de Museos*	Supervision of museums and galleries
	Consejo Superior de Deportes	Sports' Council

produce a considerable amount of documentation, research papers and books and for this purpose they have their own publications departments (*servicios de publicaciones*), which are likewise run as autonomous bodies.

The number of these bodies is not static and the tendency is to attempt to reduce them wherever possible in order to avoid duplication and to secure economies. This sometimes means the incorporation of their function within a ministerial department. Thus, in 1985 the arbitration and conciliation service, the *Instituto de Mediación, Arbitraje y Conciliación* (IMAC) and its personnel were transferred to a newly created sub-directorate general, the *Subdirección General de Mediación, Arbitraje y Conciliación*, within the Ministry of Labour and Social Security (see 11.4).

Some examples of these bodies and the ministries to which they are responsible are shown in Figure 6.5. The overall financial control and co-ordination of these bodies and other areas of public administration is dealt with in 9.7.

6.4   Health and social security

When referring to social security (*seguridad social*) in terms of administration, this is taken to include the health service as well as social assistance and welfare benefits. Together the institutions involved in these areas constitute a significant element within Spain's economic structure; in 1985 they absorbed some thirty-two per cent of the total budget for central administration, autonomous administrative bodies and social security.

6.4.1   *Background*

In order to appreciate the current structure of the institutions it is important to be aware of the proliferation of organisations which existed under the Franco regime. Before and during this period there was a mixture of public and private-sector provision in which the National Welfare Institute (*Instituto Nacional de Previsión*/INP) dating from 1908 was the main state agency. It was responsible for basic medical care and welfare payments for unemployment and family allowances. It was also responsible for co-ordinating the administration and development of the voluntary agencies. The mutual benefit agencies (*mutualidades laborales*) provided a system of medical care in the case of accidents at work, as well as retirement pensions and invalidity pensions for workers and employers in various sectors of the economy. Alternatively, employers could opt to include their workers in friendly societies (*mutuas patronales de accidentes de trabajo*) which provided for accident and sickness insurance. Given the fact that the official trade unions of the time were largely extensions of state administration, not surprisingly they played important representative and consultative roles within health and social security. Furthermore, in view of the inadequacies of the system, major companies frequently ran their own systems and their 'benevolence' was important in attracting and retaining key personnel.

6.4.2   *Reform*

With the return of democracy to Spain after 1975, it was clear that social security, in its fullest sense, was a major area in need of reform. In recognition of the urgency of this need, a new Ministry of Health and Social Security (*Ministerio de Sanidad y Seguridad Social*) was created in July 1977. Specific reference was made to the need for reform of the system in the consensus political programme agreed in October of the same year by the major parties in the so-called Moncloa Pacts (see 11.5.1). The Constitution expressly referred to the state's responsibility in the provision of social security and health services (Articles 41 and 43) and it also paved the way for the decentralisation of the administration of these functions to , regional authorities (Article 149.17). It was clearly desirable to expand and improve the provision of health and social security facilities in order to bring Spain more in line with other EEC countries. At the same time this extension had to be accompanied by a streamlining of the organisation in order to produce a more coherent and unified system. This means a reduction in the array of institutions involved and a clearer definition of the distinct areas of social security, health and social assistance.

The basic reform was contained in a Royal Decree of November 1978 dealing with official control over social security, health and employment matters. This, while seeking to rationalise the administration of the system and to reduce the number of bodies involved, did not remove the private sector provision; rather it sought to enlist the collaboration of private sector entities, such as the friendly societies (*mutuas patronales*), by establishing a register through which their activities could more properly be controlled.

Since the reform of 1978, there has been a single social security system under the Ministry of Labour and Social Security (*Ministerio de Trabajo y Seguridad Social*) which is responsible for the overall budget and general co-ordination of the various services. However, the Ministry of Health and Consumer Affairs (*Ministerio de Sanidad y Consumo*) is functionally responsible for matters of public health and health education. The 1978 reform established four main institutions: INSS, INSERSO and INSALUD, responsible respectively for social security, social services and health, and a central treasury, the *Tesorería General de la Seguridad Social*, with responsibility for financial control. In addition there are a number of other bodies of an autonomous or semi-autonomous nature involved in various aspects of these services. The institutions are referred to under their functional headings: social security (6.4.3), social services (6.4.4), health services (6.4.5) and central treasury (6.4.6).

6.4.3   Social security institutions

The National Social Security Institution (*Instituto Nacional de la Seguridad Social*/INSS) is a separate legal entity with decision-making capacity concerning the administration of the state's social security provision. It is classified as an administrative entity (*entidad gestora*). Its structure was initially established by the Royal Decree of 30 July 1979. It operates under the auspices of the general secretary of state of the Ministry of Labour and Social Security. It is responsible for administering social security benefits which include old age pensions, invalidity pensions and family allowances. It replaces many of the separate entities which existed

previously, although not all have disappeared entirely. Thus it incorporates, as supporting bodies, some of the former mutual agencies
(*mutualidades laborales*), such as those responsible for mineworkers and
diverse occupations including artists, writers and bullfighters. These
bodies lack separate legal identity and the term *laborales* has been dropped
from their title. However, it is worth noting that separate bodies have been
retained for the administration of social security benefits for civil servants
through the *mutualidad General de Funcionarios Civiles de Estado*
(MUFACE), for local government officers, through the *Mutualidad
Nacional de Previsión de la Administración Local* (MUNPAL), and for
members of the armed forces, through the *Instituto Social de las Fuerzas
Armadas* (ISFAS).

In view of the significant number of people employed in the fishing
industry, a special body, the Institute for the Welfare of Seamen (*Instituto
Social de la Marina* /ISM) was created in 1919 to provide social security
cover for seafarers. It continues to retain its separate identity as an
administrative entity or *Mutualidad del Mar* and, because of the peculiar
nature of the working conditions of those it covers, it acts as an administrative agency not only for social security but also for social services and
health.

An area of social security which has assumed increasing importance in
recent years has been that relating to unemployment both in terms of
benefits and retraining. The National Employment Institute (*Instituto
Nacional de Empleo*/INEM) was created in 1978 as part of the social
security reform. Because of the significance of its functions, it operates as
a major autonomous administrative agency.

The participation of interested parties in the running of the social
security system is specifically referred to in the Constitution (Article
129.1). This takes place through the equal representation of unions,
employers' organisations and the government on both the general council
and the executive committee of the INSS. The former is responsible for
establishing general guidelines and for approving the estimates and the
annual report, while the latter supervises the implementation of policy
decisions.

6.4.4   Social services institutions

The National Institute for Social Services (*Instituto Nacional de Servicios
Sociales*/INSERSO), like the INSS, enjoys separate legal identity and has
the fiscal benefits of an administrative entity. It exists in order to com-
plement the state's provision of social security welfare payments with a
range of social services. Thus, for example, it looks after residential homes
for children and the elderly, and is also responsible for special services and
treatment centres for alcoholics and drug addicts. To the extent that some
facilities are more specialised than others, it works through a number of

other agencies and autonomous bodies which are involved in social assistance (see 6.4.4.1 and 6.4.4.2).

INSERSO has a general council and an executive committee, the structures of which were laid down in the Royal Decree of 17 January 1980. The director general of the Institute is assisted by three directors in charge respectively of the services for the elderly, the handicapped and special services. The Institute's provincial substructure has facilitated the transfer of administrative power on a regional basis. The regional governments, therefore, have been gradually taking over the functions of INSERSO, which in turn is diminishing in significance.

In addition to the major institution described above, there are two autonomous bodies of less significance which nevertheless merit reference:

6.4.4.1 *National Institute for Social Assistance (*Instituto Nacional de la Asistencia Social/*INAS)*

This is an autonomous administrative body under the auspices of the Directorate General of Social Welfare (*Dirección General de Acción Social*) of the Ministry of Labour and Social Security. It owes its origin to the *Instituto Nacional de Auxilio Social* created in 1940, shortly after the Civil War. It is responsible for administering public assistance and supplementary benefits to those in particular need.

6.4.4.2 National Social Assistance Fund (Fondo Nacional de Asistencia Social/*FONAS)*

This is a fund administered by a board of trustees (*patronato*) which acts as an agent in the channelling of subsidies for and investments in nurseries, homes for the handicapped and old people's homes. The services themselves are provided by other state welfare institutions together with private welfare organisations, such as the Red Cross and the Catholic Church's *Caritas* organisation.

6.4.5 *Health service institutions*

The National Health Institute (*Instituto Nacional de la Salud*/INSALUD) is the third administrative entity within the social security system but, unlike the INSS and the INSERSO, this entity comes under the auspices of the Ministry of Health and Consumer Affairs. It is responsible for executing government policy throughout the health service, including hospitals, medical centres and home care. INSALUD works in collaboration with other public and private institutions rather than replacing already existing facilities. However, it has gradually extended its services to increasing numbers of the population, although this is proving costly at a time when most countries are striving to contain public health expenditure and at a time when other social security expenses are increasing. It has the same basic organisational structure as the other two administrative entities, with a general council, an executive committee and a director general. In recent years its importance has diminished as its functions have been progressively transferred to the regional governments (see 6.4.8).

The Institutional Administration of National Health (*Administración Institucional de la Sanidad Nacional*/AISNA) is an autonomous administrative body, under the Ministry of Health and Consumer Affairs, dating from 1972. It is responsible for the broad area of public health and it organises vaccination programmes and special research centres dealing with infections and rare diseases.

6.4.6   Central Treasury for Social Security (Tesorería General de la Seguridad Social)

In view of the economic importance of social security in general within the economy, this special organisation was set up under the Budget Law of 1977. Although it has its own legal identity, it is not classed as an autonomous entity or body but rather as a common service (*servicio común*). Its function is to provide a unified treasury (*caja única*) for all the income and expenditure of the social security system. Previously, with the existence of separate treasuries for each benefit agency, some were wealthy and others poor. This change promotes the concept of solidarity between the different branches of the system. It provides overall financial co-ordination and control for the three major administrative entities INSS, INSERSO and INSALUD. It manages their finances, administering the collection of social security contributions and benefit payments, as well as borrowing and investment programmes. The Central Treasury functions under the Ministry of Labour and Social Security and administrative responsibility is vested in the hands of a director appointed directly by the minister. There are a number of assistant directors who are in charge of specific areas such as resources, payments, budgets and planning. It also has regional offices in order to co-ordinate its operations within the regions.

6.4.7   Financial control

In 1985 some 25 per cent of the total social security expenditure was diverted to the health service area covering medical care and the subsidising of drugs for which the public pay 40 per cent of the cost price. The remaining 75 per cent was earmarked for pensions and the other welfare benefits (*prestaciones*). At the same time social security income has traditionally come from contributions (*cotizaciones*), with a heavy burden falling on employers. In 1979 the state only met some 6 per cent of the cost; however, as the services have expanded and costs have escalated, this proportion has risen, so that by 1985 it was approximately 21 per cent.

The economic importance of social security is such, therefore, that a special body was set up under the Budget Law of 1977 to regulate and control its expenditure. The Social Security Audit Corps (*Intervención General de la Seguridad Social*) operates within each of the social security administrative entities in order to secure proper financial management and control. Its officers prepare plans and reports on prospective expenditure, carry out analyses of budget estimates and expenditure, and co-ordinate accounting and auditing procedures throughout the system. In turn this body is responsible to the State Audit Corps (*Intervención General del Estado*/IGAE) which, as part of the Ministry of Economy and Finance, exercises overall control over state spending through delegates and inspectors working over the whole range of public administration (see 9.7.2). The social security budget is subject to parliamentary control and the accounts are scrutinised by the Audit Tribunal (see 9.7.3).

6.4.8   Recent developments

The structure described above has been subject to new tensions. On the one hand, the economic crisis has placed new demands on the system as pensions and benefits have fallen in real value and as support is required for a growing number of unemployed workers. On the other hand, the emergence of regional governments, anxious to exercise responsibilities in direct relation to their populations, has made this an obvious case in which powers are expected to be transferred.

A new Social Security Law was approved on 31 July 1985 and a new Health Law is, at the time of writing, completing its stages through the legislative process. These measures aim to rectify the most urgent needs of the moment, but they suggest a piecemeal and pragmatic approach rather than a further major restructuring along the lines of the 1978 reform. The Social Security Law seeks to achieve a redistributive effect on incomes and to concentrate aid where it is felt to be most needed.

The Health Law is designed to achieve a better distribution of resources as well as greater uniformity within the system and to ensure that health services are extended beyond the current level of 90 per cent of the population. The Law is also a further stage in the transfer of powers for health matters from central to regional government. In 1982 this power was transferred to Catalonia and one year later to Andalusia. However, the proportion of the INSALUD budget corresponding to Catalonia has already proved to be insufficient. Although the administration of these services will pass to the regions, the state retains overall responsibility for maintaining standards and, therefore, in future a new organisation, the

Interregional Health Council (*Consejo Interterritorial de Salud*), will supervise the operation of health areas throughout the respective regions.

6.5   Delegated administration (*administración periférica*)

6.5.1   Background

The present pattern for the administration of the state has its origins in the reforms carried out at the beginning of the nineteenth century, when provinces were first established. These provinces (see Figure 4.1) were clearly envisaged as institutions for the administration of central government policy and not authentic organs of local government. For many generations, indeed right up to the end of the Franco era, central government delegated administrative but not political autonomy to bodies established at provincial level as part of what came to be called the *administración periférica*. This whole operation was co-ordinated from the Ministry of the Interior which had ultimate responsibility for what were the major institutions of delegated local government, the civil governor's office (*gobierno civil*) and the town halls (*ayuntamientos*), the activities of which were tightly controlled from Madrid. In addition to these major institutions, each ministry in Madrid had its provincial offices (*delegaciones provinciales*) each endowed with its own bureaucracy.

As the process of devolving political power to the regions has developed in the post-Franco era, the *administración periférica*, logically seen as redundant except in cases where power is never likely to be devolved, has been gradually honed down. In recent years, many administrators of the state have been transferred to the bureaucracies of the new autonomous communities and, following the Law of 4 May 1983, what remain of the provincial delegations of various ministries have been incorporated into the civil governor's office of each province. However, in spite of these changes, it will probably be several years before this delegated administration disappears altogether and thus some treatment of it at this point would appear to be justified.

6.5.2   Government delegate (delegado del gobierno)

The figure of the government delegate is envisaged in Article 154 of the Constitution, which states that 'he shall direct the administration of the state in the territory of the autonomous community and shall co-ordinate this with the administration of the community itself'. The role of the delegate, who is appointed by the council of ministers on the recommendation of the prime minister, is fleshed out in a little more detail in the Law of November 1983.

The Law states that the government delegate, who is obliged to have his office in the same city as the regional seat of government, is the highest representative of the government in the autonomous community. In all official ceremonies he takes precedence over other local dignitaries, except if the president of the regional government is present (see 7.6.2). In his role as head of the state administration at regional level, he exercises his authority over the civil governors within the autonomous community and through them over all other dependent bodies. An important body which enables him to carry out his function in this respect is the co-ordinating committee (*comisión de coordinación*) which he chairs and which is made up of all the civil governors in the region plus, when appropriate, the heads of all delegated services.

6.5.3   Civil governor (gobernador civil)

The civil governor, whose role was first defined as long ago as 1812 is the provincial equivalent of the government delegate and therefore the highest representative and executive of the state administration at provincial level. He is appointed by the prime minister on the recommendation of the Minister of the Interior, following consideration in the council of ministers. Thus, as in the Franco era, he tends to be a political appointee and there is normally a wholesale replacement of all civil governors when a government of a different party comes to power. Although he exercises less power than he did under the strongly centralised Franco state, because of the long tradition attaching to his role he has maintained a good deal of prestige and certain important powers; these are reflected in a specific statute contained in the Decree of 15 October 1977.

Basically, under the overall authority of the central government and the government delegate of the region, he is responsible for the implementation of policies at provincial level for which the state is still responsible either fully or on a shared basis. His role is much more specific than that of the government delegate since for generations a whole provincial bureaucracy, the most important tier of the *administración periférica*, has been functioning under the control of the civil governor. Although this bureaucracy has recently been much reduced, as decentralisation has been implemented, the governor still retains a tight control over the elements that remain. In this context one of his most important functions relates to what, under Franco, was called the maintenance of public order and what under the 1978 Constitution is referred to as public safety and the defence of citizens' rights and liberties. Specifically he is in charge, as traditionally he always has been, of the state police and security forces that operate at provincial level. Related to this function, he plays a major role in cases of serious emergencies, such as large-scale fires, flooding, droughts and so on, which may affect the province.

Another of his most important tasks is to make recommendations to central government about what he considers to be the investment requirements of the province in the public sector. Clearly, in this regard, co-operation with the local authorities is highly desirable.

Like the government delegate, one of his major responsibilities is to ensure co-ordination at provincial level between the administration of the state and that of the local authorities, in particular the provincial council (see 8.4.1.1). In this respect he is required to provide information and statistics that will help the local authorities function more efficiently, just as they are required to provide him with information about the functioning of local institutions.

Finally, it should be pointed out that, in the single-province autonomous communities, all the powers of the civil governor have been taken over by the government delegate, who in fact now tends to occupy the building once occupied by the civil governor. In these regions, therefore, the delegate has assumed responsibility for more specific powers than his counterparts in the larger communities, since he must oversee the administration of the former delegations now absorbed into the *gobierno civil* (see 6.5.1).

6.6   Conclusion

During the late 1970s and early 1980s the government and administration of the Spanish state underwent a profound transformation and even at the time of writing (1986) the process is still not complete. As we saw in Chapter 2, the impetus for such changes came from the new Constitution which reflected a widespread desire for a new legal framework and a completely new set of principles for guiding public life. Democratisation, as well as embracing such notions as efficiency, communication and accountability, where, without doubt, considerable progress has been made, also enshrined the key concept of decentralisation, reflected in the creation of the autonomous communities. In this objective, too, a good deal has been achieved but, as will become clearer in Chapter 7, certain difficulties remain. This is at least partly due to the fact that, in the constitutional and devolution processes, the final shape of the Spanish state was left an open question; if anything the constitution makers opted for a model mid-way between a federal state, in which the communities would have had sovereign institutions, and the centralised state which Franco bequeathed them. In practical terms this has meant a certain duplication of responsibilities between central and regional authorities; at the regional level, the authorities are still hampered by the fact that they must share certain powers with central government and, to some extent, are also subject to such watchdogs of Madrid as the government delegate and the civil governor. A more rational restructuring of administration would seem to have demanded the disappearance of the civil governor and his dependencies which owe allegiance to the Minister of the Interior. Moreover, the devolution process, while envisaging the elimination of many departments of the central administration as powers were progressively transferred to the regions, has in fact led not simply to the retention but even an expansion of departments in Madrid. This has been justified on the grounds of the need for co-ordination but in reality reflects the desire to retain overall political control. A blatant example of proliferation in recent years is that, in spite of the reduction in the number of ministries from twenty-one to fifteen in 1982, over fifty new directorates general have been set up. Thus, it would seem that we have in Spain a classic case of Parkinson's Law which, if it spirals out of control, could saddle the country with an impossibly expensive and oppressive bureaucracy; this could jeopardise the healthy evolution towards the freer, more democratic model of administration envisaged by the constitution makers of 1978.

7 Regional government

7.1 Regional autonomy in the post-Franco era

The political map of Spain is now radically different from what it was only a few years ago. Instead of a unitary state divided into some fifty provinces (see Figure 4.1), the role of which was merely to administer the services of the central government, the country now has a semi-federal structure in which the powers of the state are shared with seventeen newly created autonomous communities (see Figure 7.1), each endowed with its own president, parliament, executive and high court of justice. In the modern history of Spain there is no precedent for such a major change in the structure of the state nor for such a fundamental shift of power from the centre to the periphery.

The long and complex history of the tensions between the centre and the periphery in Spain falls outside the scope of this work and is well-documented elsewhere. Suffice it to say here that, partly as a reaction to centuries of stifling centralism, culminating in the dictatorship of General Franco and partly in response to deep-seated cultural differences – particularly manifest in the case of the Basques and the Catalans – the post-Franco era has witnessed considerable popular and official support for some form of decentralisation. This has been conceived as an essential ingredient of the return to democracy. In the summer of 1977, following the UCD victory in the June elections of that year, Adolfo Suárez appointed a Minister for the Regions whose specific brief was to take some steam out of the clamours for regional autonomy and to negotiate provisional autonomy agreements with representatives of the regions.

Subsequently, between September 1977 when Catalonia's historic regional government, the *Generalitat*, was restored and the end of 1978, most of Spain's regions were endowed with institutions which, while enjoying only limited powers, represented an important symbolic first step on the road to self-government. The conversion of these provisional bodies into fully fledged autonomous organs of government had to await the promulgation of the Constitution in December 1978.

Figure 7.1 *Autonomous communities of Spain*

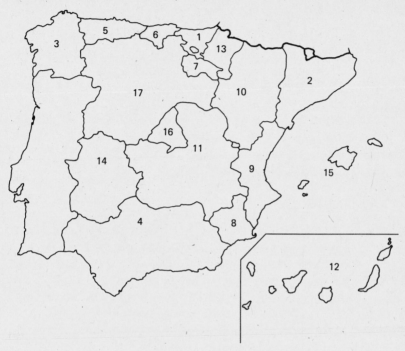

Key:

Autonomous community	Executive body	Capital	Date statute approved
1 País Vasco (Euskadi)	Gobierno Vasco	Vitoria	18.12.79
2 Cataluña (Catalunya)	Generalidad de Cataluña (Generalitat de Catalunya)	Barcelona	18.12.79
3 Galicia	Junta de Galicia (Xunta de Galicia)	Santiago de Compostela	6.4.81
4 Andalucía	Junta de Andalucía	Sevilla	30.12.81
5 Principado de Asturias	Consejo de Gobierno	Oviedo	30.12.81
6 Cantabria	Diputación Regional de Cantabria	Santander	30.12.81
7 La Rioja	Consejo de Gobierno	Logroño	9.6.82
8 Murcia	Consejo de Gobierno	Murcia	9.6.82
9 Comunidad Valenciana	Gobierno Valenciano	Valencia	1.7.82
10 Aragón	Diputación General de Aragón	Zaragoza	10.8.82
11 Castilla–La Mancha	Junta de Comunidades de Castilla–La Mancha	Toledo	10.8.82
12 Canarias	Gobierno de Canarias	Las Palmas	10.8.82
13 Navarra	Diputación Foral de Navarra	Pamplona	10.8.82
14 Extremadura	Junta de Extremadura	Mérida	25.2.83
15 Islas Baleares	Gobierno de la Comunidad de las Islas Baleares	Palma de Mallorca	25.2.83
16 Comunidad de Madrid	Consejo de Gobierno	Madrid	25.2.83
17 Castilla y Léon	Junta de Castilla y León	Valladolid	25.2.83

7.2   Autonomy in the 1978 Constitution

During the sixteen-month constitutional debate, the autonomy issue was by far the most controversial. In some way a balance had to be struck between the fears of the parties of the Right that any reference to the 'nationalities' of Spain represented a threat to national unity and the obvious preference of the Left for a federal-type solution. Certain parliamentarians were equally concerned that autonomy might be a disguise for mere administrative decentralisation, without any effective decision-making power being devolved to the regions. Many regionalists were unhappy about the distinction, drawn in Article 2, between the 'nationalities' and the 'regions' of Spain, especially when Transitional Provision 2 of the Constitution suggested, although it did not actually state, that the former corresponded to the Basque Country, Catalonia and Galicia, which would be able to accede to autonomy through an accelerated procedure.

Not surprisingly, the formula eventually agreed on was very much a compromise between the various political groups represented in Parliament, a compromise that applied to both the procedure for attaining autonomy and the powers to be exercised by the new regional institutions. However, with the possible exception of the Basque Nationalists, who urged their electorate to abstain in the constitutional referendum, arguing that the pre-existence of Basque rights or *fueros* had not been expressly recognised, all major parties could accept the basic proposition of Article 2. This is stated as follows:

The Constitution is based on the indissoluble unity of the Spanish Nation, the common and indivisible motherland of all Spaniards, and recognises and guarantees the right to autonomy of the nationalities and regions of which it is composed and the common links that bind them together.

This basic principle is developed in considerable, if not always clear, detail in Section VIII of the Constitution entitled, 'The Territorial Organisation of the state'. Article 143.1 spells out the territorial basis for the establishment of self-governing regions:

Exercising the right to autonomy recognised in Article 2 of the Constitution, adjoining provinces with common historical, cultural and economic characteristics, the islands and the provinces with a historical regional identity will be able to accede to self-government and form autonomous communities in accordance with the provisions of this section of the Constitution and of their respective statutes.

7.3   Three routes to autonomy

A consideration of the three routes to autonomy is relevant in that, at least until the whole process is complete, the method by which autonomy has been obtained has an important bearing on the nature and extent of the self-government secured. The eventual decision to provide three possible routes in fact represents part of the compromise reached in the course of the constitutional debate. At the heart of this issue were the claims of Basques and Catalans, and to some extent the Galicians and Andalusians, that, for historical and cultural reasons, they merited preferential status.

7.3.1 Rapid route (Transitional Provision 2 of the Constitution)

According to this Provision those regions which had in the past voted in a referendum in favour of autonomy would be permitted to proceed by a relatively simple process towards full autonomy. The already constituted pre-autonomous bodies would draw up a draft statute of autonomy which, following scrutiny by the Constitutional Committee of the Congress (see 2.1), would be submitted to a referendum in the regions concerned. The regions qualified to apply for autonomy via this route were: the Basque Country (*País Vasco* or *Euskadi*), Catalonia (*Cataluña* or *Catalunya*) and Galicia.

7.3.2 Slow route (Article 143)

Initially it was envisaged that, apart from the above three regions (the so-called 'historic nationalities'), this would be the normal route for all the regions in their progress towards autonomous status. This would involve a positive initiative on the part of all the provincial councils (see 8.4.1.1) and two-thirds at least of the municipal councils (see 8.3.2.1) in each region to set in motion the autonomy process. Subsequently a statute of autonomy (*estatuto de autonomía*) would be drawn up by an assembly comprising members of the provincial councils as well as deputies and senators elected in the provinces of the region concerned. This statute would be passed to the *Cortes* for approval as an organic law (see 4.7.1.1). When approved, the region would be able to assume responsibility for the limited areas of decision-making listed in Article 148 of the Constitution. Only five years after the approval of its statute could a region proceed towards the full autonomy enjoyed from the outset by the historic nationalities. Since all the regions proceeding towards autonomy by this route did so between January 1982 and February 1983, no application to accede to full autonomy could be anticipated before January 1987.

7.3.3 Exceptional route (Article 151.1)

During the constitutional debate some regional representatives, particularly those from Andalusia, argued that the above two-tier arrangements made no provision for a region like Andalusia which, while not qualifying as a historical nationality, could still claim widespread popular support for full autonomy, as evidenced by mass demonstrations in its favour. Thus, a compromise solution was suggested involving an alternative route which, providing certain conditions were fulfilled, would allow such a region to follow an accelerated procedure towards full autonomy.

These conditions included the need for the initiative to be supported not only by all the provincial councils concerned but also by three-quarters of the municipal councils. To back this initiative a popular referendum would have to be held and this would require the affirmative vote of an overall majority of the electoral roll in each province. Only when these steps had been taken could the region follow the procedure outlined in 7.3.2 and even then a second referendum was required to approve the actual text of the statute. Clearly there were political interests at work here determined to ensure that, at least in the short term, full autonomy was to be granted to no more than a privileged few. As we have seen, however, in the long term, all the regions would theoretically have the right to attain the same level of autonomy.

7.3.4   *Navarre (Navarra)*

This region merits special attention because of the unusual path which it has followed to autonomy. Navarre, an independent kingdom until the early sixteenth century before it was annexed by the joint Kingdom of Castile and Aragón, has subsequently enjoyed more autonomy than any other part of Spain, even surviving the centralising tendencies that occurred in the nineteenth century. Because it supported Franco in the Civil War the region was able to retain its ancient rights (*fueros*), including the privilege, unique in Spain at that time, of being able to raise its own taxes. Culturally the Navarrese of the north, many of whom speak Basque, feel a kinship with the three Basque Provinces to the west, while those of the south feel more affinity with Castile or simply prefer to retain their separate identity. For this reason, when other regions were deciding their future status within the new Spanish state, the people of Navarre found themselves deeply divided over whether to form their own autonomous community or join the community of the Basque Country. This dilemma is reflected in Transitional Provision 4 of the Constitution which offers the region the option of merging with the Basque Country at a later date should it so decide. This remains a long-term possibility. In the meantime, however, the political leaders of Navarre have negotiated with the state a pact which grants them autonomy, more or less along the lines of Article 143, but includes their historic right to levy their own taxes. This pact culminated in the Organic Law on the Restoration and Development of the Autonomous Government of Navarre (*Ley Orgánica de Reintegración y Amejoramiento del Régimen Foral de Navarra*).

7.4   Establishment of the autonomous communities

The first regions to attain autonomy under the 1978 Constitution were the Basque Country and Catalonia, where successful referendums were held in October 1979 and the statutes of autonomy of which were ratified in the *Cortes* by an organic law of December of that year. In March of the following year elections were held to the Basque and Catalan Parliaments, as a result of which the first regional governments of the post-Franco era were sworn in. On the same day a referendum was held in Galicia to approve that region's statute of autonomy. Elections, however, were not held until October 1981 when, simultaneously, the referendum to approve the Andalusian statute was held. The delay in holding these polls was partly due to the attempted *coup* of February 1981, which came close to destroying Spain's hard-won democracy.

A more significant effect of the *coup*, however, was that it strengthened the case of those who had been urging caution with regard to the autonomy process. The controversial Law on the Harmonisation of the Autonomy Process (*Ley Orgánica de Armonización del Proceso Autonómico*/LOAPA), one of four Agreements on Autonomy (*Acuerdos Autonómicos*) related to devolution approved in July 1981, was in essence a post-*coup* pact between the ruling UCD party and the opposition PSOE to ensure that the whole process was brought under tighter control. One of the major provisions of this law was that Andalusia was to be the first and the last region to accede to autonomy by the exceptional route; all the remaining regions would have to settle for the slow route laid down in Article 143. As it happened, this did not present serious problems since regional awareness and demands were undoubtedly less intense in the other regions, with the possible exception of Valencia and the Canary Islands. Thus, following the approval of their statutes of autonomy between late 1982 and early 1983, elections to the Parliaments of the remaining thirteen regions took place in April 1983, simultaneously with the local elections scheduled for that period. By the summer of 1983 Spain's newly created autonomous communities, which would still have to wait a long time before the powers they had inherited were officially devolved to them, could at least see their new institutions in place and beginning to function. A whole new tier of government and administration was slowly being created.

It should be pointed out that, in the case of the six single-province communities that emerged in the course of this process, the provincial tier of government merged with the institutions of the new autonomous communities. Thus, for example, the *Diputación Foral de Navarra*, formerly a provincial-level body, is now upgraded to a regional-level institution. The six regions concerned are: Asturias, Cantabria, La Rioja, Madrid, Murcia and Navarre.

7.5   Nature and implications of autonomy

Autonomy is not the easiest term to define and has a variety of different senses. In the Spanish case, however, whatever the limitations of the new decentralised structure and whatever state control over regional institutions still exists, autonomy is undoubtedly of a political nature. A serious attempt has been made to create alternative region-based centres of political power which, while in the last resort subservient to the central power, enjoy a generous degree of freedom to run their own affairs. It is generally accepted that political autonomy consists of a capacity to take decisions and to implement them on the basis of adequate resources. For it to be effective, political autonomy must include statutory, legislative and, above all, at least some financial autonomy. These three aspects will now be examined separately.

7.5.1   *Statutory autonomy*

All seventeen autonomous communities are now subject not only to the Constitution but to their own statutes of autonomy which govern all aspects of political life at regional level. In effect they constitute regional constitutions. Having been approved in the *Cortes* as organic laws, they can only be amended by an overall majority in both Houses of Parliament and only after a complicated procedure can they be overruled by Madrid. At the simplest level, a statute enables a region to organise its own institutions of self-government and establish the parameters of its own particular relationship with the central authorities.

It is interesting to note that, although the statutes have many features in common, because each is the result of a long process of political negotiation, they all have individual features which reflect their own special relationship with Madrid. The Basque Statute, as we shall see (7.5.3.2), enshrines the restoration of the economic agreements (*conciertos económicos*), involving certain tax-raising privileges, while the Catalan Statute grants the region considerable freedom in matters related to education, culture and language. As we have already seen (see 7.3.4), the Navarrese Statute (or *Fuero*) is also in many ways unique.

7.5.2   *Legislative autonomy*

In common with federal systems, with which the new structure of the state has much in common, the autonomous communities, endowed with their own legislatures, have the right to draw up and approve laws, as well as the right to execute and administer them either directly or through the provincial authorities. As we shall see, the areas of competence in which a community can legislate depend on the level of autonomy achieved, at least in the short term, and on the content of a given statute. Whatever their limitations, however, the regional parliaments had all begun to function by the summer of 1983 and already in each case a large corpus of legislation has been approved and published in the regional equivalents of the Official State Gazette (*Boletín Oficial del Estado*/BOE).

7.5.3   Financial autonomy

7.5.3.1   General scheme

Authentic autonomy clearly implies control over financial resources, and the Constitution (Article 156) recognises the right of the autonomous communities to financial autonomy. This, however, has to be exercised within the state's overall responsibility for taxation and for ensuring that all Spaniards have equal opportunities. As foreseen in Article 157.3, the details of these financial arrangements were spelt out in the 1980 Organic Law on the Financing of Autonomous Communities (*Ley Orgánica de Financiación de las Comunidades Autónomas*/LOFCA). The LOFCA established a special Council for the Fiscal and Financial Policy of the Autonomous Communities (*Consejo de Política Fiscal y Financiera de las Comunidades Autónomas*), composed of the finance ministers from the communities together with the state finance minister and the minister for public administration. This is a consultative body which looks at the co-ordination of policy in regard to public investment, costs of services, public debt and the distribution of resources to the regions. The rights of the respective parliaments to control their own budgets and responsibilities of their respective finance departments are also laid down in the various statutes of autonomy.

The precise details of revenue vary according to the nature of the functions of the authorities concerned. However, the ultimate aim is to achieve a ratio of public-sector spending as between the state, the autonomous governments and the local authorities in the region of 50:25:25. Currently, as the transfer of powers has not been completed, this ratio falls short of its target, being, in 1985, approximately 80:10:10.

Fifteen of the autonomous communities operate under the same basic guidelines which start from the premise that the state will guarantee to cover the cost of services which are transferred over a set transition period. During this time the state's contribution should diminish as the right to retain more taxes is granted to the regions. After six years a fixed quota will then be paid from the state's annual budget, renewable every five years. The annual share in the state's budget is therefore in proportion to the services which have been transferred as well as to the tax income which regions are allowed to retain. In 1985 more than fifty per cent of the state's education budget and twenty-five per cent of its public works budget were transferred to the autonomous communities. By this date also, nine communities (Andalusia, Aragón, the Canary Islands, Castilla–La Mancha, Castilla y León, Catalonia, Extremadura, Galicia and Valencia) had been given the right to retain the taxes referred to in Figure 7.2.

In addition, financial resources are transferred in relation to the specific services of the numerous autonomous bodies referred to in Chapters 6 and 9, which include the budgets of the social security organisations INSALUD and INSERSO, although by 1985 only two regions, Andalusia and Catalonia, had seen this function transferred to them.

Article 157.1(c) of the Constitution also foresaw the creation of an Inter-regional Compensation Fund (*Fondo de Compensación Inter-territorial*/FCI) as a means of ensuring adequate finances for the disparate regions. This has now begun to function and the intention is that a minimum of thirty per cent of the amount designated by the state for public investment should be channelled to the regions in accordance with a 'needs' formula based on population density, income, emigration and unemployment levels *inter alia*. In 1985 Andalusia and Galicia received by far the highest proportion of the fund, twenty-seven per cent and ten per cent respectively.

Apart from revenue proceeding directly or indirectly from central government sources, the autonomous communities also derive income from their own local taxes, rates and surcharges on state taxes. Moreover, they have the right to borrow money. The main sources of revenue are summarised in Figure 7.2.

7.5.3.2 Basque Country and Navarre

While fifteen of the autonomous communities rely largely on the state to transfer funds in their direction, the Basque Country and Navarre (see 7.3.4), enjoy the benefits of their historic rights (*fueros*). Two special economic agreements, the *concierto económico* for the Basque Country and the *convenio económico* for Navarre, grant the three Basque provinces of Alava, Guipúzcoa and Vizcaya, and the single province of Navarre, the right to levy and collect all taxes except customs duties and the taxes on petroleum products and tobacco. These rights have to be exercised in conformity with the general state system of taxation, using the same terminology, criteria and classification of activities. The same rate of taxation has to be used as that imposed by the state in the case of personal income tax, company tax and sales taxes (to be replaced by VAT). While there is some flexibility allowed with the remaining taxes, the overall tax level cannot be lower than the state level.

From the income which is derived from taxation, the authorities in the Basque Country and Navarre have to deduct an annual quota (*cupo*) to be paid to the state in respect of those services and powers which the latter retains. This quota is agreed for a five-year period but is subject to annual adjustment to take account of inflation.

Figure 7.2. *Sources of revenue for autonomous communities*

A   *Central government funds*
1   For services transferred
2   For autonomous bodies
3   From the Inter-regional Compensation Fund (FCI)
4   Retention of certain taxes:
    Inheritance tax
    Wealth tax
    Capital transfer tax
    Luxury tax
    Gaming duties

B   *Own sources*
1   Taxes (*impuestos*, *tributos*) on property, products and activities
2   Charges (*tasas*) for services ranging from publications to health services
3   Surcharges (*recargos*) over and above state taxes
4   Borrowing: short-term, from banks; long-term, through issue of bonds
5   Investments and industrial, commercial and agricultural services
6   Others, such as fines, donations and legacies

Full details of all tax revenues have to be submitted to the Ministry of Finance in Madrid in order to enable the overall co-ordination of the fiscal system to take place. Furthermore, the accounts of these two communities, together with those of the other fifteen, are subject to scrutiny by the audit tribunal (see 9.7.3).

7.6   Institutions of autonomy

Article 152 of the Constitution lays down that in statutes of autonomy approved under the rapid route (that is, the four regions which first gained full autonomy), the institutions of the autonomous community will be: a legislative assembly or parliament, an executive or governing council, a president and a high court of justice (see Figure 7.3). Interestingly, in the case of the slow-route autonomous regions, no institutions are specified, and Article 147 merely states that their statutes should contain 'the titles, structure and location of the autonomous institutions'. However, the texts of the four Agreements on Autonomy signed in 1981, including the LOAPA (see 7.4), assume that all autonomous regions will have the same institutional structure, and in practice this has been the case. To a very great extent, these institutions are a regional reflection of national institutions and, like the latter, they must be organised along democratic lines.

7.6.1   *Regional assembly* (asamblea regional)

Except for the fact that it is composed of a single chamber, each regional assembly or parliament is more or less a mirror-image of the Madrid

Figure 7.3 *Regional institutions*

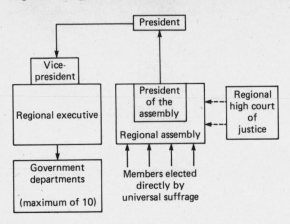

Congress. As with the latter its members, known as deputies (*diputados*), are elected by universal, free, direct, equal and secret suffrage in accordance with the same system of proportional representation and seat allocation as operates for the general elections (see 4.3.1). Thus the number of seats contested may vary between 135 for densely populated Catalonia to 35 for thinly populated Cantabria. The constituency in multiprovincial regions is the province, while the single-province regions operate as one constituency, unless the major parties (i.e. those represented in the Madrid Parliament) agree unanimously to adopt a different system, for example, one based on districts (*comarcas*).

The normal life-span of the assembly is four years after which elections must be held. The dates for these elections are fixed well in advance by the central government which can, if it wishes, decide, as it did in May 1983, to combine regional with local elections.

Since the first elections in Andalusia, the Basque Country, Catalonia and Galicia took place on different dates, indeed in different years, these are likely to remain spaced out in the future, although there is nothing to stop the government deciding to make general elections coincide with one of these dates, as it did in the case of the Andalusian elections in June 1986. Since the first elections for the remaining thirteen communities took place on one date, in future these will all be held at the same time.

The internal organisation of each Assembly is also similar to that of the Madrid Congress and is enshrined in a *reglamento* similar to that drawn up for the Lower House in Madrid. Each has its own president, who controls the everyday running of the assembly; in this task he is helped by the presiding council (*mesa*) consisting of himself, often one or two vice-presidents and several secretaries, as well as a team of *letrados*. Each has established a standing committee (*diputación permanente*) which looks after the affairs of the regional assembly when it is not in session. More-over, each assembly has created its own bureaucracy to deal with a wide range of issues from relations with the regional executive to publications and public relations.

As in Madrid, the regional assembly works through plenary sittings (*plenos*) and committees (*comisiones*) and its ordinary working sessions are from September to December and from February to June. Extra-ordinary sessions can be called by the president at the request of the stand-ing committee, a fifth of the deputies or a specific number of parliamentary groups or, indeed, by the regional executive itself.

The powers and functions of the regional assembly are clearly laid down in the appropriate statute of autonomy. It has the right not only to draw up regional laws but to submit them to a vote and approve them without reference to Madrid. The procedure for initiating and approving legis-lation is very similar to that operating at the national level; the majority of draft laws (*proyectos de ley*) emanate from the executive. As well as these legislative powers, the assembly exercises a function of control, both economic and political, over the executive, which is thus made account-able to it. In addition, as we shall see, one of the important functions of the assembly is the right to nominate the president of the autonomous community concerned. Furthermore, it must elect from among its ranks the senators who are to represent the community in accordance with Article 69.5 of the Constitution. The assembly also enjoys two further powers: first, the right to present bills (*proposiciones de ley*) to the national Congress (see 4.7.2) and, second, the right to present appeals (*recursos de anticonstitucionalidad*) to the constitutional court where it considers that there has been an infringement of the Constitution affecting the rights of the autonomous institutions (see 2.5.2.1).

7.6.2 *President* (presidente)

The president of the autonomous community, who is also the president of the regional executive, is designated by the regional assembly from among its members and appointed by the king. In practice, of course, what hap-pens is that the leader of the majority party or coalition is elected following the presentation of his programme to parliament and a vote of investiture, as in Madrid. Essentially, the president has three functions:

(i)   He is the symbolic head of the region and as such he represents the com-munity in its relations with the monarch, the government in Madrid and foreign dignitaries.

(ii) He is head of the regional executive (see 7.6.3). In this prime ministerial capacity, in collaboration with his ministers (*consejeros*), he has the responsibility for taking the important political decisions affecting the community as well as the obligation to ensure that official policy is trans-

Figure 7.4. *Composition of* Junta de Andalucía

Regional Ministry of	Consejería de
Internal Affairs	*Gobernación*
President's Office	*Presidencia*
Economy and Development	*Economía y Fomento*
Finance	*Hacienda*
Territorial Policy and Transport	*Política Territorial y Transportes*
Agriculture and Fisheries	*Agricultura y Pesca*
Labour and Social Security	*Trabajo y Seguridad Social*
Health and Consumer Affairs	*Salud y Consumo*
Education and Science	*Educación y Ciencia*
Culture	*Cultura*

lated into effective action. In this capacity, like his counterpart at national level, he is the titular head of both the regional executive and administration.

(iii)   The president nominates and dismisses the members of the regional executive. He may appoint as his vice-president one of his ministers in charge of a particular department or a political colleague with no ministerial responsibility. The vice-president can assume powers delegated to him temporarily or permanently by the president and stands in for him when the latter is ill or absent.

Leaving aside the judicial aspects, the president can normally only be dismissed if he loses the confidence of the regional assembly. This can only be demonstrated by a constructive motion of censure presented to the assembly by the opposition, which must include the name of an alternative president. If the motion is approved, by an overall majority, this candidate is automatically sworn in as the new president of the autonomous community.

7.6.3 *Regional executive* (consejo de gobierno)

The regional executive consists of the president, the vice-president(s), where relevant, and the ministers, who collectively perform all the executive and administrative functions of the autonomous community. It is always accountable to the assembly, of which the president and his ministers are invariably members. The Constitution does not lay down how these ministers are to be appointed; while the normal procedure is for the president to name his ministers, usually from elected regional deputies, it is theoretically possible for the regional assembly itself to assume this responsibility. Like their counterparts at national level, these ministers are individually accountable to the president for the performance of their own ministries and collectively responsible to the regional assembly for the overall policies of the regional executive. Unlike the deputies, they receive a fixed salary plus expenses. Although the rank of regional deputy is obviously compatible with that of *consejero*, the latter is not allowed to hold office in any other branch of public administration. Like its counterpart at national level, the regional executive normally meets once a week under the chairmanship of the president. As well as approving draft laws to be sent to the assembly, one of its major functions is to issue decrees (*decretos*) and resolutions (*resoluciones*) which do not require the approval of the assembly. Likewise, the ministers themselves are authorised to issue orders (*órdenes*) over relatively minor matters relating specifically to their own departments.

7.6.4 Regional ministries (consejerías)

For economic reasons the 1981 Agreements on Autonomy laid down that, at least in the case of the slow-route autonomous regions, no more than ten ministries would be allowed in each autonomous community. Neither the Constitution nor the statutes of autonomy specify which ministries are to be created in each region and in fact in each case it has been left to the regional executive to decide on the structure of public administration. Thus, as can be seen from the example of the *Junta de Andalucía* (see Figure 7.4), functions that at the national level are separate, have been combined.

Within the various regional ministries, however, the internal structure is very similar and to a large extent reproduces the national pattern, with under-secretaries, director generals, and so on. It is interesting to note that Article 4.2, Clause 5 of the first of the Agreements on Autonomy states emphatically that 'in the autonomous communities there will be no more staff appointed other than those strictly necessary for the immediate support of the political bodies concerned'. The same Clause goes on to stress that posts below and including the level of director general will be filled from among the ranks of professional civil servants. In spite of this stricture, however, political appointments have undoubtedly been made at these levels and, moreover, regional bureaucracies have tended to expand as regional governments, savouring political power for the first time, have seemed to vie with each other in creating a whole series of official and autonomous bodies dependent, to a greater or lesser extent, on the department of regional administration.

7.6.5 High Court of Justice (Tribunal Supremo de Justica)

Just as a new tier of legislature and executive has been created at regional level, so an additional level of judicial authority has been established for each of the autonomous communities. To a large extent this is logical: since legislative power has been granted to these communities, it follows that there should be in each case a High Court to which disputes involving regional law can be referred. However, it should be stressed that this body is in a sense less autonomous than the parliament and the governing council of the community concerned in that it falls within the ultimate authority of the Supreme Court of Justice in Madrid.

7.7   Powers of the autonomous communities

It is in the key area of powers (*competencias*) devolved to the autonomous communities that we see most clearly where contemporary Spain, at least for the moment, seems to differ from the classical federal state. In the latter, the regions tend from the outset to assume control over a clearly defined area and inherit clearly structured institutions. In Spain, however, not only has each region been free to decide whether or not to request autonomous status, but it has been, and will be, able to decide on the level of autonomy required and, where applicable, the time-scale of progression to full autonomy.

According to the Constitution, the powers granted to the communities will depend on the route by which autonomy has been achieved. Basically the slow-route autonomous communities can assume responsibility for areas of responsibility listed in Article 148 of the Constitution. In reality these include little more than one might expect of a local authority in a fairly centralised state like the UK. As we have seen (7.3.2), these thirteen areas must wait at least until 1987 before they can advance to full autonomy. However, the Constitution fails to make clear what extra powers would be granted at that time and what the limits to autonomy (*techos autonómicos*) would be. In the case of the four rapid-route autonomous regions, experience has in fact shown that the nature and extent of these powers may vary quite significantly from one region to another. This is partly because the particular demands and requirements of one region have differed considerably one from another. However, it is also related to the imprecise wording of Article 148.2 of the Constitution which states that 'after five years and following reform of their statutes, these autonomous communities will be able progressively to extend their powers within the framework of Article 149', but gives no indication what these new powers will be.

Yet Article 149 lists what are called the 'exclusive powers of the state' which include such areas of competence as foreign affairs, defence, customs and international affairs, areas which even under a federal system would never be devolved to a regional authority. Clearly regional authorities could only assume responsibility for some of the powers listed in

Article 149, although which fall within this category and which do not is far from clear. Nevertheless, by examining closely Articles 148 and 149, and bearing in mind the statutes of the rapid-route regions, it is possible to formulate a more precise distinction between the various levels of competence.

7.7.1 *Exclusive powers of the autonomous communities*

Article 148 of the Constitution lists a series of powers to which slow-route regions can accede. These include: the organisation of their own institutions of self-government; town-planning; housing; public works; forestry; environmental protection; museums; libraries; cultural affairs; the regional language (where applicable); tourism; sport and leisure; social welfare; health and hygiene; and non-commercial ports and airports.

7.7.2 *Shared powers*

By implication rather than prescription, Articles 148 and 149 also indicate a number of areas in which power is shared between the national and regional institutions. These include: agriculture and cattle-rearing, which must be organised 'according to the overall structuring of the economy', the encouragement of economic development, which must be carried out 'within the objectives laid down by national economic policy', and the maintenance of historic buildings. In fact, as we shall see, such shared powers refer to areas over which, in the last analysis, the state claims ultimate sovereignty. Authority to share these powers is granted by way of basic legislation (4.7.1.5).

7.7.3 *'Devolvable' powers*

The so-called exclusive powers of the state are indicated in Article 149 of the Constitution. However, it is precisely by way of this list that a slow-route region is authorised, should it so wish, to extend its powers in the future: it would then enjoy these powers in common with the rapid-route communities. Again it is case-law, or rather the individual statutes of autonomy, rather than the Constitution, which gives us some clue as to which of these powers may be acquired in this way. By implication these can be divided into two groups:

7.7.3.1 *Delegated powers*
Such powers, which in no way imply a ceding of sovereignty on the part of the central powers, include such areas as: the overall system of communications, ports and airports that are 'of general interest'; post and telecommunications; control of air-space and air transport; and academic and

professional qualifications. Such powers can only be delegated by act of Parliament, in practice through framework laws (see 4.7.1.4).

7.7.3.2 *Normally exclusive powers of the state*

This section includes four areas of competence which are normally associated with national institutions only: justice, fiscal affairs, public security and international affairs. These areas are listed in Article 149 and therefore fall, theoretically, under the exclusive powers of the state. However, in certain respects they are in the process of being assumed by the rapid-route regions.

With regard to fiscal matters, Article 156.2 of the Constitution lays down that 'the autonomous communities shall be able to act as delegates or collaborators of the state in the levying, management and allocation of the latter's tax resources'.

Article 157, which includes a list of a region's financial resources, refers to the possibility of a community raising its own taxes. In practice, as we have seen, only the Basque Country and Navarre have so far achieved genuine autonomy in this respect (see 7.5.3.2).

With respect to public security, Article 149 allows the fully autonomous regions to create their own regional police forces. The first region to take advantage of this provision was the Basque Country which in 1980 created its own force, the *Ertzantza*. These forces are administratively and financially dependent on the regional government but in the last resort are accountable to their political masters in the Ministry of the Interior in Madrid. Moeover, in no region so far have regional police replaced any security forces under the direct control of the state.

As far as international affairs are concerned, the involvement of the autonomous communities is limited to such matters as the right to request information on treaties that might directly affect them, the right to make proposals relating to international matters and the right to participate in decisions of this nature through their regional representatives in the Senate.

7.7.4   *Exclusive powers of the state*

In view of the flexible nature of the Constitution, particularly in so far as it refers to the communities and their potential rights, it is difficult to be categorical about which powers belong exclusively to the latter and which to the state. However, again by implication rather than by prescription, it can probably be safely assumed that the state will always retain responsibility for such obviously national affairs as: nationality; immigration; political asylum; defence and the armed forces; customs and tariff barriers; foreign trade; the monetary system; general economic planning;

the authorisation of elections and referendums; the overall administration of justice; and the signing of international agreements and treaties.

7.7.5 Transfer of powers

Obviously the approval of the statutes of autonomy and the establishment of the institutions of self-government were only the first steps taken in the long and complicated process of transferring real powers to the seventeen autonomous communities. Subsequently, in each ministry mixed committees (*comisiones mixtas*) of bureaucrats, one half representing the state and the other half the communities, have been established and charged with the onerous task of transferring not only the powers themselves but the human, material and financial resources required to convert such powers into reality. General guidelines for the transfer of powers were laid down in Section IV of the Harmonisation Law, the LOAPA (referred to in 2.5.2.3 and 7.4). The Law clearly states that the royal decrees (*reales decretos*) by which these transfers are effected shall contain precise references to the transfer of the appropriate funds. It also protects the rights of civil servants transferred in this process: state functionaries who are transferred to the bureaucracies of the autonomous communities will continue to belong to the same professional corps, remain on the same grade and retain all their financial, career and professional rights (Article 32).

The process of transfers began soon after the elections to the Basque and Catalan parliaments in March 1980. Partly because of lack of clarity in the Constitution and the statutes of autonomy and partly due to underlying political problems, this process has not always been smooth. In the case of the slow-route regions, more progress has been made for the simple reason that, for the moment at least, fewer powers are being transferred; indeed, at the time of writing eight of the thirteen regions concerned had completed the process. In the case of the Andalusians, Basques, Catalans and Galicians, however, considerable work remains to be done and is often hampered by political differences; this is particularly true in the Basque Country and Catalonia, where, since 1980, the nationalist parties have been in power.

7.8 Controls over autonomy

7.8.1 Normal control

According to Article 153a the constitutional court (see 2.5.2.3) has the final word in adjudicating the constitutionality of any regional legislation. Article 161.2, for example, grants the government the right to challenge any measures adopted by the autonomous community; the challenge automatically leads to the suspension of these measures until the Court, within a period of five months, has either confirmed or lifted the suspension. Through the council of state (see 5.7), the government exercises ultimate control over the powers which it is allowed to delegate to the autonomous communities (Article 153b). The administrative divisions of the regional high courts of justice have ultimate jurisdiction over the regional administration (Article 153c). The Audit Tribunal (9.7.3) exercises ultimate control over economic and budgetary matters (Article 153d).

7.8.2   Extraordinary control

According to Article 155 of the Constitution, if an autonomous community fails to carry out its obligations under the Constitution or if it acts in a way likely to harm the general interests of the state, the government (with the agreement of the president of that community or, where this is not forthcoming, following an overall majority in the Senate), can adopt the measures necessary to oblige it to carry out its obligations or to desist from allegedly harmful activities. As yet, this extraordinary means of control has not been invoked and no ruling has appeared which indicates what precisely these 'necessary measures' might involve.

7.8.3   Financial control

It should already have become apparent that this is a major, if not the major, way in which the state exercises control over the activities of the regions. With the exceptions of the Basque Country and Navarre, the other regions only enjoy a limited capacity for the self-generation of funds and the greater part of funds spent at regional level derive from central coffers. The Inter-regional Compensation Fund is also administered centrally (see 7.5.3).

7.8.4   Other controls

Although they do not appear in the Constitution under the heading of control, there are two other *de facto* controls over the activities of the communities:

7.8.4.1   Agreements of co-operation (acuerdos de cooperación)
The joint *Cortes* have the right to authorise co-operation agreements between autonomous communities (see 4.6.2.2). This ruling appears in the same Article and conveys the same tone as the clause forbidding the federation of the same (Article 145).

7.8.4.2 Harmonisation (armonización)

According to Article 150.3 the state can approve laws which establish the necessary principles to harmonise the legislation of autonomous communities even in areas of devolved competence, should the national interest so require it. The necessity for such legislation has to be approved by an overall majority of the two Houses of Parliament. It was through this Article that the controversial LOAPA was introduced in 1981 (see 7.4). Article 4 of this law made it perfectly plain that in the case of powers devolved under Article 149 of the Constitution, currently involving only the rapid-route regions, state law would always prevail over the legislation and regulations approved by the autonomous communities. Article 6 of the same law permits the government and the joint *Cortes* to request the provision of information on activities even within the exclusive competence of the communities. The most stringent requirement, however, appears in Article 8 which states that when the communities exercise state powers delegated or transferred to them through an organic law, 'the authorities of the autonomous communities must always regulate their activities to conform to the instructions given by the relevant state authorities'. Failure to comply with this would lead to a possible suspension of the transfer or delegation and a reassumption of state control in that area.

7.9   Conclusion

It is clear that the process of devolving political power to the regions is far from complete and daunting problems remain to be surmounted. At the root of many basic problems are theoretical and constitutional considerations. It may well be that in the end Adolfo Suárez and the constitution makers will not be thanked for adopting an open-ended, *laissez-faire* approach in which fundamental matters, such as the final form of the Spanish state, were avoided and serious political problems were glossed over by imprecision in Section VIII of the Constitution. It is far from clear at the time of writing whether Spain is moving slowly towards a federal state or is likely to remain basically a regional state comparable to Italy. Neither is it clear what the limits are for regions that may wish to transfer to full autonomy, especially when the experiences to date of the rapid-route regions do not bode well in this respect. Even more daunting are the economic and administrative implications of devolution. Not only is the whole process of transferring powers, department by department, sector by sector, inevitably going to be very protracted, but the sheer cost of creating an extra tier of authority, involving seventeen extra governments and administrations, is bound to impose severe strains on an already fragile economy. In theory, as a result of devolution, areas of the central bureaucracy that have been transferred to the new regional authorities should have been either closed down or substantially reduced; as yet, however, there is little evidence of this happening and, if anything, the ministries in Madrid are continuing to expand, albeit under the pretext of rationalisation and the assumption of a co-ordinating role.

The acid test of the autonomy process, however, is likely to be political and cultural and relates to that much used, if not abused, word 'solidarity'. Sadly, during recent years 'insolidarity' between the regions and peoples of Spain seems to have been the order of the day. This has been exemplified in the constant squabbles between Madrid and the Basque governments and by the apparent resentment shown by Basques and Catalans when the distribution of the Inter-regional Compensation Fund seems to have favoured the poorer regions, Andalusia for example. One of the basic questions lying at the heart of the autonomy issue, a question which could make or break the whole operation, is the extent to which substantial powers can be granted to the 'region-based' communities (e.g. Castilla y León, Murcia) without giving offence to the 'nation-based' communities (e.g. Basque Country, Catalonia) which, for a whole series of historical, cultural and economic reasons, feel that they merit preferential status. If the former were to be given powers in any way comparable to those enjoyed by the Basque Country and Catalonia and if substantial resources were transferred to them at their expense, what then would be the reaction of these historical nationalities? This and many other questions relating to autonomy remain, for the moment, unanswered.

8   Local government

The institutions making up what is most accurately referred to, at least in Spain, as 'local administration' but is often called 'local government', include the municipal and provincial authorities. In legal documents these institutions are known collectively as local corporations (*corporaciones locales*). Since power has been devolved from Madrid to the autonomous communities, these local institutions are now politically dependent on the new regional authorities which were examined in Chapter 7 but financially to a large extent dependent on central government.

8.1   Background

The Franco regime, in combining political repression with excessive bureaucratic centralism, presided over the effective demise of local democracy. During the Franco era local institutions were basically instruments for administering the policies of central government and enjoyed no real autonomy. Such was the degree of central control that mayors, for example, were directly appointed by Franco's minister for home affairs or the civil governor of the province concerned, both of whom were directly appointed by Franco. Moreover, local elections were rigidly controlled by the dictator's single party, the National Movement (see 1.2) which ensured that, to those few seats open to direct election, only officially sponsored candidates were elected.

Furthermore, additional problems have been created by the fact that over the last thirty years, as we have seen (in 1.3), Spain has experienced unprecedented demographic, social and economic changes that were not accompanied by necessary corresponding changes in the territorial structure and administration of the country.

Thus the governments elected since 1977 have been confronted not only with the need to democratise government at all levels but also with the necessity of overhauling an anachronistic system of local administration. In order to underpin them, both sets of reform required a much higher level of economic support than had been available in the past.

8.2   Reform of local government

As at the national level, political reforms have taken precedence over administrative and economic change. Even here, however, change has been slow to be enacted. Apparently for reasons of political self-interest, Adolfo Suárez was reluctant to hold local elections before April 1979, a month after the second round of general elections. Thus between 1977 and April 1979 a situation of often dangerous tension existed between the democratically elected central government and the non-reformed local institutions, still manned by Franco appointees. However, fully democratic local elections based on the Election Law of March 1977 were eventually held, first in 1979, then in May 1983. As a result the political map of local government was re-drawn.

Administrative reform, however, has lagged well behind political change. Although Calvo Sotelo's UCD government introduced limited changes in October 1981, basically local government was being run according to outmoded norms and practices. For a fundamental reappraisal of local administration, Spaniards had to wait until April 1985 when the Socialist government of Felipe González approved the Basic Law on Local Government (*Ley Reguladora de las Bases de Régimen Local/* LRBRL). This law lays down the ground rules for the organisation of local government within the framework of Spain's new democracy.

In some ways, and especially to those expecting substantial reform, the document is a disappointment in that the traditional pattern of administration is largely maintained. For example, the provincial tier of government, so maligned by the Left because of its associations with state centralism, is preserved and in some ways strengthened. However, it should in fairness be pointed out that this battle had already been lost during the constitutional debate, when the Left made substantial concessions to its political opponents in the interests of the consolidation of democracy. Even prior to the approval of the Constitution, it was clear that consensus politics was winning the day: it ensured the survival of the provinces as the electoral constituency in the Election Law of March 1977 and also in the Local Election Law of August 1978, both of which were incorporated into the updated Organic Law on Elections (*Ley Orgánica del Régimen Electoral General*) of June 1985. Thus it came as no surprise that Article 137 guaranteed that local administration would be based on provinces as well as municipalities.

In one important way the new Law breaks new ground in local government legislation: it has outlined the services it expects local authorities to carry out, either on their own or in collaboration with other authorities, according to their size of population. Never before in the history of Spanish local government have such specific guidelines been laid down nor have such flexible arrangements been agreed in terms of sharing responsibilities between the different tiers of administration.

8.3   Municipal government

The 8,022 municipalities, centred in the town halls (*ayuntamientos*), have a much longer history and a higher level of popular acceptance than the provinces. These reasons plus the fact that, except in times of dictatorship, such bodies have been popularly elected, possibly explain why there is more stress on municipal than provincial autonomy in the Constitution. It is interesting to note, however, that the Basic Law on Local Government goes some way towards rectifying this, perhaps hoping to secure more popular support for the provinces.

Article 140 of the Constitution states: 'The Constitution guarantees the autonomy of the municipalities. They shall enjoy full legal status. Their government and administration are the responsibility of their respective town halls, made up of the mayors and councillors . . . '

8.3.1   *Municipal institutions*

The basic institutions at municipal level are: the full municipal council (8.3.2.1) and the municipal commission (8.3.2.3), each headed by the mayor (8.3.2.2). These are statutory bodies the existence of which is legally required. However, each town hall has the freedom to create any additional permanent or *ad hoc* entities that it considers necessary for the efficient running of municipal affairs. Clearly, the overall pattern will vary considerably from the large urban authorities to the small rural ones with responsibility for only a few hundred citizens. In fact the freedom of action of these authorities in this respect is partly determined by the Election Law of June 1985, which establishes the number of councillors to be elected in each municipality according to the latter's population (Article 179).

Figure 8.1 shows the organisation of the institutions of the Town Hall of Málaga, a fairly typical, large urban municipality, serving a population of over half a million.

8.3.2   *Major municipal bodies*

8.3.2.1   *Municipal council* (pleno del ayuntamiento)
The seat of municipal government is the town hall (*ayuntamiento*), a term which is also used, both officially and popularly, to refer to the whole body of municipal institutions and sometimes the municipal council. The Basic Law on Local Government uses the term *ayuntamiento* in the broader sense and the full council is referred to as *el pleno del ayuntamiento* or, for

Figure 8.1 *Municipal government of Málaga*

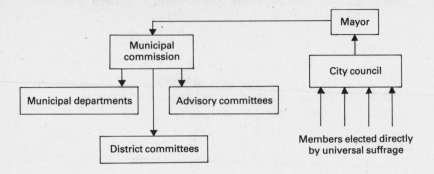

short, *el pleno*. This is the rule-making, elected body of municipal government and roughly corresponds to an English city, or town, council.

The *pleno* is made up of councillors *(concejales)* who are elected, like politicians at the national and regional levels, by universal suffrage. A system of proportional representation operates similar to that used for the Congress and the D'Hondt system is employed for the allocation of seats. Electors vote in constituencies called *términos municipales*, the area served by each town hall, not for individual councillors representing wards or districts (as in the UK), but for municipality-wide lists on which there is a ranking order headed by each party's nominee for the post of mayor. The number of councillors per municipality is fixed in proportion to its population, although to safeguard the existence of small rural authorities a minimum of five per municipality has been laid down in the 1985 Election Law. If councillors die, resign or are dismissed, their places are taken by the following names on the list of the political party concerned, thus obviating the need for by-elections. Councillors serve for a period of four years and there is no limit to the number of terms of office they may serve. The council cannot be dissolved and elections, controlled by the central government, are called on a regular four-year basis.

In normal circumstances ordinary sessions of the full council must be held at least every three months; in fact, the Málaga *pleno* meets every month. Extraordinary sessions, in the case of emergencies, can be called either by the mayor or by at least a quarter of the council members. Councillors must be given a minimum of two days' notice of ordinary sessions and the agenda for the meeting, with accompanying documentation, must be in their hands that same day. The quorum for meetings is a third of the full membership and this must be maintained throughout the meeting. Agreements may be reached on the basis of a simple majority; if voting produces a tie, the mayor, acting as chairman, may use his casting vote (*voto de calidad*).

The municipal council does not have the authority to draft major laws but does have the right to draft and approve regulations (*ordenanzas*) which must conform to legislation emanating from either the *Cortes* or the regional parliament. One of its major functions is to control and oversee the work of the municipal commission (see 8.3.2.3). Moreover, the *pleno* is empowered to approve and, where appropriate, modify the budgets presented to it by the commission, to prioritise expenditure and to approve the accounts. Naturally the council has the right to establish its own internal organisation, including the appointment, payment and dismissal of full- and part-time staff. As with its provincial counterpart, it may have recourse to the appropriate courts to ensure that the commission is operating legally. It may also approve a motion of censure against the mayor (see 8.3.2.2).

In two important ways, however, the municipal council is different from and indeed more powerful than its provincial counterpart. First, it has the power to determine its own revenue by raising its own taxes to supplement the grants from national and regional governments. Second, it has the right to participate in supramunicipal bodies, to create submunicipal bodies, to alter the municipal boundary and to create or eliminate municipalities in consultation with higher authorities.

8.3.2.2 Mayor (alcalde)

Unlike some of his British counterparts, whose role has become honorary and decorative, a Spanish mayor always plays an active political as well as representational role. Indeed, there is so much prestige and tradition attached to his role that in provincial capitals like Málaga he tends to be regarded as a more important figure than the president of the provincial council (see 8.4.1.2).

The mayor is elected by members of the full council meeting at its first session following local elections. He is normally head of the majority party in the council and must have headed the electoral list of the party concerned. It is possible, of course, for the leader of a minority to become mayor if a candidate is acceptable to a coalition of parties and the latter is able to win a majority in the council. This occurred in Seville, for example, in 1979, when the leader of the Andalusian Socialist Party, Luis Uruñuela, became mayor. The Constitution allowed for the direct popular election of mayors but, following several years of speculation, the new Electoral Law of 1985 opted solely for the method outlined above.

The mayor combines several functions in one person: he is the chief representative and president of the municipality, chairman of the full council, head of the municipal commission (see 8.3.2.3) and head of the municipal administration. He is, moreover, the highest representative of the state at municipal level. The mayor's main function is to direct municipal government and administration and it is his responsibility to convene and chair sessions of the *pleno*, the municipal commission and other municipal bodies. He must also direct, inspect and promote municipal works and services. He also has the right to issue edicts (*bandos*) on minor matters without consulting the council. It is his duty to impose fines and other sanctions on those who flout these edicts or other orders of the council.

One of his major roles is that of head of the municipal police force (*policía municipal*), which is run from the town hall, usually through a Department of Security and Citizen Protection. The mayor must adopt urgent measures in the case of local emergencies or catastrophes (flooding, large-scale fires, explosions etc.) when there is a grave risk to public safety, and he must immediately inform the *pleno* of his actions.

The mayor also enjoys wide powers of appointment: he has the right to appoint not only the members of the municipal commission from among the members of the council, but also his deputy mayor(s) (*teniente(s) de alcalde*), who must be a member/members of the commission. Moreover, the mayor can appoint members of other municipal organisations and must appoint all staff who are empowered to use fire-arms. In fact, in his name at least, all the employees of the town hall are appointed – although in practice posts are often filled by the heads of the departments concerned from civil servants qualified in particular fields.

One of the more pleasurable functions of the mayor, in his representational role, is to receive and often entertain visiting dignitaries to the town or city concerned; visitors may range from the king and queen to foreign statesmen and members of national and international trade or cultural delegations. As one would expect, he is also much in demand to act as chairman for many local organisations and to open and close a whole range of events from large fairs to Holy Week processions in the big towns and cities to school functions and talent contests. It is not surprising, then, that the local population tend to identify with him far more than with either the civil governor or the president of the provincial council, as he is in much more daily contact with the people. Since public relations are such an important aspect of his role, most mayors are assisted by a non-political head of protocol (*jefe de protocolo*).

8.3.2.3 *Municipal commission* (comisión municipal de gobierno)

This body normally exists only in municipalities with over 5,000 inhabitants. It consists of the mayor, the deputy mayor and a number of councillors, not exceeding a third of the total of the latter, appointed by the mayor and subject to dismissal by him. Normally all the members of the commission belong to the majority party.

The principal task of this commission is to assist the mayor in the exercise of his duties. In practice, especially in the large authorities, each member is given responsibility for a particular area of administration (8.3.3.1), and/or for a particular district of the municipality (8.3.3.2).

Figure 8.2. *Municipal departments of Málaga*

Legal and Administrative Department	*Area Jurídico-Administrativa*
Economic Department	*Area Económica*
Public Works and Services Department	*Area de Obras y Servicios Urbanos*
Health and Social Affairs Department	*Area de Salud y Servicios Sociales*
Security, Traffic and Transport Department	*Area de Seguridad, Tráfico y Transportes*
Staffing and Internal Affairs Department	*Area de Personal y Régimen Interior*
Department of Operational Services	*Area de Servicios Operativos*
Supplies and Commerce Department	*Area de Abastecimientos y Actividades Comerciales*
Town Planning Department	*Area de Urbanismo*
Culture and Citizen Participation Department	*Area de Cultura y Participación Ciudadana*
Tourism Department	*Area de Turismo*
Information and Institutional Relations Department	*Area de Información y Relaciones Institucionales*
Parks and Gardens Department	*Area de Parques y Jardines*

8.3.3   Other municipal bodies

It should again be stressed that, while the above institutions are statutory, the following have only optional status and their existence or otherwise depends on the size of the municipality.

8.3.3.1 Municipal departments (delegaciones o áreas)
In all but the smallest authorities, municipal administration has been divided up into units specialising in particular spheres of interest and usually headed by an elected councillor. The internal departmental structure of the Town Hall of Málaga, shown in Figure 8.2, is not dissimilar to that found in other large municipalities.

The heads of these departments are responsible, under the mayor, for appointing and dismissing their administrative, technical and secretarial staff within the guidelines established by the Basic Law. However, appointments at this level must be made according to administrative and professional and not political criteria. Thus, below the level of head of department, the local government officers may belong to any or no political party and normally remain in post when there is a change in the council.

8.3.3.2 District delegations (delegaciones de distrito)
While clearly, even in small municipalities, local administration needs to be subdivided into functional units, the existence of territorial divisions and their number depends exclusively on the size of the municipal authority. A small municipality may have no such divisions, while Málaga has eleven. In the latter case, each of these areas is the responsibility of a nomi-

nated councillor or delegate (*delegado*) who may or may not be a member of the commission, but who will almost always be a member of the ruling party. Local residents with complaints, who are reticent about approaching the town hall directly, may seek help from their *delegado* or from the local committee over which he presides (see 8.3.3.3).

8.3.3.3 District committees *(juntas municipales de distrito)*

These are non-elected bodies, usually composed of respected citizens who reside in the district and who are appointed by the *delegado* with the approval of the *pleno*. The responsibility of the members is to represent the interests of local residents (*vecinos*) and channel their complaints, problems, and so on, to the council.

8.3.3.4 Advisory committees *(comisiones informativas)*

These non-elected bodies are found in only some of the larger municipalities. In Málaga, for instance, there are nine such committees headed either by members of the commission or councillors from the ruling party. Each committee consists of a chairman and five members representing the major political groups on the council and the independents, in rough proportion to their share of seats on the council. To a very large extent, these committees mirror the departmental organisation of the town hall. For example, some of the major committees in Málaga are: Finance; Works and Public Services; Town Planning; Security; and Health and Social Services. The main function of these advisory committees is to enable councillors of all political persuasions to participate in an advisory role in specific areas of policy in which they may have a special interest or expertise. They also serve as channels of communication between the commission and the minority political groups.

8.3.4   Open assembly *(concejo abierto)*

In municipalities of less than one hundred inhabitants, a system of open assembly operates. Article 29 of the Basic Law recognises these cases and also allows such an arrangement to exist where geographical location or other factors make their establishment advisable. In order to establish such a system, the majority of the inhabitants concerned must send a petition to the town hall concerned which must approve the request by a two-thirds majority before final approval is granted by the regional government.

Under such a system the government and administration of the municipality is the responsibility of a mayor who is elected by a neighbourhood assembly (*asamblea vecinal*) composed of all the voters. The latter have the right to take decisions and vote on all matters affecting the municipality.

8.3.5 Responsibilities of the municipal authority

Each municipality is required to carry out certain minimum functions in accordance with legislation emanating from the central or regional government. Article 26 lays down what these responsibilities are, depending on the size of the *término municipal*.

8.3.5.1
All municipalities are responsible for public lighting, cemeteries, refuse collection, street cleaning, supply, sewers, road access, pavements and food and drink inspection.

8.3.5.2
Municipalities with a population of over 5,000 are in addition responsible for public parks, public libraries, markets and sewage treatment.

8.3.5.3
Municipalities with a population of over 20,000 are in addition responsible for social services, police and fire services, sports facilities and abattoirs.

8.3.5.4
Municipalities with a population of over 50,000 are in addition responsible for urban transport and environmental protection.

One must distinguish between the above responsibilities, which are the compulsory minimum in each case, and additional services, outlined in Article 25, for which the municipal authority can claim either exclusive or shared rights. Exclusive rights include public security and traffic control, the promotion and management of housing, cultural activities and the care of historic buildings; rights shared with the regional government include collaboration in the provision of educational facilities, in the management of local education and in the provision of primary health care.

Municipalities which find themselves unable to provide the basic services required by law may be granted official dispensation by the regional government, in which case the latter is likely to charge the provincial council (see 8.4.1.1) with the task of providing them (Basic Law, Article 26, Sections 2 and 3). On the other hand, the central or regional authorities may decide to delegate additional powers to municipalities deemed capable of exercising them. In such circumstances they must be persuaded that either efficiency or public participation is thereby enhanced. Some of the areas in which the municipalities are encouraged to assume additional powers are: education; culture; housing; health; the promotion of opportunities for women; and the protection of the environment. Obviously,

Figure 8.3 *Provincial government of Málaga*

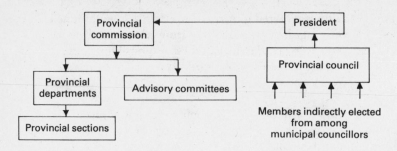

funds would be made available by the state or the regional authority to enable the municipality to exercise such powers (see 8.6).

The interests of all local authorities, especially in relation to their financial dealings with the state, are represented by the Federation of Municipalities and Provinces (*Federación de Municipios y Provincias/* FEMP) which has become an important pressure group defending local government in both financial and legal respects.

8.4   Provincial government

The provinces (see Figure 4.1) were established as the main units of the *administración periférica* (see 6.5) through which the central government hoped more easily to impose its policies. According to Article 141.1 of the Constitution the province is defined as follows: 'The province is a local entity with its own legal status, consisting of a group of municipalities and representing a territorial division designed to carry out the activities of the state.'

Thus we can discern a certain duality in the role of the province: on the one hand, as an entity which brings together several municipal authorities, it clearly has a local function and in fact in this respect it is dependent on the new regional authorities. On the other hand, it is also evident that the provinces retain their traditional role as outposts of central government and one assumes that this applies to areas of competence which are not yet devolved or cannot constitutionally be devolved to the regional authorities. When fulfilling this role, they are clearly operating as part of the reduced *administración periférica* and are subject to the ultimate control of the civil governor (see 6.5.3).

8.4.1   *Provincial institutions*

The basic institutions at provincial level are: the full provincial council (8.4.1.1) and the provincial commission (8.4.1.3), each headed by a president (8.4.1.2). These are statutory bodies which must exist in all provincial capitals, although the council, like the municipal council, is free to create other bodies should it so decide. Figure 8.3 shows the organisation of the major institutions of the Provincial Council of Málaga, although the pattern varies very little from one province to another.

8.4.1.1 *Provincial council* (pleno de la diputación provincial)

The seat of provincial government is the county hall (*diputación provincial*), a term which is also used to refer to the whole body of provincial institutions as well as the full provincial council. The Basic Law on Local Government uses the term *diputación* in the broader sense and the full council is referred to as *el pleno de la diputación*. This is the rule-making body of provincial government.

The provincial council is made up of provincial deputies (*diputados provinciales*) who, except in the case of the three Basque Provinces (see 8.4.2) are elected indirectly by the municipal councillors elected in the preceding municipal elections. As with the latter, seats are allocated according to a system of proportional representation. Initially, a fixed number of seats is established for each province, the electoral board (*junta electoral*) of which allocates seats to each *partido judicial*. The latter, which is a territorial division for the administration of justice and contains several municipalities, is the constituency for these elections. The allocation is not rigidly proportional since, however small its population, every *partido* has one deputy while no single constituency can have more than three-fifths of the total for the province. Provincial deputies hold office for four years and, provided that they are re-elected as municipal councillors, they may be re-elected as deputies. The procedure for meetings of the council is exactly the same as that outlined for municipal councils (see 8.3.2.1).

The provincial council does not have the authority, any more than the town halls, to draft major laws. In certain areas it enjoys the right to draft orders or regulations (*ordenanzas*) which flesh out and must conform to laws emanating from the *Cortes* or the regional parliament. One of its principal functions is to control and oversee the work of the provincial commission (see 8.4.1.3) which is accountable to it. The council may have recourse to the courts to ensure that the commission is operating within the limits laid down by national and regional law. Another major function is to approve annually a provincial co-operation plan concerning municipal works and services; the municipalities are obliged to participate in this plan.

8.4.1.2 *President of the provincial council* (presidente de la diputación provincial)

The president of the council is elected by all the members of the full council from among those members at its first meeting. Any provincial deputy is eligible to be the president. He tends to be a person of standing from the majority party on the council and is often a mayor of an important municipality, though this is not a requirement.

The president is the chief representative of the *diputación*, chairman of the *pleno* and head of the provincial commission with responsibility for the government and administration of the province. It is his duty to convene and preside over sessions of the full council, the commission and any other provincial institutions that may be established by the *diputación*. One of his major duties is to direct, inspect and promote the services and works of the provincial government, including those delegated to it by the regional government. The president must also see that the decisions of the council are enacted and published in the *Official Provincial Gazette* (*Boletín Oficial de la Provincia*). One of his major functions is to appoint vice-presidents of the council as well as the members of the provincial commission from among the provincial deputies. All the staff of the *diputación* are officially appointed in his name.

In the early years of the Franco era, the civil governor was the highest representative of the state at provincial level (see 6.5.3) and he presided over meetings of the provincial council. From 1957, however, the new post of president of the provincial council was created in an attempt to distinguish between the functions of the civil governor's office and the provincial authority. However, the president tended to live under the shadow of the civil governor. Under the new democratic arrangements, however, this process is being reversed and the president is acquiring more prestige while the governor's role is being slowly reduced in significance.

8.4.1.3 *Provincial commission (*comisión provincial de gobierno*)*
The commission consists of the president of the council, his vice-president(s) and a number of provincial deputies whose number may not exceed one-third of the legal total for the province. As we have seen in 8.4.1.2, the members are appointed by the president and are subject to dismissal by him. The principal task of the commission is to assist the president in his duties and to carry out the tasks which may be delegated to it either by the president or by act of the national or regional parliament. The president may, and frequently does, delegate responsibilities for specific tasks to individual members of the commission; indeed, he may also delegate in this way to deputies who do not belong to the commission.

8.4.1.4 *Provincial departments (*delegaciones or áreas*)*
As with the municipal tier of government, the administration of the *diputación* is divided up into several departments (*delegaciones*) each headed by a delegate (*delegado*) who is certainly a provincial deputy and may well be a member of the commission. In the case of the Province of

Figure 8.4. *Provincial departments of Málaga*

Department of General and Economic Services	*Area de Servicios Generales y Económicos*
Department of Health	*Area de Salud*
Department of Social Services	*Area de Servicios Sociales*
Department of Culture, Education and Sport	*Area de Cultura, Educación y Deportes*
Department of Municipal Co-operation	*Area de Cooperación Municipal*

Málaga, the *Diputación* consists of five major departments (*áreas*), as shown in Figure 8.4, each of which are subdivided into a number of divisions (*secciones*). The Department of General and Economic Services (*Area de Servicios Generales y Económicos*), for example, consists of twenty-one sections ranging from finance and revenue to the emergency fire and rescue services.

8.4.2   Special arrangements

Within the above arrangements there are three exceptions to the rule which are outlined in the Basic Law: the Basque Provinces; the single-province autonomous communities, including Navarre; and the Balearic and Canary Islands.

As we have already seen in 7.5.3.2, the three Basque Provinces, Alava, Guipúzcoa and Vizcaya, which were recognised as 'historical territories' in the *concerito económico* negotiated with the central government in 1981, have been able to recover their long-lost privileges, which relate particularly to the levying of taxes. Such privileges are not available to any other provinces, with the exception of Navarre. The *diputaciones forales*, as they are called, whose members are directly elected at the same time as municipal councillors (see 8.3.2.1), exercise these rights in addition to those described above, thus making them much more powerful than most provincial councils. Indeed, in addition to the long-standing friction between Madrid and Vitoria (the seat of the Basque government), tension has now arisen between those advocating virtually autonomous provinces (Alava, Guipúzcoa and Vizcaya) reflecting, in fact, a past historical reality, and the supporters of a strengthened Basque government (see 10.5.1).

The single-province autonomous communities, as we have seen in 7.4, have assumed all the powers, responsibilities and resources of the former provincial authorities. Provincial institutions, as such, therefore, have now ceased to exist and these areas are run by regional bodies which enjoy political as well as administrative autonomy.

The organisation of the Islands (*Islas*) is laid down in Article 41.4 of the Constitution and, in much more detail, in the statutes of autonomy of the

Balearics (*Islas Baleares*) and the Canaries (*Islas Canarias*), each of which forms a separate autonomous community. The problem here is the geographical separation of certain units belonging to the came community. In the case of the Balearics, this has been solved by devolving substantial powers to the three island councils, known as *consejos insulares*, of Mallorca, Menorca and Ibiza–Formentera. Each of these councils is composed of the national deputies elected in these islands who are empowered to head the government and administration thereof. Article 39 of the statute spells out in some detail the powers which they may exercise in addition to those normally exercised by a *diputación provincial*.

In a similar way, the government and administration of the Canaries is entrusted to seven island councils (*cabildos insulares*) which also enjoy greater powers than their equivalent provincial councils on the mainland. Unlike their counterparts in the Balearics, the members (*consejeros*) of the *cabildos insulares* are elected by universal suffrage at the same time as the municipal elections.

8.4.3   Responsibilities of the provincial authority

According to Article 36 of the Basic Law on Local Government the major powers of the *diputación* are as follows: (i) to co-ordinate municipal services and to ensure an adequate and complete provision of services across the whole province; (ii) to give legal, economic and technical assistance to the municipalities, particularly to those of limited economic and administrative capacity; (iii) to provide public services of a supramunicipal nature; and (iv) to develop support for and administer interests that are peculiar to that province.

All the above powers refer to the provincial authority in its role as a local authority and, as such, depend basically on the institutions of the appropriate regional government. However, Article 31(b) of the Basic Law on Local Government makes it clear that one role of the province is to share in the co-ordination of local administration, collaborating with regional and central authorities.

8.5   Other local government entities

As well as the provincial and municipal tiers of government and administration, the Basic Law on Local Government envisages the creation, where appropriate, of both submunicipal and supramunicipal bodies. The aim of the former is to provide an outpost of local administration in small communities separated from the seat of local government within the *término municipal*.

The major example of the former unit is the *entidad local menor* which may be established at village, hamlet or parish level. The institutions of this body are the 'suffragan' mayor (*alcalde pedáneo*) and the neighbourhood council (*junta vecinal*) which is composed of all the electors of the area concerned who, through a majority system, elect one of their number as mayor. The size of the council will vary according to the size of the population. In reality, these bodies are subject to the local *ayuntamiento*, though the latter may devolve certain concrete responsibilities to them.

The purpose of the supramunicipal bodies is to represent and promote the common interests of several municipalities; two examples of these are the district and the metropolitan area.

8.5.1 District (comarca)

Some areas of Spain, for example Catalonia, would have preferred this traditional administrative and political division of the region which, in different political circumstances, might have replaced the provinces both as electoral constituencies and as administrative units. It is significant that the political parties in certain regions, notably the Socialist party, have adopted the *comarca* rather than the province as the base for their immediate subregional institutions. Article 42 of the Basic Law permits the creation of *comarcas*, provided that two-fifths of the municipalities concerned are not expressly opposed to the idea. Interestingly, it is possible for a *comarca* to be formed from municipalities within more than one province provided that both provincial councils approve. Such arrangements, including the territorial limits, the organs and their composition, are subject to approval by laws emanating from the regional parliament.

Similar in many ways to the *comarca* is the *mancomunidad*, usually a larger association of municipalities.

8.5.2 Metropolitan area (área metropolitana)

The *área metropolitana*, as its name suggests, may be established in large urban areas where the joint co-operation of adjacent municipalities is essential to providing a fair, rational and well co-ordinated service across an area that is likely to have many common economic and social problems. Regional law determines the organs of government and administration to be established and ensures the equal representation of all the municipalities involved.

8.6 Financing

Naturally the key factor in the revitalisation of local government and administration in Spain is finance and resources. Article 142 of the Constitution states that local authorities will be financed by their own taxes and from a share in those levied by the state and the autonomous communities. According to national and regional legislation, local authorities have a right to supplement the grants due to them from higher levels of government by raising their own revenue from local sources. The major part of this local revenue comes from taxes of various kinds, such as the Spanish equivalent of rates, licences for property, businesses and vehicles, income from public transport, fines for driving, parking and other offences as well as revenue from local cultural and historical attractions. Obviously these sources constitute only a small fraction of the global financial needs of any municipal authority.

Every year each local authority is obliged by law to approve and publish a single budget covering all revenue and expected expenditure during the coming financial year. During a fixed period of time this budget is on view to members of the public who have the right to make complaints; subsequently the budget is published in the official *Gazette* of that authority. Final approval of the budget must be given by the full council of the appropriate authority before 31 December prior to the financial year concerned; if approval is not granted, the budget for the previous year stands.

In line with the policy of greater accountability of both public and private organisations in Spain, the accounts of local authorities must be scrutinised each year by a special audit committee, the *Comisión Especial de Cuentas*, of each local authority. This body is made up of members from the various political groups represented in the full council. Like the annual budget, the accounts must be available to the public before being approved by the council. In addition the accounts must be submitted to the State Audit Tribunal (see 9.7.3).

8.7   Conclusion

From the foregoing it can already be seen how, in many ways, local administration in Spain has been or is being transformed in comparison with the rigid and ossified structure and practices of the past. Some of the most important moves in this direction relate to the more flexible arrangements between different tiers of administration and to the tightening up of accounting practices as well as legislation to ensure that devolved responsibilities will be accompanied by devolved resources. In one other important way, too, the system is slowly being modernised and that is in the field of communication and public involvement.

At least as far as the man in the street is concerned, this is perhaps the most obvious way in which, both in theory and in practice, local government is being modernised. Article 69 of the Basic Law in fact states: 'The local corporations shall provide the fullest information about their activities and facilitate the involvement of all citizens in local life.' Article 70 lays down that sessions of the *plenos* must be open to the public and, of course, to the media, with the exception of meetings of the commissions.

Decisions taken by the local authorities must be made public, including the annual budget. All citizens have the right to obtain copies of the decisions taken by local councils and any background to such agreements, as well as a right to consult archives and registers. Another form of popular involvement is the referendum, which mayors and presidents of provincial councils may call, on matters of 'a local nature which are of special interest to local residents', with the exception of financial matters.

Article 72 is worth quoting in full because it shows how those concerned with the reform of local government are determined to encourage more open government and more popular involvement in local affairs:

The local authorities favour the development of associations for the defence of the general or sectorial interests of residents, they provide them with the fullest information about their activities and, as far as possible, they make public resources available to them, give them access to the economic aid required to meet their objectives, and they encourage their participation in the running of the authority . . .

While this right might be interpreted as a skilful political move to ensure that local pressure groups, like the once very militant neighbourhood associations (*asociaciones de vecinos*) are brought into the fold, in the long term such offers (provided they are backed up by action and public funds), could well be of great benefit to the health of local government in Spain.

There is little doubt that the sort of reforms outlined above, plus the fact that local elections are now carried out in a fully democratic manner, have begun to reawaken a genuine interest in local affairs in recent years. In the main, local authorities, particularly at the municipal level, have responded to this and have been much more prepared than in the past to provide information on the activities and plans of the councils, as well as to stimulate more involvement in local activities – be they economic, political or cultural. It will be a long time, however, before the depressing legacy of centuries of neglect is finally eradicated.

9   Public sector enterprises

The involvement of the Spanish state in the economy is expressly recognised in the 1978 Constitution. Although Article 38 declares that Spain is
to have a market economy, the right of the state to intervene in the
economy, when the public interest is at stake, is confirmed in Article 128
which refers to the right to public ownership of resources and essential
services. Article 129 refers to diverse forms of participation in public
ownership and this appears to acknowledge the complex mixture of
organisations inherited by post-Franco governments. The pragmatic
approach to economic policy during the Franco era led to the creation of
a series of entities which seemed to possess a momentum of their own,
often removed from their original objectives and the prevailing needs of
the time. These entities enjoyed considerable autonomy which was compounded by the fact that responsibility rested at various times with
different ministries. In many cases senior posts were the reward for loyal
service to the regime and the significance and direction of many enterprises
was due to the nature of the undertaking's chairman, be he a military or
political figure or a technocrat. In attempting, therefore, to understand the
institutions which pertain to the public sector, it is important to appreciate
that often their structures and traditions are vestiges of the previous regime
and that proper control and accountability are relatively new concepts.

Classification of the public sector may take various forms according to
whether it be for legal, administrative or financial purposes. However, the
1977 Budget Law (*Ley de Presupuestos*) divided the public sector into
three subsectors, all of which are dealt with in this volume. These subsectors are: autonomous administrative bodies (see 6.3), public sector
financial institutions (see Chapter 13) and public sector enterprises
(*empresas públicas*). In turn, the public sector enterprises may be considered under different groupings. Here, however, they will be examined
according to the headings used in the public sector accounts (see Figure
9.1).

Figure 9.1. *Public sector enterprises*

1. Autonomous commercial, industrial and financial bodies	*Organismos autónomos comerciales, industriales y financieros*
2. Companies under the National Institute for Industry	*Empresas del Instituto Nacional de Industria*
3. Companies under the Directorate General for State Assets	*Empresas de la Dirección General del Patrimonio*
4. Companies under the National Institute for Hydrocarbons	*Empresas del Instituto Nacional de Hidrocarburos*
5. Other public sector entities	*Otros entes públicos*

9.1 Autonomous commercial, industrial and financial bodies (*organismos autónomos comerciales, industriales y financieros*)

These bodies are organised like the administrative bodies described in 6.3. They, too, are dependent on particular ministries and because of the nature of their responsibilities they are given a considerable degree of autonomy in their day-to-day running. They are distinguished from these other bodies in that they have a commercial, industrial or financial role which makes a more independent structure appear more appropriate. Although they do not have the legal status of public limited SA companies (see 12.3) they can, to all intents and purposes, be considered as public sector enterprises.

In 1985 there were more than eighty of these bodies and some idea of the range of ministries and fields of operation involved can be seen from the examples provided in Figure 9.2. Several ministries have provision for housing for their civil servants and their dependants and these housing schemes are run by a housing trust (*patronato de casas*) which corresponds to the specific ministry. This, for example, is particularly important in the case of the armed forces and hence the Ministry of Defence has a housing trust for each branch of the forces. Numerically important, too, are the port authorities (*juntas de puerto*) which are responsible for the facilities around Spain's extensive coastline.

The most significant body of this type in economic terms is the National Institute for Industry (*Instituto Nacional de Industria*/INI). This is a state holding company responsible in turn for more than seventy public sector companies (see 9.2). It has a staff of some 660 people and it is constituted as an autonomous body under the auspices of the Ministry of Industry and Energy from which it receives its general policy guidelines and to which it is responsible in the discharge of its duties. It has its own board with a chairman, vice-chairman and secretary appointed by the Minister of Industry and Energy, together with twenty-one members from various

Figure 9.2. *Examples of autonomous commercial, industrial and financial bodies (1985)*

Ministry responsible	Autonomous body	Function
Ministry of Economy and Finance	*Fábrica Nacional de Moneda y Timbre*	Mint
	Instituto de Crédito Oficial (ICO)	Co-ordination of official credit (see 13.8)
	Consorcio de Compensación de Seguros	Insurance underwriting (see 13.12.1)
Ministry of Public Works and Town Planning	*Junta del Puerto de Algeciras*	Port authority
	Confederación Hidrográfica del Duero	Irrigation authority
	Instituto para la Promoción Pública de la Vivienda(IPPV)	Housing finance
Ministry of Industry and Energy	*Instituto Nacional de Industria* (INI)	Holding company
Ministry of Agriculture Fisheries and Food	*Servicio Nacional de Productos Agrarios* (SENPA)	Agricultural market regulation
	Instituto para la Conservación de la Naturaleza (ICONA)	Forestry, conservation and state parks
	Fondo de Ordenación y Regulación de Producciones y Precios Agrarios (FORPPA)	Intervention agency for price regulation
	Empresa Nacional de Seguros Agrarios (ENESA)	Agricultural insurance (see 13.12.2)
Ministry of Transport Tourism and Communications	*Caja Postal de Ahorros*	Post Office Savings Bank (see 13.5.1)
	Aeropuertos Nacionales	Civil airports
Ministry of Culture	*Teatros Nacionales*	National theatres

other ministries, reflecting the diverse range of activities in which INI companies are engaged.

The Ministry of Agriculture has a number of significant commercial and financial bodies under its auspices in addition to the administrative bodies already referred to in 6.3. These are involved in the whole range of price support and intervention schemes which are an integral part of the agricultural sector and as such they are responsible for significant budgets. They have been modelled largely along the lines of those of other EEC countries and have been steadily coming into harmony with the various intervention agencies of the Common Agricultural Policy.

From time to time attempts are made to rationalise the large number of autonomous bodies in order to produce more efficiency and greater economies. Hence the Housing Development Agency (*Instituto para la Promoción Pública de la Vivienda*/IPPV), was created in 1981 to replace three other bodies: the *Instituto Nacional de la Vivienda*, the *Instituto Nacional de Urbanización* and the *Administración del Patrimonio Social*

Urbano. Likewise, in 1981 the Insurance Compensation Consortium (*Consorcio de Compensación de Seguros*) was reformed and it took over responsibility for underwriting third-party vehicle insurance from three other bodies (see 13.12.1). Further attempts to reduce the number of autonomous entities are likely to follow in the future.

9.2 Companies under the National Institute for Industry (*Instituto Nacional de Industria*/INI)

The creation of the National Institute for Industry in 1941 needs to be viewed against the economic background of the immediate post-Civil War years (see 1.2). During the ensuing years of autarky the aim of the INI was to provide the basis for an economy oriented towards economic self-sufficiency. It was involved in sectors in which private interests could not or would not invest. It pursued a policy of import substitution and it took over responsibility for all defence and strategic industries. Since those early days its role has changed in the light of different economic and political circumstances.

As a holding company the INI possesses shares in a number of companies which in turn are constituted as public limited liability SA companies (see 12.3). Its holding is not static since, according to the policy of the time, it may be acquiring or disposing of companies or it may be increasing or decreasing its shareholding in existing companies within the group. On 1 January 1985 it participated directly in some sixty-three companies which in turn directly controlled 150 subsidiaries. Even where the INI does not hold a majority of shares, its influence is usually decisive. It forms a major industrial group within the economy, employing over 200,000 workers and contributing about 10 per cent of Spain's gross domestic product. In some sectors of the economy the INI companies produce most, if not the entire, output. Thus 75 per cent of ships built in Spain are constructed by the INI and 100 per cent of aluminium. In other sectors it represents considerably less, producing approximately a third of total steel, electricity and industrial vehicles.

Some, but by no means all, INI companies are recognisable by the prefix *Empresa Nacional* or EN in their name. Otherwise they are indistinguishable externally from other SA companies and many of them have their shares quoted on the stock exchange. Government influence, however, is strong, particularly as the chairmen and most of the board members are state appointees. Indeed, in the past much criticism has been levelled at the choice of retired military and political figures in key sectors of Spanish industry. The INI itself has been no exception to this practice and personalities have been important in determining the direction its policies have taken. Nevertheless, in recent years serious attempts have been made to ensure a more technical and business-like approach to the running of the holding as a whole. The government exercises control over the planning of the activities, investments and financing of the group through its approval of programmes for each enterprise (*Programas de Actuación, Inversiones y Financiación*/PAIF). The *Cortes* is then required to approve a budget for INI and to agree to borrowing limits. Ultimately the State Audit Tribunal checks and audits the accounts of the INI itself and the companies in which it participates. At the same time the reporting procedures between the INI and the group have been considerably strengthened. The INI's own team of inspectors and auditors are anxious to see that guidelines are adhered to and that there is no repetition of the more *laissez-faire* practices which earned the holding a bad name at the height of the Franco era.

The INI has traditionally been associated with firms with financial problems, characterised by low productivity, over-manning, obsolete equipment, substantial losses and large borrowings with subsequent high debt repayments. To some extent, this has been inherent in the nature of the sectors in which the holding has been most heavily involved but it also reflects vicissitudes in policy and control. At times it was expected to play a subsidiary role to the private sector and to manage firms in crisis sectors such as textiles. On other occasions it was encouraged to take a more aggressive stance and to promote new advanced technology sectors in the fields of electronics and computers. From 1975 to 1982 it seemed to be largely concerned with safeguarding employment by taking over or increasing its holding in companies in diverse sectors which were making heavy losses and in imminent danger of closure. These included companies in shipbuilding (*Hijos de J. Barreras*), capital goods (Babcock and Wilcox), tourism (*Viajes Marsans*) and the motor industry (SEAT). The latter is an example of a company which has seen its INI participation rise and fall on a number of occasions. Currently the majority of SEAT shares are held by Volkswagen.

Since 1982 the government has used its INI holdings to promote its industrial rationalisation policies more energetically. To a large extent this has been an inevitable consequence of the concentration of its participation precisely in those sectors which have excess capacity. Thus, in the case of shipbuilding and iron and steel, which were responsible for almost half of the total group losses in 1984, the government has drawn up rationalisation programmes (*planes de reconversión*) which have led, *inter alia*, to the closure of an entire steel works, that of *Altos Hornos del Mediterráneo* (AHM) at Sagunto and the slimming down of the labour force employed in the shipyards owned by *Astilleros Españoles* (AESA).

The companies are organised in sectorial divisions, each headed by a director with a management team. The divisional structure is shown in Figure 9.3, together with some examples of the companies which make up the group and the percentage INI shareholding in 1984.

The INI's major investment has tended to be concentrated in the Basque

Figure 9.3. *Examples of companies under the National Institute for Industry (1984)*

Division (no. of companies)	Example of company	% INI shareholding	No. of employees in the division
Electricity (2)	Empresa Nacional de Electricidad, SA (ENDESA)	97.3	14,601
Iron and steel (4)	Empresa Nacional Siderúrgica, SA (ENSIDESA)	97.5	26,701
Mining (3)	Empresa Nacional Hulleras del Norte, SA (HUNOSA)	100.0	23,336
Defence (4)	Empresa Nacional Bazán de Construcciones Navales Militares, SA (Bazán);	100.0	27,942
	Construcciones Aeronaúticas, SA (CASA)	71.6	
Shipbuilding (4)	Astilleros Españoles, SA (AESA)	100.0	19,376
Capital goods (5)	Aplicaciones Técnicas Industriales, SA (ATEINSA)	85.8	7,775
Aluminium (2)	Empresa Nacional del Aluminio, (ENDASA)	63.5	7,257
Food processing (1)	Empresa Nacional para el Desarrollo de la Industria Alimentaria, SA (ENDIASA)	100.0	4,160
Electronic and data processing (6)	Sociedad Española de Comunicaciones e Informática, SA (SECOINSA)	55.3	3,290
Motor vehicles (2)	Empresa Nacional de Autocamiones, SA (ENASA);	100.0	32,213
	Sociedad Española de Automóviles de Turismo, SA (SEAT)	94.8	
Ball bearings (2)	SKF Española	97.0	1,398
Fertilisers (4)	Empresa Nacional de Fertilizantes, SA (ENFERSA)	100.0	4,283
Air transport (2)	Iberia, Líneas Aéreas de España, SA (Iberia);	99.5	26,018
	Aviación y Comercio, SA (AVIACO)	67.0	
Sea transport (2)	Compañía Trasatlántica Española, SA (Trasatlántica)	93.9	1,348
Miscellaneous companies (8)	Viajes Marsans, SA (Marsans)	100.0	10,287
Regional development (8)	Sociedad para el Desarrollo Industrial de Galicia, SA (SODIGA)	54.0	173
Foreign trade and finance (4)	Sociedad de Inversiones Mobiliarias en el Exterior (SIMEX)	100.0	177

Source: INI, *Annual Report*, 1984

Country, Catalonia and Madrid. However, in a move to promote industrial development in other generally poorer regions, a number of special industrial development corporations have been established since 1972. These have the prefix SODI (*Sociedad de Desarrollo Industrial*), which means Industrial Development Corporation, followed by the first letters of the region concerned. The following seven corporations existed in 1985: SODIGA (Galicia); SODIAN (Andalusia); SODIEX (Extremadura); SODICAN (Canary Islands); SODICAL (Castilla y León); SODICAMAN (Castilla–La Mancha); and SODIAR (Aragón).

The INI generally holds just over 51 per cent of the shares, the other shareholders being savings banks, commercial banks and the *Banco Exterior*. The regional authorities also now have shareholdings and are represented on the boards of these corporations, a logical step in view of the emphasis on decentralising public sector involvement and encouraging local initiatives. The SODI aim to take a minority holding in new enterprises and to provide sufficient financial assistance and technical back-up in order to support job creation. Their involvement is regarded as being of a temporary nature with the intention of leaving successful ventures in the hands of private enterprise once they have proved viable. At the end of 1984 they participated in some 300 companies employing a total of just over 11,000 people.

9.3   Public sector companies under the Directorate General for State Assets (*Dirección General del Patrimonio del Estado/ DGPE*)

The DGPE functions under the auspices of the Ministry of Economy and Finance and it is responsible for administering the state's direct shareholding in companies. It operates at a similar level to the INI in that it seeks to co-ordinate the activities of a large number of diverse enterprises. In this case, however, the shares are held by the state directly rather than indirectly through a holding company, as is the case with the INI.

The *grupo patrimonio*, as it is known, consists of companies from a variety of economic sectors: communications, finance, services, transport, agriculture and textiles. There are some twenty-four companies in the group, although the number is not rigid as companies may cease to operate or be sold off and new companies created. In turn these companies hold shares in some eighty other companies, many of which they effectively control. In an attempt to provide greater cohesion and to facilitate analysis, the DGPE now groups the companies under broad sector headings, as can be seen in Figure 9.4.

These companies also differ considerably in size measured by various criteria such as number of employees, turnover, total assets, direct investment, and so on. Whatever criteria are adopted three companies dominate the group: the telephone company (*Telefónica*), the tobacco distributor (*Tabacalera*) and the overseas trade (*Banco Exterior*). Together these represent 75 per cent of turnover, 69 per cent of profits and 83 per cent of employment within the group. Some, on the other hand, are extremely small and are confined to very specific objectives. Thus, the somewhat

Figure 9.4. *Companies under Directorate General for State Assets (1984)*

Sector	Company	% of state holding	No. of employees
Banking	Banco de Crédito Agrícola	100.0	351
	Banco de Crédito Industrial	100.0	530
	Banco de Crédito Local de España	100.0	288
	Banco Hipotecario de España	100.0	884
Export Finance	Banco Exterior de España	51.4	8,873
	Compañía Española de Seguros a la Exportación (CESCE)	50.2	325
Agriculture	Mercados en Origen de Productos Agrarios, SA (MERCORSA)	52.0	120
	Empresa de Transformación Agraria, SA (TRAGSA)	20.0	1,900
Industry			
Textiles	Hilaturas y Tejidos Andaluces, SA (HYTASA)	100.0	1,495
Textiles	Intelhorce, SA	100.0	2,205
Textiles	Hilaturas Gossypium, SA	53.2	840
Footwear	Industrias Mediterráneas de la Piel, SA (IMPIEL)	96.4	2,070
Tobacco	Tabacalera, SA	53.5	8,554
Mercury	Minas de Almadén y Arrayanes, SA (MAYASA)	100.0	1,045
Salt	Nueva Compañía Arrendataria de las Salinas de Torrevieja, SA	25.0	513
Services			
Telephones	Compañía Telefónica Nacional de España (CTNE)	31.5	66,029
Shipping	Compañía Trasmediterránea, SA	95.7	2,891
Shipping	Remolques Marítimos, SA (REMASA)	66.6	133
News agency	Agencia EFE, SA	33.3	714
Tunnel project	Sociedad Española de Estudios para la Comunicación Fija a través del Estrecho de Gibraltar, SA (SECEGSA)	100.0	12
Discovery of America anniversary activities	Sociedad Estatal de Ejecución de Programas Conmemorativos del V Centenario del Descubrimiento de America, SA	100.0	10
Commerce			
Duty free shops	Almacenes, Depósitos y Estaciones Aduaneros, SA (ALDEASA)	100.0	377
Film making	Cinespaña, SA	99.4	9

Source: DGPE, *Annual Report*, 1984

weightily titled *Sociedad Estatal de Ejecución de Programas Conmemorativos del V Centenario del Descubrimiento de América*, SA was established in 1981 in order to prepare for the five hundredth anniversary, in 1992, of the discovery of America. In 1983 it employed ten people. The *Sociedad Española de Estudios para la Comunicación Fija a través del Estrecho de Gibraltar*, SA (SECEGSA) was also created in 1981. It employs twelve people and its main functions are the study and promotion of a tunnel across the straits of Gibraltar.

The DGPE is of long standing and a plaque unveiled by General Franco in 1974 marking the centenary of its foundation still stands in the ministry corridors. One of the main purposes of the DGPE was to ensure the appropriate transfer to the state of tax revenue due from the sale of certain commodities which were placed in the hands of monopoly distributors. This has been the case of *Tabacalera*, SA responsible for tobacco distribution since 1945, and its monopoly is due to come to an end as a result of Spain's entry into the EEC. Similarly the DGPE was responsible for CAMPSA, the petroleum products entity which was transferred to the newly created INH in 1981 (see 9.4). The national telephone and telecommunications network is clearly a major concern of the state and hence the *Compañía Telefónica Nacional de España*, SA (CTNE) (generally known as *Telefónica*), comes under the auspices of the DGPE. The state's interest in the world's major mercury mines at Almadén were for a long time in the hands of an autonomous body until in 1981 it was reconstituted as a state company known as *Minas de Almadén y Arrayanes*, SA (MAYASA) under the auspices of the DGPE.

In other cases the DGPE proved a convenient agent for activities which did not fit clearly into the framework of other ministries. It was also supposed to ensure a more independent outlook than might arise from sharing control among various competing ministries. In general, the management of the companies in the group is decentralised as each is constituted as a separate public limited liability company in its own right. Each company has its own board of directors (*consejo de administración*) which exercises its functions, as in any other company, in accordance with the respective articles of association. However, as the state generally holds the majority of shares (in some cases the totality), board membership is usually made up largely of government appointees. Even where the state does not hold all the shares, the other shareholders are frequently drawn from other parts of the public sector. Furthermore, on occasions a specific government representative or delegate (*delegado del gobierno*) is appointed to safeguard the state's interests in key sectors, as is the case with both *Telefónica* and *Tabacalera*. This also applies to the salt mining concern, *Nueva Compañía Arrendataria de las Salinas de Torrevieja*, SA, where the state only holds thirty-eight and a half per cent of the shares but where the representative happens to be the director general of the DGPE himself.

While the larger companies can provide full managerial functions for themselves, some of the smaller concerns can benefit from access to shared facilities and the support of group management services. On the other hand, the desire to secure greater accountability at all levels of government since the restoration of democracy in Spain has increased the need for greater co-ordination and steps have been taken since 1977 to exercise greater control than was previously the case. The DGPE has a formal set of management guidelines and regular reporting procedures. These were reinforced by rules designed to define more clearly the complex inter-relationships between the state, the company and the shareholders. Although some measure of standardisation in the presentation of financial data appears to have been achieved, the move towards overall harmonisation in planning and management is proving more difficult and time-consuming.

In recent years the DGPE has also been seen to take a more active role in carrying out government economic policy. Thus it has been involved in the industrial rationalisation of the textile industry through its participation in HYTASA, *Intelhorce*, SA and *Hilaturas Gossypium*, SA. These companies have been heavy loss-makers and considerable restructuring has been required, this has proved to be a painful experience for those involved, especially as the two former companies are located in Andalusia, where unemployment is particularly high.

The role of the DGPE in the public sector was enhanced when it was given responsibility for the RUMASA group of companies following the expropriation of this conglomerate in February 1983. The complex network of companies required careful scrutiny to distinguish fact from fiction and help was required from international auditing firms to complete the task. The government held firm to its avowed intention of returning companies to the private sector as soon as possible and the DGPE took advice from a special commission established to adjudicate the various bids. Thus, within two years the reprivatisation process had been largely completed with some 220 firms sold to private interests and a further 502 firms put into liquidation. At the time of writing only a few companies remain in the hands of the DGPE.

This process has not been without controversy and the trial of the founder of the RUMASA group, José María Ruíz Mateos, extradited to Spain from Germany in December 1985, is likely to add further fuel to this. Reprivatisation appears to have been an expensive exercise and it has led to over 5,000 redundancies. Moreover, there has been criticism of the fact that some of the leading companies in the group have been sold off to foreign investors as was the case with the *Banco Atlántico*, sold to the Arab Banking Corporation, and *Galerías Preciados*, sold to the Venezuelan Cisneros group. There was a feeling in trade union circles at least, that not only had the carve up of the banking entities between the existing powerful 'big seven' strengthened their position, but the state had also lost an opportunity to further its interests in this sector of the economy.

9.4 National Institute for Hydrocarbons (*Instituto Nacional de Hidrocarburos*/INH)

The INH was founded in 1981 as a state holding company along the lines of the INI in order to combine that part of the energy sector which had pre-

Figure 9.5. *Companies under the National Institute for Hydrocarbons (1984)*

Company	Activity	% of INH holding	No. of employees
Hispanoil	Prospecting and	100.0	262
Empresa Nacional de Investigación y Explotación de Petróleos, SA (ENIEPSA)	production of hydrocarbons	100.0	415
Empresa Nacional de Petróleos, SA (EMP)	Transport and refining of crude	99.9	5,422
Compañía Ibérica Refinadora de Petróleos, SA (Petrolíber)	oil	82.7	800
Compañía Arrendataria del Monopolio de Petróleo, SA (CAMPSA)	Distribution and marketing of petroleum products	97.5	8,629
Butano, SA	Distribution and	100.0	3,428
Empresa Nacional del Gas, SA (ENAGAS)	marketing of natural gas	100.0	538
Asfaltos Españoles, SA (ASESA)	Transport and refining of crude oil	50.0	50
Productos Asfálticos, SA (PROAS)	Distribution and marketing of petroleum products	25.0[a]	279
Aplicaciones de Energía, SA (APLESA)	Engineering and research	100.0	31

[a] Another company within the group, ASESA, owns a further 50 per cent of the share capital.
Source: INH, *Annual Report*, 1984

viously been under the control of the INI, with two companies, CAMPSA and *Petrolíber*, which has previously been under the auspices of the *Dirección General del Patrimonio*. It is structured and run in a similar way to the INI. This new grouping, however, came as a setback for those who believed in a positive and expansionary role for the INI by taking away from it a major sector with profit-making capacity. It appeared to heighten the belief that the INI was left to concentrate on crisis sector management.

Nevertheless it presents a model for a more rational structure for state enterprises by bringing together those companies closely identified with a specific sector. This is particularly significant in the case of energy in view of the post-1973 crisis and Spain's heavy reliance on imported oil as a source of energy.

The INH was therefore set up to co-ordinate and control all the public sector enterprises operating in oil, natural gas and petrochemicals. It was considered to be a way of facilitating the implementation and achievement of an energy policy and of promoting technological research and development.

In 1985 it directly controlled ten companies and indirectly controlled twenty-five. It was also a minority shareholder in a further twenty-one companies. Through the companies it controlled, it employed over 22,200 employees and it represented over 1 per cent of Spain's gross domestic product. The companies controlled by the INH were responsible for 46 per cent of Spain's petrochemical products, 42 per cent of the crude oil refined and 100 per cent of the natural gas produced in Spain. The ten companies in which the holding company had more than a 50 per cent stake in 1984 are indicated in Figure 9.5.

The number of companies in such a volatile sector is clearly not static and rationalisation initiated in 1985 has already led to the mergers of *Hispanoil* and ENIEPSA, and EMP, *Petrolíber* and INH's holdings in ASESA. In addition to those companies directly controlled by INH, there are some forty-five companies in which it has minority or indirect share-holding.

The position of CAMPSA is currently being altered. It has operated as a state-run monopoly since its foundation in 1927 as a means of securing a proper tax return to the state from this key resource. However, in the light of EEC legislation its monopoly status can no longer be retained and it is being restructured, with parts being transferred to private sector and other state-owned refineries. In 1985 INH's effective holding in CAMPSA was thus reduced by more than 30 per cent.

9.5   Other entities

There are a number of other public sector entities which do not come under the auspices of the holding companies described above nor are they classified as autonomous commercial, industrial or financial bodies. Instead more flexibility and greater independence is granted to so-called state companies (*sociedades estatales*) operating in particular spheres of activity. These include Spanish Railways (*Red Nacional de Ferrocarriles Españoles*/RENFE) and Spanish Radio and Television (*Radio Televisión Española*/RTVE). These have their own separate legal identity and autonomous status regulated by government legislation and decrees. Their budgets have to be approved by the *Cortes* and they are also subject to the financial controls outlined in 9.7. Control of the television network has been a controversial issue, especially as at the moment there is no alternative to the state-run network. The legal framework is now regulated by a Law of 10 January 1980 which, among other aspects, seeks to secure independence by having an elected board of management, six members being appointed by each House of Parliament. In the case of RENFE, nationalised in 1941 and granted its own statute in 1964, the Minister of

Transport is responsible for appointing the members of the board who then choose a chairman and executive director. The Minister also approves the budget and borrowing requirements and he generally oversees its operations. In addition, the Ministry of Economy and Finance also has its own representative (*delegado*) on the board. The government now agrees the major policy guidelines and investment plans in the form of a forward contract-plan (*contrato-programa*).

9.6   Co-ordination

The very fact that there are so many different entities, each with some degree of autonomy, makes co-ordination difficult to achieve. This is further compounded by the fragmentation of decision-making between different ministries, leading to diffusion in authority. At times there is no clear demarcation between the holding companies themselves. Thus the INI has major shareholdings in some of the companies within the DGPE group. Similarly the Official Credit Institute (*Instituto de Crédito Oficial/* ICO), itself an autonomous financial entity, is responsible in turn for four official credit institutions (*entidades oficiales de crédito/*EOC) which are under the jurisdiction of the DGPE (see 13.8). The INI and the DGPE both operate in diverse sectors of the economy and their companies are also very varied in size and experience. Furthermore, as many of the enterprises are a mixture of private as well as public capital, there may often be a conflict of interests. Thus, although the state may be the majority shareholder, decisions may be strongly influenced by the private sector, which may include foreign investors.

It is not surprising, therefore, that concern has been felt for a long time about the accountability of public sector enterprises. To whom are they answerable and what guarantee is there that money is being wisely spent? The nature of the Franco regime meant that for a long time public criticism was difficult and only rare scandals, such as that involving the misappropriation of official credit by the *Matesa* company in the 1960s, cast any light on the activities of some areas of the public sector.

9.7   Financial control

Clearly, therefore, some moves to correct these anomalies were to be expected in the post-Franco era and the *Cortes* now takes more interest in the allocation of resources than was previously the case. In the first instance, budgets within the public sector are subject to substantial parliamentary scrutiny before being approved. Thereafter, control is exercised in a number of ways: internal audit; treasury control; external audit; and independent audit.

9.7.1 Internal audit

In recent years the three state holding companies have strengthened their control over the companies in which they participate. Thus the INI, for example, has a strong audit section with its own team of auditors who standardise reporting procedures and check the financial records and statements of the respective companies.

9.7.2 Treasury control

The Ministry of Economy and Finance has a department, the State Audit Corps (*Intervención General de la Administración del Estado*/IGAE) with more than 200 inspectors who are in regular, if not permanent, contact with the various entities of the public sector. There are also separate corps for the supervision of the regional and local authorities. Reports are submitted from the Ministry of Economy and Finance to the ministry responsible for co-ordinating the particular entity concerned and copies are sent to the council of ministers. If it is suspected that any criminal irregularities have taken place, a report is submitted from the IGAE to the Directorate General for Litigation (*Dirección General de lo Contencioso*) of the Ministry of Economy and Finance. This department will then decide whether or not to recommend that the papers be forwarded to the state prosecutor (*fiscal*).

9.7.3 Audit Tribunal (Tribunal de Cuentas)

Parliament delegates the detailed examination and control over all public sector accounts to the Audit Tribunal which was entrusted by the Constitution (Article 136) with responsibility for the financial scrutiny (*fiscalización*) of all state and public sector accounts. Article 153 of the Constitution also gave it responsibility for the accounts of the regional governments. Some of these have since created their own audit tribunals without prejudice to the power of the State Audit Tribunal. Thus, in Catalonia there is the *Sindicatura de Cuentas* and in Galicia, the *Consejo de Cuentas*. Navarre, because of its traditional economic privileges (see 7.5.3.2), has its own independent system, the *Cámara de Cómputos*, which handles the accounts of local authorities without recourse to the *Tribunal de Cuentas*. Indeed they rejected a demand to submit accounts to the State Audit Tribunal in 1985 on the grounds that this would merely duplicate the existing provisions.

The Audit Tribunal seeks to confirm whether the various bodies have legally and efficiently discharged their responsibilities in accordance with the Constitution and the law. It presents an annual report to the *Cortes* or to the legislative assemblies of the regional governments as the case may be. It is an independent body the members (*consejeros de cuentas*) of which have the same status as members of the judiciary. They have to be suitably qualified as auditors, lawyers or economists with a minimum of fifteen years' professional experience. Six members are appointed by each chamber of parliament and the twelve in turn propose one of their number to the king for approval as chairman (*presidente*). Members are appointed for nine years and the chairman holds office for three years.

9.7.4   Independent audit

In recent years it has become common for many of the major public sector enterprises to have external audits by independent auditors usually drawn from the major international accounting firms. This reflects an increased reliance on external foreign sources of finance and the need to indicate credit-worthiness, as well as being a measure of the increasing involvement of state enterprises in foreign trade.

9.8   Conclusion

Although some steps have been taken towards the rationalisation of the vast array of public sector companies with the creation of the energy sector holding company INH, considerable overlap still exists between the various bodies responsible for the co-ordination of the sector as a whole. At the same time, the regulation of public sector companies remains long overdue despite the fact that ·the need to restructure, control and co-ordinate the public sector was highlighted in the various social pacts between the government, political parties, employers and unions (see 11.5). Thus, although the Moncloa Pacts of 1977 made reference to the need for a special statute for public sector enterprises (*Estatuto de la Empresa Pública*), progress has been slow and the proposal has not yet got beyond the preliminary draft stage.

Nevertheless, the public sector in general has become subject to much more scrutiny. There now appears to be a clear acceptance that greater accountability is required at all levels of society and that auditing in both the public and private sector must be taken seriously. Since the PSOE came to power in 1982, there has been an increasing emphasis on investigative audits and more than 300 public sector enterprises have been the subject of state audits. Perhaps not surprisingly, the general public – long suspicious of financial irregularities during the Franco era – has shown considerable interest in the findings of the various auditing bodies outlined above. This interest has been stimulated by the discovery of deficiencies in a wide spectrum of activities ranging from the state railways to the Prado Museum. However, this greater openness, although at times painful in its exposure of failures, may go a long way towards restoring the long-tarnished image of Spain's public sector.

10 Political parties

10.1 Political parties, past and present

Like many democratic institutions in Spain, political parties have often experienced a precarious existence. For long periods they have either been outlawed or seen their activities severely curtailed. For much of the nineteenth and twentieth centuries the political scene was dominated by the military, which conferred upon itself the right to intervene in political life whenever it judged that stability was threatened. Since the beginning of the nineteenth century, neither democracy itself nor political parties in particular have had the most favourable opportunities to take root; prior to the post-Franco era, the party system was subject to severe economic, social and political pressures that prevented it from establishing and consolidating itself as it had done in other countries of Western Europe.

After the Civil War, Franco abolished all political parties, except his own subservient National Movement which was an amalgam of loyal right-wing groups (see 1.2). With the exception of the PSOE, the PCE, the PNV and the ERC (see Figures 10.1 and 10.5), all the parties that had occupied the political stage in the 1930s sank without trace. However, in the wake of the Political Reform Law of 1976 (see 1.4), there occurred a veritable explosion of political parties, at national and regional level, all eager to participate in the first democratic elections for over forty years, scheduled for 15 June 1977. In total it is estimated that there were some 200 parties in existence at the time, ranging from the extreme Left to the extreme Right.

Some of these, on the Left, had emerged clandestinely in the late 1960s and early 70s to enjoy a risky existence under Francoist repression; some in the Centre and on the Right had begun to form as political associations under the pseudo-democratic legislation of Arias Navarro, who in 1974 legalised political groupings under the limited umbrella of the National Movement. The majority, however, were formed as a consequence of the Suárez reform between late 1976 and the spring of 1977 (see 1.4).

Figure 10.1. *National political parties in Spain (1986)*

Name of party	Ideology	Founder(s)	Year founded	Leader(s), 1986
Partido Socialista Obrero Español – PSOE	Socialist	Pablo Iglesias	1879	Felipe González
Partido Comunista de España – PCE	Communist	Antonio García Daniel Anguiano Mesto García	1920	Gerardo Iglesias Antonio Hernández Mancha
Alianza Popular – AP[a]	Conservative	Manuel Fraga	1976	Antonio Hernández Mancha
Partido Demócrata Popular – PDP[a]	Christian Democrat	Oscar Alzaga	1982	Oscar Alzaga
Partido Liberal – PL[a]	Liberal	Pedro Schwartz	1982	José Antonio Segurado
Centro Democrático y Social – CDS	Social-Democrat	Adolfo Suárez	1982	Adolfo Suárez
Partido Reformista Democrático – PRD	Liberal	Miguel Roca	1983	Miguel Roca Antonio Garrigues

[a] From 1982 to 1986 these three parties fought as a coalition known as the Popular Coalition (*Coalición Popular* / CP)

10.2   Constitutional and legal position

Bearing in mind the vicissitudes of political parties in the past, the constitution drafters of 1978 inserted specific guarantees about their existence and their rights within the country's new Constitution. Article 6 states as follows: 'Political parties express political pluralism, they contribute to the formation and expression of the popular will and they are the major instrument of political participation.'

There is little doubt that reference to political parties, like that to the trade unions (see Chapter 11), was deliberately incorporated in order to pre-empt attempts to restore any kind of pseudo-democracy that limited or prohibited the participation of parties in the political process. Hence, in order to preserve and legitimise their vital role, they have been, as it were, institutionalised. Moreover, the Law on Political Parties (*Ley de Partidos Políticos*) of 4 December 1978 spells out in detail the rights and obligations of parties, their mode of functioning, which must be democratic, their legal status and their financial rights *vis-à-vis* the state. With regard to finances, Article 6 of this Law states that each party will receive an annual amount from the state related to the number of seats obtained in each House of Parliament and to the number of votes cast for each party list. Thus in Spain, unlike the UK, for example, political parties are not dependent on the subscription fees of their members, on trade unions or on big business. There is no law, however, to prevent any of these organisations from directing funds to the party of their choice.

According to Article 2.1 of the above law, political parties become fully legal twenty-one days after their leaders have presented documentation containing personal details and the party statutes at the Ministry of the Interior, on the official register of which they must appear.

10.3   National parties

The major national parties are now examined in detail, particular attention being paid to the Socialist Party, the Communist Party and the Popular Alliance. Passing reference will be made to other parties operating nationally (see 10.4). The Union of the Democratic Centre (*Unión de Centro Democrático*/UCD) is not examined here since, although it played a vital part in the rebirth of party politics during the restoration of democracy (see 1.4), it no longer plays a part in the institutional reality of present-day Spain, having been disbanded in the spring of 1983. Inevitably, however, reference will be made to it when considering other parties and when assessing the electoral performance of all the parties concerned (see 10.8).

10.3.1 Spanish Socialist Workers' Party (Partido Socialista Obrero Español/PSOE)

10.3.1.1 Origins
The PSOE was founded in May 1879 by a group of print-workers in Madrid under the leadership of Pablo Iglesias. It is the oldest party in Spain and one of the oldest in Europe. From an early stage (1888) it had established its own trade union, the UGT (see 11.3.1), which helped it to grow into a mass party by the 1930s. Its major bases of support were the industrial areas of the north (the Basque Country and Asturias) and Madrid but, by the time of the Second Republic – which it helped to establish – it was widely supported all over the country.

10.3.1.2 Ideology
The PSOE was traditionally a working-class party committed to the emancipation of the working classes and the destruction of the capitalist system. To a large extent, it drew its inspiration from Marx but in practice it has never been exclusively Marxist. It has, however, been subject to tensions between the exponents of pure Marxism and the advocates of social democracy. This was most recently illustrated in May 1979 when at its XXVIII Congress, against the wishes of its general secretary, Felipe González, a resolution was passed affirming the Marxist nature of the party. Following González's resignation, the party adopted a collective leadership until an extraordinary congress was summoned the following September. On this occasion a moderate resolution, supported by

González, was approved; this resolution described Marxism as 'a theoretical instrument for the analysis of social reality', an analysis which 'comprehends the various contributions, Marxist and non-Marxist, which have helped to make Socialism the great alternative for emancipation of our time'. Consequently González was re-elected general secretary in a decision that was to prove historic in terms of improving the party's electoral credibility. Subsequently, the PSOE moved some way towards the centre of the political spectrum in a deliberate attempt to widen its electoral appeal.

10.3.1.3 Policies

Reflecting the above changes, the party's manifestos from 1977 to 1986 showed a gradual progression from a 'traditional' socialist programme – with a strong element of state intervention, for example – to a much more pragmatic platform. While the 1977 manifesto appealed for radical changes in economic direction, including the nationalisation of a wide range of private organisations and firms, the 1982 and 1986 programmes barely mentioned nationalisation and stressed the need to strengthen both the private and public sectors of the economy. In common with the Socialist parties of the EEC, of which Spain has now become a member, it accepts that the mixed economy is here to stay. To a large extent, the accent has been on the modernisation and streamlining of existing institutions, an efficient and honest bureaucracy, a properly managed economy, an extended health service, a more equitable and more modern education system, for example, rather than on sweeping changes. Education is an area to which the Socialists attach great importance but where the hand of pragmatism can very obviously be seen: whereas the resolutions of the XXVII Congress in 1976 were foreseeing the day when grants to private schools would be stopped and private education allowed to wither away, party policy since 1980 has been to preserve the private sector, including financial aid, while bringing it more closely under the scrutiny and control of the state. However, in certain social areas the party has presented a more definite left-wing image: it argued consistently in favour of a more liberal divorce law than the one approved by the *Cortes* in 1981, and in 1985 it pushed through a limited abortion law while in government. It has also designed a whole series of measures to improve the legal and social status of women.

Historically, the PSOE, even in its early post-Franco manifestos, was committed to the establishment of a federal Republic. In two senses this ideal has been modified in recent years. In the first place, convinced of the democratic commitment of King Juan Carlos, the party has come to accept that the winning of the 'democracy versus dictatorship' battle was more important than winning the 'republic versus monarchy' contest. Second, although still theoretically committed to federalism, the party has accepted the compromise formula, enshrined in the Constitution, of the state of the autonomous communities (*estado de las autonomías*) and indeed has played a major part in consolidating and developing the process of decentralisation initiated under the governments of the UCD.

In terms of foreign policy, the party has consistently argued, on political as well as economic grounds, for Spain's full membership of the EEC and saw its ambition realised in January 1986 when Spain, with Portugal, was finally admitted. Clearly more long-term in nature, but no less consistent, is the party's determination to restore Gibraltar to Spanish sovereignty; the party took the first step towards normalising relations and preparing the way for serious negotiations with the UK when in February 1985 it reopened the frontier with Gibraltar, closed since 1969. In one key area, however, pragmatism has once again won the day and that is over the question of NATO, which Spain joined in May 1982. At the time, this decision was vigorously opposed by the party and, in the campaign for the 1982 elections, the party committed itself to holding a referendum to allow the people to decide on Spain's future status within the Atlantic Alliance. However, not long after assuming power at the end of 1982, the PSOE government became convinced that to remain in NATO was in Spain's best long-term interests. Thus the government found itself in the embarrassing position of recommending to the electorate that the country should remain a member of the organisation. However, the outcome of the referendum was a comfortable majority in favour of the government's policy.

10.3.1.4 Structure

The most obvious feature of the internal structure of the PSOE is its federal nature. The party consists of autonomous federations or regional parties based on the autonomous communities. These federations are in turn made up of provincial and local branches known as *agrupaciones*. Another characteristic of party organisation, which endeavours to give a good example of democracy, is that at each level there is a decision-making body or congress which elects an executive committee to carry out its policies, as well as a management and control committee to monitor the activities of the latter. In each case the executive organ is responsible in both a political and financial sense to the congress.

The basic unit of the party is the local branch (*agrupación local*). This consists of the local assembly (*asamblea local*), which performs both a decision-making and monitoring role, and the local committee (*comité local*), which acts as the executive. At the provincial level the provincial congress (*congreso provincial*), elected directly from local assemblies, elects the provincial executive committee (*comité ejecutivo provincial*) which is overseen by the provincial committee (*comité provincial*). A very similar pattern exists at the level of the autonomous community, where the

Figure 10.2 *Simplified structure of PSOE at national level*

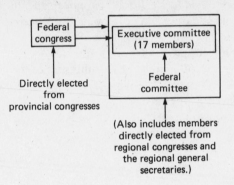

party institutions are the regional congress (*congreso regional*), the regional executive committee (*comité ejecutivo regional*) and the regional committee (*comité regional*). The autonomous nature of the regional parties, which have their own general secretaries, is often reflected in the adoption of a distinct name, usually an addition to the PSOE acronym. Thus the Andalusian Party is known as the PSOE–A, the Catalan as the PSC–PSOE and the Galician as the PSG–PSOE. In practice, the autonomy supposedly enjoyed by these regional parties is often limited by the not infrequent intervention in the appointments of regional party leaders by the national party.

As can be seen in Figure 10.2, the major organs of the PSOE at national or federal level are the congress; the executive committee; and the federal committee, which will now be examined separately.

Federal congress(congreso federal*):* This is the sovereign body of the party the major task of which is to formulate the official policy which it is expected that the parliamentary party will support in the *Cortes* and which a Socialist government will implement. It meets in ordinary session every two years and in extraordinary session when, as in 1979, circumstances dictate it. The congress is composed of delegates directly elected by the provincial congresses on the basis of proportional representation. The other organs of the party listed below are elected by secret ballot within this congress. Motions to the congress are presented by the provincial branches (*agrupaciones provinciales*).

Executive committee (comisión ejecutiva): It is the function of the executive committee to carry out the policies or resolutions agreed either by the federal congress or by the federal committee (see below), taking whichever decisions are considered necessary to implement such policies. Its seventeen members are elected by the federal congress every two years. They include the president and the general secretary (i.e. the leader) of the party, a deputy secretary, six executive secretaries (*secretarios ejecutivos*) and eight departmental secretaries (*secretarios de áreas*), each responsible for specific areas, such as internal organisation, international relations, trade union affairs and public relations. A similar structure is found in the executive committees of the regional parties. The executive committee is convened either by the general secretary, by the secretary for organisation or at the request of a simple majority of its members. In theory, at least, the president and the general secretary have no overriding authority, but in practice their views carry enormous weight.

Federal committee (comité federal): Between congresses this is the highest authority in the party. It is composed of the executive committee, the general secretaries of the regional parties, representatives of these parties elected in their regional congresses and representatives directly elected by the federal congress. The major functions of the federal committee are: to organise the party's electoral campaign, to oversee the activities of the executive committee, to check the statutes of the regional parties or federations and to appoint and dismiss the director of the party's fortnightly journal, *El Socialista*. It is to this body, too, that the Socialist Youth Organisation, the *Juventudes Socialistas*, is responsible.

Of all the major national parties, the PSOE, in the relatively short time of its legal existence, has become the most firmly rooted in Spanish society and the most institutionalised at local level. While the influence of the national leadership is considerable, largely thanks to the power it exercises at so many levels, local Socialists have increasingly been able to make an impact on both the party and on political life in general.

10.3.2 *Communist Party of Spain* (Partido Comunista de España/ PCE)

10.3.2.1 *Origins*
The Spanish Communist Party traces its origins to April 1920 when, influenced by the Bolshevik revolution of October 1917, several members of the PSOE's Youth Organisation and other dissidents decided to adhere to the newly formed III (Communist) International and found a new party. From its inception the party announced itself to be Marxist and revolutionary and its policies were aimed at bringing down the capitalist system. Throughout its history the party has been subject to schisms, the most recent occurring in the wake of the general elections of 1982 (10.8.2).

10.3.2.2 *Ideology*
Until the 1960s, this revolutionary Marxist party believed that the road to power was not by the ballot box but by revolution. This, it argued, would come about when the Franco regime – inevitably in the party's view – crumbled. However, under the influence of Santiago Carrillo, who had led

the party from exile since 1960 and had promoted Eurocommunist ideas, the PCE redefined its objectives in a more pragmatic way. Subsequently it advocated democracy as the route to power. Although ideally it would have preferred the establishment of a government of national unity, combining all the democratic forces of Spain, it was finally persuaded to accept the gradual route to change proposed by the government of Adolfo Suárez. Thus, once-hated institutions like the monarchy, the Church and the army were accepted as necessary elements within the new Spain, in which the PCE itself was determined to play a part. Moreover, while retaining a nominal commitment to Marxism, the party modified a number of its economic policies to the extent that, in the short term at least, it advocated the reform rather than the elimination of the existing structure. In short, like the PSOE, it attempted to present a more pragmatic, modern and democratic image to an electorate that wished to forget the traumas of the Civil War and was not interested in revolution.

In line with the above changes, in its Manifesto Programme of 1975 and in subsequent manifestos, the party affirmed its commitment to democracy, while retaining its long-term goal of the establishment of socialism in Spain. It also declared its willingness to withdraw from power if ever defeated at the ballot box, a promise which many on the Right still view with suspicion. A key decision came in the IX Congress of 1978 when the party agreed to drop the reference in its statutes to Leninism in a further attempt to separate the PCE from Soviet Communism in the popular mind. In spite of its theoretical preference for a republic, it has accepted the reality of the monarchy; and like the PSOE it has postponed its long-term goal of a federal system and given its support to the *Estado de las Autonomías* in spite of its historical preference for centralism.

10.3.2.3 Policies

In terms of economic policy, PCE manifestos do not read very differently from those of the PSOE. However, in certain ways, the party's approach is more radical: for example, more stress is laid on the need to reverse the current unemployment figures by means of a massive plan of public investment; the party would also go further than the PSOE in terms of nationalisation, taking into public ownership the so-called 'large monopolistic companies' – the banks, finance houses and insurance companies. A greater effort would be made to create a free health service paid for out of the national budget; and more attention would be paid to the needs of agricultural workers.

One interesting feature of their policies is that, while wishing to strengthen the state system of education, the PCE recognises the right to existence of the private schools – no doubt a concession to the new middle classes, which it is trying to woo. The party supported the introduction of a very liberal divorce law, civil marriage, family planning centres, a radical abortion law and measures designed to end discrimination against women.

With regard to foreign policy, the party has been a consistent supporter of entry into the EEC. Like every other party, it supports Spain's claim to Gibraltar; conversely it has also championed the return to Morocco of the North Africa enclaves of Ceuta and Melilla. As part of its theoretical commitment to non-alignment and the eventual suppression of the two military power blocs, the PCE has consistently opposed entry into NATO and, in the campaign leading up to the referendum of March 1986, advocated Spain's withdrawal, as well as the removal of the American bases from Spanish soil.

10.3.2.4 Structure

The present structure of the PCE dates from the new statutes drawn up at the end of the IX Congress of 1978. The structure established in that Congress has basically been maintained since then, although the XI Congress of December 1983 introduced some minor modifications. In line with the prevailing Eurocommunist mood, the IX Congress advocated a new type of party that would be more broadly based, would encourage more free discussion within the ranks and introduce democratic secret ballots for all the main organs of the party. One of the major changes was the replacement of the traditional party cell (*célula*), which tended to be dominated by doctrinaire intellectuals, by the branch (*agrupación*). This is the basic unit of the PCE and may exist either on a territorial level like those of the PSOE or at the level of a centre of work, such as a large firm, or a centre of learning or study, like a university. In the Madrid region, for example, out of a total of 165 basic branches (*agrupaciones de base*) 132 are currently territorial, 25 are based on centres of work and 10 have been established on a sectorial basis.

Like the PSOE, the Communist Party claims to be federal in structure and, in the same way as the Socialist Party, it is organised at local, provincial and regional, as well as national, level. The basic branch (*agrupación de base*) consists of a decision-making body, the local assembly (*asamblea local*) and of an executive, the local committee (*comité local*) elected by the local assembly. The structure at provincial level is more or less identical, except that the decision-making body is the provincial conference (*conferencia provincial*) which elects an executive known as the provincial committee (*comité provincial*). Provincial conferences are composed of the delegations from the local assemblies. Both local and provincial committees, each led by an elected secretary, are encouraged to set up working parties (*grupos de trabajo*) to examine specific issues. In line with the party's centralised structure, the local committee is responsible to the higher level committees rather than to the local

Figure 10.3 *Simplified structure of PCE at national level*

Directly elected from regional and provincial congresses

Includes delegates from regional congresses

assembly, in spite of the fact that in theory the assembly is the supreme organ.

Since the regional branches of the Communist Party are supposed to be autonomous, it is not surprising to find that the structure at this level closely mirrors that of the party at national level. Thus the regional party is endowed with the following institutions: the regional congress (*congreso regional*), composed of delegates from the provincial conferences, which itself elects a regional committee (*comité regional*); the latter, in turn, elects the members of both the regional conference (*conferencia regional*), which also consists of delegates from the provincial committees, and the regional executive committee (*comité ejecutivo regional*). These four bodies perform functions similar to their national counterparts described below. It should be stressed that regional parties, based on the autonomous communities, are theoretically autonomous, and free to organise themselves internally, as well as to establish their own names and symbols. Thus the Andalusian Communists were able to establish the Communist Party of Andalusia (*Partido Comunista de Andalucía*/PCE–PCA) and the Galicians the Galician Communist Party (*Partido Comunista Gallego*/PCE–PCG). At this point it should be mentioned that in Catalonia the Communist movement is represented by the United Socialist Party of Catalonia (*Partit Socialista Unificat de Catalunya*/PSUC); this 'independent' party, founded as long ago as 1936, has struggled hard to maintain a separate identity from the Madrid-dominated PCE.

As can be seen in Figure 10.3, at the national level, the principal organs of the party are: the congress; the party conference; the central committee; and the executive committee, each of which will now be examined in turn.

*Congress (*congreso*):* This is the sovereign body of the party. It is composed of delegates elected at regional congresses (50 per cent) and of delegates elected in the provincial branches. The congress meets in ordinary session every three years, convened by the central committee. An extraordinary congress may be held at any time at the request of either the central committee or by regional parties representing at least 50 per cent of the total membership of the party. One of the major functions of the congress is to draw up and approve party policy and to debate the reports presented by the central committee, as well as to adopt resolutions appertaining to this report. The congress is responsible for deciding the number of members to be elected to the central committee and carries out elections to the same on the basis of a secret, direct and personal vote among the members of the congress. Amongst the members who are elected, of course, is the leader or general secretary (*secretario general*) of the party. Another important function of the congress is to draw up the statutes of the party which must be approved while the congress is in session.

It should be stressed that the delegates to the congress are chosen according to majority principles so that even numerically strong minority groups have little chance of their point of view being represented at a higher level.

Party conference (conferencia del partido): This is made up of the members of the central committee, the delegations of the regional parties in proportion to the number of members they represent, the political secretaries of the provincial parties as well as representatives of the leadership of the PSUC. Delegates from the Communist Youth Organisation (*Unión de Juventudes Comunistas de España*) are also allowed to attend, but without a vote. The conference of the party is convened only by the central committee. It meets every year and is empowered to take decisions affecting the whole party, excluding matters that are the exclusive arena of the congress. Its major purpose is to ensure that between congresses the central committee provides information about, and a forum for debate on matters within its competence. Very roughly, it is the equivalent of the PSOE's federal committee but with fewer powers (see 10.3.1.4).

Central committee (comité central): In reality this is the major political and executive organ of the party. Indeed, Article 45.10 of the party statutes states categorically that 'the central committee is the organ of government, representation, administration and treasury of the party'. It meets at least six times a year according to statute, convened either by the executive committee or at the request of one-third of its members. As we have already seen, its members are elected every three years at the party congress. One of its major functions is to ensure the application of the policies agreed in the congress, as well as to direct the political activities of the PCE members of the Senate and the Congress. It also draws up and approves the election programmes and selects candidates for party representation in state institutions. It is responsible for managing the financial affairs of the party and for approving its annual budget. The central committee also has important powers of appointment; it appoints the directors of the party's principal publications *Mundo Obrero* and *Nuestra Bandera*, the president and general secretary of the party and the members of the executive committee.

Executive committee (comité ejecutivo): Between meetings of the central committee, the ongoing functions of the party are exercised by this body, which meets every fortnight or whenever the national political situation or the internal affairs of the party demand it. This body is made up of the president, the general secretary and deputy-secretaries (should there be any), plus any other members appointed by the central committee. One of its major functions is to direct the activity of the party's parliamentary group and the political orientation of the party journals mentioned above. It also decides on the dates for meetings of the central committee, for which it draws up the agenda.

From the foregoing it should be clear that, while operating basically along democratic lines, in accordance with the Constitution, the PCE keeps a very tight control from its political centre, which in practice means the central committee.

10.3.3 *Popular alliance* (Alianza Popular/*AP*)

This is by far the largest party within the alliance of parties which until recently fought both national and regional elections as the Popular Coalition (*Coalición Popular*/CP), comprising AP, PDP (see 10.3.5), PL (see 10.3.6) and various regional parties (see 10.6.1/2/3).

10.3.3.1 *Origins*
Sociologically the Alliance has its origins in the Franco regime. It is typified and, until his retirement in 1986, it was dominated by its president, Manuel Fraga, who, following his career as a minister of Franco, was undoubtedly converted to democracy, but retained a very authoritarian approach to politics. The party came into being in October 1976 as a loose coalition of seven right-wing parties, most of which were led by ex-Franco ministers like Fraga. At that time it clearly intended to maintain certain features of Francoism, albeit within a democratic framework. Subsequently, it has been modified in terms of both composition and ideology as it has tried to find a permanent space within the political spectrum.

10.3.3.2 *Ideology*
Bearing in mind the fluctuating history of this party and its tendency to be dominated from the top by a small number of influential individuals, it is not surprising that a definition of its ideology proves to be a difficult task. At one end of the spectrum, some of its founder members held views that fell little short of Francoism, while Christian Democrats like Oscar Alzaga of the Popular Democratic Party (*Partido Demócrata Popular*/PDP) (see 10.3.5 and 10.8.3) and the former general secretary, Jorge Verstrynge, present a more moderate, liberal image. At times Fraga has tried, primarily for electoral reasons, to steer the Alliance towards the Centre; at others he has spoken of the need to create an alliance of the broad Right (*la gran derecha*). The neo-Fascist members of the party, most of whom have now

deserted him, originally gave it a dubious image which cast doubts on the party's commitment to democracy. More recently, however, such charges have seemed less and less justified and the party now seems to have stabilised its position as European Conservative, with a strong element of Christian Democracy. With the disappearance of the UCD, it became the undisputed challenger for power on the right of the political spectrum.

10.3.3.3 Policies

During the transition, while accepting the need for a democratic state based on the rule of law and the wisdom of making certain concessions to the regions, AP stressed at all times the overriding necessity for a strong state the unity of which would be guaranteed by the monarchy, an institution to which the party has been consistently committed. As the political heir of Francoism, the party lays great stress on public order and assigns an important role to the armed forces in the protection of the state and its institutions. AP was also the only major party to insist during the constitutional debate that there be an explicit reference to the role of the Catholic Church. To some extent, the party still shares some of Franco's fears about the disintegration of the state due to excessive separatist or nationalist demands and, although it would find it very difficult to turn back significantly the tide of decentralisation, AP might well try to have Section VIII of the Constitution reformed (see 7.2).

Economically the party favours a social market economy as once advocated by the UCD, but in the case of AP the stress is much more on the market and the values of enlightened capitalism, the freedom to establish firms, private initiative and risk-taking entrepreneurship. It is very hostile to excessive state involvement in the economy, particularly nationalisation and high rates of taxation. Ideally the party would like to see a high-wage economy linked to improved levels of production and incentives for workers. Paradoxically, perhaps, the party favours a state-financed national health and social security system. Not surprisingly, AP favours creating circumstances that stimulate foreign investment and, unlike the parties of the Left, is not suspicious about the increasing role of multinational companies in the Spanish economy.

The Alliance, as might be expected, defends traditional values and social policies. It stresses the need to maintain the private sector of education; not only are individuals and entities to enjoy the right to found and run such centres but parents must have the right to send children to the school of their choice. Its hostility to greater state control over education was demonstrated in its obstructive opposition to the PSOE's new education law, the LODE, during 1983 (see 2.4.3.3). The party is very conservative in its attitude to policies concerning the family; although there is an acceptance of a restricted form of divorce, AP is totally opposed to abortion and, indeed, is hostile to birth control and family planning.

With regard to foreign policy, the party is firmly committed to membership of the EEC. It is equally committed to the Atlantic Alliance and in 1982 supported the UCD in its decision to take Spain into NATO; having always argued that the military and economic agreements signed with the USA from 1953 onwards tended to be unfavourable to Spain, the party has consistently favoured full integration into the Alliance, including its military structure. This remains the party's position in spite of the fact that, in order to embarrass the government of Felipe González, Fraga urged his followers to abstain in the March 1986 referendum (see 1.4). Like the other major parties, AP is keen to strengthen existing economic and cultural links with Latin America, although obviously Fraga and his allies are much less enthusiastic than the parties of the Left about countries such as Cuba and Nicaragua.

10.3.3.4 Structure

In spite of its attempts to present itself in populist terms, AP remains a voters' rather than a members' party and has never become a mass party. To some extent, the way in which the party is structured and led reflects this. Basically, like the PCE, the party is tightly controlled from the top and has no pretensions to be federal in structure. Unlike the parties of the Left, its activities at local level are geared more to electoral success than to building up party membership and the encouragement of grassroots' participation.

At the municipal level there is no equivalent of the PSOE's local assembly, only a local committee (*junta local*) composed of party 'notables' who make little effort to mobilise mass support. Since the provincial congress (*congreso provincial*) is composed of groups of such notables indirectly elected from various *juntas*, it is not surprising that the provincial steering committee (*junta directiva provincial*) which it elects tends to be an exclusive club of party personalities rather than a body elected by genuine delegates from the grassroots of the party. In the same way, regional deputies are automatically co-opted to the regional steering committee (*junta directiva regional*), which is elected by members of the regional congress (*congreso regional*). Members of the latter are indirectly elected from the various provincial congresses.

In addition to these bodies, both the provincial and regional steering committees have an executive committee. An interesting feature of the structure, which reflects the centralised nature of the party, is that, although the provincial executive committee (*comité ejecutivo provincial*) is elected by the provincial steering committee, the regional executive committee (*comité ejecutivo regional*) is elected from the various provincial executive committees, thus reinforcing the tendency to promote party personalities.

As can be seen in Figure 10.4, at the national level, the principal organs

Figure 10.4 *Simplified structure of AP at national level*

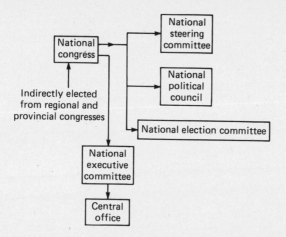

of the party are: the national congress; the national steering committee; the national executive committee; the national political council; and the national election committee.

National congress (congreso nacional): This is the sovereign body of the party. It meets in ordinary session every two years and in extraordinary session whenever the national steering committee, by an overall majority, decides to convene it. It is composed of *ex officio* members of both the national steering committee and the national political council (see below), no more than fifty members designated by the national executive committee on the recommendation of the president of the executive (in practice the president of the party), and delegates indirectly elected from the provincial congresses. The major tasks of the congress are: to decide on the ideological orientation of the party; to draw up and approve its statutes; and to approve or censure the actions of the party organs, including the steering committee.

National steering committee (junta directiva nacional): This is the most important party body between congresses. One part of its membership is elected by the national congress and the other by the regional and provincial congresses. To a certain extent, it can be compared to the PSOE's federal committee in that it performs a monitoring and disciplinary function, ensuring on behalf of the congress that party policies agreed in the latter are carried out by the other organs of the party and that the party statutes are obeyed.

National executive committee (comité ejecutivo nacional): As its name implies, this is the principal executive and administrative body of the party. It is composed principally of members elected by the national congress, as well as *ex officio* members, such as AP senators and deputies in the

Cortes and several nominees of the president of the party. The president and general secretary of the party hold those same ranks within the executive committee, and indeed within the national steering committee. The executive committee meets on a regular basis with a brief to stimulate, co-ordinate and control all the activities of the party in line with party policy as laid down by the national congress and is empowered to draft all the necessary regulations and guidelines to ensure that this is put into effect. One specific task of the executive is to elect the members of the party's central office (*oficina central*), one of the main functions of which is to draft party propaganda and to promote the image of the party through its public relations department.

National political council (consejo político nacional)*:* Amongst the changes to organisation which the party introduced at its V Congress in 1982 was the creation of this body, the main function of which is to provide an advisory political service for the other institutions of the party. The political council, like the other organs of the party, is elected every two years by the congress.

National election committee (comité electoral nacional)*:* As its name implies this body, elected by the national congress, ensures that the party machine is geared up to fight elections at all levels.

It should be noted that, parallel with AP, there exists the Popular Alliance Federation (*Federación de Alianza Popular*) which includes several minor national and regional groupings. The Federation also includes a youth organisation known as the *Nuevas Generaciones*, the New Generation.

10.3.4 *Democratic and Social Centre* (Centro Democrático y Social/*CDS*)

This Social Democratic party was founded by Adolfo Suárez in July 1982. It gained only two seats in the Congress in the elections of October of that year, and, even in November 1985, in the Galician regional elections, it won no seats and only three per cent of the vote. However, in the general elections of June 1986 it made substantial progress, winning 19 seats in the Congress with 9.23 per cent of the popular vote and securing for the first time its own parliamentary group (see 4.4.5)

10.3.5 *Popular Democratic Party* (Partido Demócrata Popular *PDP*)

This Christian Democratic Party was founded by Oscar Alzaga in July 1982. It has nearly always fought subsequent elections in conjunction with AP and has thus shared that party's changing fortunes. In the general elections of 1982 its share of the Popular Coalition's 106 seats in the

Congress was sixteen and in 1986 it gained twenty-two out of 105. Depending on the future success of AP, it may be tempted to ally with other centrist groups like the CDS or the PRD (see 10.3.7). In fact, shortly after the 1986 general elections the party decided to withdraw from the Coalition and its deputies now form part of the mixed group (see 4.4.5 and Figure 4.3).

10.3.6 Liberal Party (Partido Liberal/*PL*)

This party was founded as the Liberal Union (*Unión Liberal*/UL) in 1982 as a result of a merger of two liberal groupings, one led by Pedro Schwartz and the other by Enrique Larroque. Like the PDP, it has fought subsequent elections as part of the Popular Coalition. It won five seats in the Congress in October 1982 and twelve in June 1986. Following manoeuvrings between various liberal groups, the party was reconstituted as the Liberal Party in December 1984 under the leadership of José Antonio Segurado. However, it is still often referred to as the UL.

10.3.7 Democratic Reformist Party (Partido Reformista Democrático/*PRD*)

This reforming liberal grouping was founded by the Catalan nationalist leader, Miguel Roca, in November 1983 with the aim of embracing like-minded national and regional parties. Roca's Catalan nationalist party, the CiU (see 10.5.3), was the first party to join in this grand design along with the liberals of Antonio Garrigues. In the Galician regional elections of November 1985, the PRD's ally, the Galician Coalition, came third after AP and the PSOE, polling over thirteen per cent of the vote (see 10.5.7). However, this new party did badly in the general elections of June 1986, winning no seats in the Congress and its future is currently in doubt.

10.4 Other national parties

10.4.1 Progressive Federation (Federación Progresista/*FP*)

This left-wing progressive party, led by the former PCE member and well-known economist Ramón Tamames, was founded in 1983 and formed part of the IU coalition for the general and regional elections of 1986 (see 10.8.2).

10.4.2 Council for Communist Unity (Mesa para la Unidad de los Comunistas/*MUC*)

This Communist breakaway group was founded in 1985 by Santiago

Carrillo following his withdrawal from the PCE. It won no seats to the *Cortes* in June 1986.

10.4.3 Workers' Revolutionary Organisation (Organización Revolucionaria de Trabajadores/ORT)

This far-left revolutionary party, linked to the union, the *Sindicato Unitario* (see 11.3.5), was founded in 1969. It has so far had no success in elections at either national or regional level.

10.4.4 Party of Spanish Labour (Partido del Trabajo Español/ PTE)

The PTE traces its origins to the late 1960s when a group of militants broke away from the PCE under Eladio García Castro. Its trade-union wing is the *Confederación de Sindicatos Unitarios de Trabajadores* (see 11.3.4). In electoral terms it has so far had no success, but particularly in Andalusia has made an impact on the labour scene.

10.5   Regional parties

In a country where the regional issue has dominated politics on so many occasions, it is not surprising that political parties have emerged to defend the political interests of communities which are conscious of possessing separate identity. In fact it was only at the turn of the century, coinciding with increased local cultural activity and, in some areas, the beginnings of industrialisation, that parties were formed and nationalism assumed a more political character.

10.5.1 Basque Nationalist Party (Partido Nacionalista Vasco/ PNV)

This basically conservative, Catholic and at times radically nationalist, party was founded in 1895 by Sabino Arana with the aim of promoting the Basque language and culture and of providing a vehicle of political expression for the Basque people. Until the 1970s it was the only nationalist party in the Basque Country (*Euskadi*). The basis of its support has traditionally been the lower-middle class, the peasantry and the clergy. Its ideology, reflecting a variety of interests, has varied from outright independence from Spain to an accommodation with Madrid within a system of autonomous government.

In the post-Franco era, partly under pressure from extreme nationalists, it has fought the Madrid government every inch of the way in its demands for a generous degree of autonomy within the Spanish state. In the regional

Figure 10.5. *Regional political parties in Spain (1986)*

Name of party	Ideology	Founder(s)	Year founded	Leader(s) 1986
Partido Nacionalista Vasco –PNV	Basque nationalist (Christian Democratic)	Sabino Arana	1894	Xabier Arzallus
Esquerra Republicana Catalana –ERC	Catalan nationalist (Republican)	Francesc Macià	1931	Heribert Barrera
Partido Andalucista –PA	Andalusian nationalist	Alejandro Rojas-Marcos	1973 (as ASA)	Salvador Pérez Bueno
Convergència i Unió –CiU[a]	Catalan nationalist	Jordi Pujol	1978	Miguel Roca
Euzkadiko Ezquerra –EE	Basque nationalist left	Francisco Letamendía	1976	Juan María Bandrés
Herri Batasuna–HB	Radical Basque nationalist	Telesforo Monzón	1978	Jon Idígoras

[a] This party was formed from the *Convergència Democràtica de Catalunya*, founded by Jordi Pujol in 1974, and the *Unión Democràtica de Catalunya*, founded in 1931.

elections of 1980 and 1984 the party emerged the clear victor. However, in the general elections since 1977 the party has consistently been defeated by the PSOE, which is particularly strong in the industrial heartland around Bilbao, with its strong immigrant vote. In the 1986 general elections the party's performance was particularly disappointing as it lost two of the eight seats which it had won in 1982 (see Figure 10.6). This was probably at least partly due to the serious schism which affected the party during 1985 and 1986 and led to the creation of a breakaway party known as Basque Nationalists (*Eusko Ta Alkartasuna*/EA) in September 1986 and led by the former president of Euskadi, Carlos Garaicoechea. This grouping favours strengthening the role of the Basque government in Vitoria, while the historical PNV, led by Xabier Arzallus, wants to strengthen the provincial authorities and adopt a more intransigent attitude to Madrid (see 8.4.2).

10.5.2 *Basque Homeland and Freedom Party* (Herri Batasuna/HB)

This party was founded in 1978 as a coalition of left-wing nationalist parties the declared aim of which was to establish the separate Basque and Socialist state of Euskadi. This is an aim shared with ETA (*Euskadi Ta Askatasuna*/Basque Homeland and Freedom) the political arm of which HB clearly is. Following the PNV's struggle to have Basque rights more explicitly recognised in the Constitution and to secure a more generous autonomy for Euskadi, this coalition shot to prominence in the general elections of 1979, when it sent three deputies to the Congress in Madrid (subsequently they have consistently refused to occupy their parliamentary seats). This was followed by a spectacular performance in the regional elections of 1980 when the party came second to the PNV, gaining eleven out of the sixty seats in the Basque Parliament. This success was largely maintained in the general elections of 1982 and the regional elections of 1984. The party came close to parity with the PNV in the general elections of 1986, winning five seats in the Congress compared to the PNV's six. Although support for the party is variable (weak in Alava, strong in Vizcaya), it can claim the support of an average 15 to 20 per cent of the Basque electorate.

10.5.3 Convergence and Union (Convergència i Unió/CiU)

The nucleus of this centre–right coalition is the Catalan Convergence Party of Catalonia (*Convergència Democrática de Catalunya*/CDC) founded in 1974 by the present President of Catalonia, Jordi Pujol. This coalition was founded to fight the general elections of 1979 and has subsequently more or less coalesced as a single party. To some extent, it can be regarded as an updated manifestation of the first Catalan nationalist party, the Catalan Regionalist League (*Lliga Regionalista Catalana*) founded at the turn of the century by Catalan industrialists and businessmen. Unlike the PNV, the CiU does not have a radical nationalist party breathing down its neck and urging it to adopt a more extremist line towards Madrid. Although it has pressed hard for generous terms for the *Generalitat*, its relations with Madrid have generally been good. Economically it gives strong encouragement to private enterprise. The CiU has followed the pattern of the PNV in yielding to the national parties in general elections, taking second place, but in the regional elections of 1980 and 1984 the party swept to convincing victories. Perhaps the most interesting feature of this party is that it appeals to a broad cross-section of Catalan voters, including many non-Catalan speakers from outside the region; its secret has been to present a modern, progressive image and to convey an impression of efficiency as a government. Currently the party is led by Miguel Roca (see 10.3.7).

10.5.4 Andalusian Nationalist Party (Partido Andalucista/PA)

This party was founded as the Andalusian Socialist Alliance (*Alianza Socialista de Andalucía*/ASA) in 1973, became the Socialist Party of Andalusia (*Partido Socialista de Andalucía*/PSA) in 1976 and finally changed its name to the above in 1984. It was founded by Alejandro-Rojas Marcos as a radical socialist and regionalist (later nationalist) party. Its most striking success was in the general elections of 1979 when it sent five deputies to the Madrid Congress and in 1980 when two of its candidates were elected to the parliament of Catalonia. Subsequently its fortunes declined rapidly, even in regional and local elections. It won no seats in the general elections of 1982 or 1986 and in the regional elections of 1986 lost one of the three seats in the regional assembly which it had won in 1982.

10.5.5 Basque Left (Euzkadiko Ezkerra/EE)

Euzkadiko was founded by Francisco Letamendía in 1977 from a group of radical nationalist parties committed to a Marxist view of society but preferring to use legal channels to gain power and opposed to ETA terrorism. It has managed to send at least one deputy (two in 1986) to the Congress as a result of all the general elections held since 1977 and it has polled an average of 10 per cent of the vote in regional elections.

10.5.6 Catalan Republican Left (Esquerra Republicana de Catalana/ERC)

This Catalan nationalist party was founded in 1931 by Francesc Macià. During the Second Republic it replaced the more conservative *Lliga Regionalista Catalana* (see 10.5.3) as the major force of Catalan nationalism. As its name implies, the party has a strongly republican orientation. In the post-Franco period it has been eclipsed by the coalition led by Jordi Pujol (see 10.5.3), both in general and regional elections. However, it remains the second most important Catalan nationalist party and retains a certain prestige because of its long struggle for democracy and opposition to Franco. The first president of the restored *Generalitat*, Josep Tarradellas, a former Catalan minister under the Republic, belonged to the ERC.

10.5.7 Galician Coalition (Coalición Galega/CG)

This party was founded as recently as 1985 by Pablo González Mariñas and joined the grand coalition conceived by Miguel Roca (see 10.3.7). In its first appeal to the electorate, in the regional elections of November 1985, the *coagas* as they are known popularly, gained thirteen out of the seventy-one seats contested and garnered 13 per cent of the vote, leaving longer established Galician nationalist parties like the Galician Left (*Esquerda Galega*/EG) well behind.

10.6 Other regional parties

In recent years other small regional parties have contested both general and regional elections. The first three in the list that follows at different times fought elections on behalf of the AP–PDP–PL coalition.

10.6.1 Regionalist Aragonese Party (Partido Aragonés Regionalista/*PAR*)

This party was founded by Hipólito Gómez and sent one deputy to the Madrid Congress in 1986. It is well represented in the regional parliament of Aragón.

10.6.2 Valencian Union (Unión Valenciana/*UV*)

This party was founded in 1982 by González Lizondo and sent one deputy to the Congress of Deputies in 1986.

10.6.3 Union of the Navarrese People (Unión del Pueblo Navarro/*UPN*)

The UPN was founded by Jesús Aizpún. As a separate party, it sent one deputy to the Congress of 1979 – though none in subsequent general elections. However, thirteen of the fifty deputies elected in 1983 to the Navarrese regional parliament are from this party.

10.6.4 Canary Independence Association (Agrupación Independiente Canaria/*AIC*)

This grouping, which advocates independence for the Canary Islands, was formed to fight the general elections of 1986, when it suceeded in securing the election of one deputy to the Congress and two senators.

10.6.5 Party of the Communists of Catalonia (Partit dels Comunistes de Catalunya/*PCC*)

This is a radical Communist grouping independent of both the PCE and PSUC (see 10.3.2). So far it has had very little electoral success.

10.6.6 Galician Left (Esquerda Galega/*EG*)

Galician Left is a moderate nationalist party which has no seats in the national Parliament but which won two seats with nearly 6 per cent of the popular vote in the 1986 elections to the regional parliament.

10.7   Membership and financing of major national parties

10.7.1 Spanish Socialist Workers' Party

Official figures for party membership are notoriously unreliable in Spain, especially in the case of parties like the PCE and AP whose fortunes have, in any case, fluctuated quite considerably since parties were legalised in 1977. The PSOE, however, has less cause to be embarrassed about such statistics than the above-mentioned parties and its official figures for membership are probably a reasonable approximation to the true situation. In its case there is little doubt that there was a dramatic increase between 1976, when membership was claimed to stand at only 8,000 and 1983 when it was estimated to have reached 140,000. Since then, the pace of increasing membership has declined somewhat but, despite many unpopular measures implemented by the Socialist government, between 1982 and 1986 more people did join the ranks of the party. In January 1986 the party claimed over 167,000 members. An interesting statistic, which can also be generally applied to other parties, is that only 10 per cent of that membership corresponds to women in spite of the party's attempts to promote their causes.

Apart from state grants, the party's revenue, like that of most other parties, comes from membership fees. In fact, a fixed percentage of income rather than a flat-rate subscription fee is recommended, though not always received, by the party. There is little doubt that in the early 1970s, at a crucial time in its development, the party received both moral and financial support from the German Social Democratic Party (SPD). According to a survey carried out in early 1985, the PSOE, in spite of increasing membership, was seriously in debt and has relied on extended credit from financial institutions.

10.7.2 Communist Party of Spain

In the case of the PCE, there is little doubt that, in spite of the party's attempts to hide the fact, its membership has declined steadily since the time of the transition, when it could boast over 200,000 members distributed fairly evenly over the whole of Spain. Indeed, in recent years this decline has accelerated, exacerbated by the de facto establishment of two breakaway groups. These are the Communist Party of the Spanish People (Partido Comunista del Pueblo Español/PCPE) of Ignacio Gallego set up in 1983 and the Council for Communist Unity (Mesa para la Unidad de los Comunistas/MUC), established by Santiago Carrillo in 1985. According to the party's own figures party membership now stands at approximately 100,000, but many commentators doubt whether it has many more than half that number. What is certain is that, whatever its membership, compared with other parties the PCE can boast a higher number of hard-core, dedicated workers both at national and local level.

The party has always been very secretive about its finances. It claims to receive no financial support from Communist countries or organisations outside Spain, but to finance itself only from subscriptions and the now much-reduced grant from the state. Since the party's disastrous electoral performance in 1982 and only marginal improvement in 1986 (see 10.8.2), the PCE's finances are undoubtedly in a state of crisis.

10.7.3 Popular Alliance

According to its own figures, AP's membership rose from 60,000 prior to the 1982 elections to 125,000 soon after, an increase that should be treated with healthy scepticism. Clearly, from 1983 onwards AP benefited considerably from the collapse of the UCD, but it is doubtful whether such a top-heavy party with little grassroots organisation has as many as 100,000 members. In the financial sense, too, the party benefited from the demise of the UCD since the Employers' Organisation, the CEOE (see 12.11), transferred its allegiance from the UCD to AP. However, in spite of this and additional state help following its electoral boost in 1982, the party is still in some financial difficulties.

10.8   Electoral achievements

The performance of the major national and regional parties in the four general elections of 1977, 1979, 1982 and 1986 are given in Figure 10.6. Fears expressed prior to the 1977 elections that the large number of parties contesting the elections might lead to a dangerous fragmentation of Parliament and to weak coalition governments like those of the 1930s, were not borne out by events. In the first place, many small groups eventually merged with each other before the elections; Suárez's UCD, formed in April 1977, was a good example of this phenomenon. In the second place, the elections themselves had a reducing effect on the complex panorama of parties. As can be seen in Figure 10.6, only four major parties made any significant impact on the electorate in these four elections. In fact less than a dozen parties – of which several were region-based – secured parliamentary representation. An interesting statistic is that in the elections of 1977 and 1979, the PSOE and the UCD together polled 63.8 per cent and 65.5 per cent of the vote respectively, while in 1982 and 1986 the PSOE and AP together polled totals of 74.3 per cent and 70.1 per cent, thus appearing to confound those who predicted party and parliamentary instability.

10.8.1 Performance of the Socialist Party

Since 1977 the PSOE has gone from strength to strength in electoral terms. In 1977 and 1979 it established itself as the main opposition to the ruling UCD, in spite of apparent disadvantages *vis-à-vis* the PCE which had led the anti-Franco struggle within Spain. In the elections of 1982 the party

Figure 10.6. *Results of general elections in Spain (1977–86)*

Party	1977 elections Seats	% of votes	1979 elections Seats	% of votes	1982 elections Seats	% of votes	1986 elections Seats	% of votes
National								
UCD	166	34.62	168	35.02	12	7.14	—	—
PSOE	118	29.27	120	30.49	202	48.40	184	44.06
PCE–IU	20	9.38	24	10.74	4	4.13	7	4.61
AP–CD–CP[a]	16	8.33	9	5.96	106	26.18	105	26.00
CDS	—	—	—	—	2	2.89	19	9.23
PRD	—	—	—	—	—	—	0	0.96
Regional[b]								
PDC–CiU	10	3.70	9	2.50	12	3.69	18	5.02
ERC	1	0.80	1	0.70	1	0.70	0	0.42
PNV	7	1.70	7	1.50	8	1.89	6	1.53
EE	1	0.50	1	0.50	1	0.48	2	0.53
HB	—	—	3	0.96	2	1.01	5	1.15
PSA–PA	0	0.3	5	1.81	0	0.40	0	2.8

[a] *Coalición Popular*'s full initials are AP – PDP – PL, representing the three parties that formed the coalition (see 10.3.3).
[b] The percentage votes shown for the regional parties are expressed in national, not regional, terms where the figures would be much higher.
Source: El País, June 1977–June 1986

won a resounding victory securing over 48 per cent of the vote and 202 seats out of 350 in the Congress, more than enough to give it an overall majority over all other parties. This success was repeated in 1986 when the party gained 44 per cent of the vote, enough to secure 184 seats. At other levels, too the success of the party, at least since 1979, has been no less formidable. Although denied victory in the regional elections of the Basque Country, Catalonia and Galicia, it has established a vital power base through the PSOE–A in Andalusia, completely dominating the regional elections of May 1982 and June 1986. In May 1983 its candidates swept to power in all but one of the remaining autonomous communities.

The party's dominance of the local election scene was equally spectacular both in 1979, campaigning in alliance with the PCE, and in 1983, campaigning on its own. At the regional level, in early 1986 the PSOE held 512 out of a possible total of 1,139 parliamentary seats, while at the local level 2,620 mayors, out of a total of 8,022, were members of the party and 23,100 councillors out of a total of 68,990 also belonged to the PSOE. In spite of the contradictions and ambiguities which many people perceived in the party's performance in government between 1982 and 1986, support for the party was largely retained during this period.

10.8.2 Performance of the Communist Party

In spite of its history of implacable opposition to the Franco regime over four long decades, when its members suffered considerable persecution, the PCE managed to gain only 9.3 per cent of the vote and twenty seats in the Congress in the elections of 1977. However, building on this surprisingly low base, the party succeeded in increasing its share of the vote to 10.7 per cent and its number of seats to twenty-four in 1979, coming in third place ahead of AP. Shortly afterwards, in alliance with the PSOE, the party performed well in the local elections, where it consolidated its third place. Since 1979, however, largely due to continuing internal wrangling, the party's fortunes have been steadily on the wane. Its performance in the first round of regional elections in 1980 and 1982 were disappointing for the party leadership; even in its stronghold of Andalusia, it won only eight seats out of 109 and in the Basque elections of 1984 it polled a mere 4 per cent of the vote, which put the party in seventh place, after all the Basque nationalist parties. As can be seen in Figure 10.6, the party did so badly in the general elections of 1982 that it won only four seats, representing 4.13 per cent of the vote. In the 1983 local elections and in the regional elections of 1983, 1984 and 1985, the continuing decline of the PCE was confirmed.

In had clearly suffered greatly from the internal struggles between the pro-Soviet group of Gallego, the supporters of Carrillo, who were hostile to internal party reform, and the supporters of the present leader, Gerardo Iglesias, who defends the Eurocommunist reforming line that was once espoused by Carrillo himself. However, the realignment of the Left, which took place in the run-up to the NATO referendum in March 1986, gave rise to the birth of a new left-wing coalition including the PCE, the FP of Ramón Tamames (see 10.4.1), the PCPE of Ignacio Gallego (see 10.7.2), and several 'green' parties, among others. The United Left (*Izquierda Unida*/IU), as it was called, managed to gain seven Congress seats in the general elections that followed in June.

10.8.3 Performance of the Popular Alliance

In view of the general reaction against Francoism, it is not surprising that in the 1977 elections the party fared badly, polling only 8.3 per cent of the vote, gaining only sixteen seats in the Congress and coming in fourth place after the UCD, the PSOE and the PCE. While Suárez continued to gain credit for dismantling the dictatorship and drawing up a new Constitution, AP could not hope to challenge the UCD's dominance of the Centre–Right. Thus, in the elections of 1979 the party, which, in conjunction with other right-wing groups, campaigned as the Democratic Coalition (*Coalición Democrática*/CD), performed even more disastrously than in 1977, seeing its share of the vote reduced to less than 6 per cent and its number of seats reduced to nine. Its performance in the 1979 local elections was equally disappointing, as was its showing in the first regional elections in 1980.

However, profiting from the gradual decline of the UCD from 1980 onwards, the party strengthened its position in all subsequent elections. Its greatest success was to win the Galician elections in 1981, polling 30 per cent of the vote. In the Andalusian elections of 1982, the party again defeated the UCD, coming second to the PSOE with 17 per cent of the vote. This was followed up by its commendable performance in the 1982 general elections when it came second to the PSOE, winning 26.2 per cent of the vote and securing 106 seats in the Congress. This success was repeated in the local and regional elections of May 1983, as well as in the second round of elections to the Basque and Catalan parliaments in 1984 and to the Galician parliament in November 1985, when it increased its hold over the region. However, following the 1986 general elections, in which it polled a similar percentage of votes and seats, it would seem that AP has reached its political ceiling. Following its disastrous performance in the Basque regional elections of November 1986, which came hard on the heels of the defection of the PDP (see 10.3.5) and the expulsion of Jorge Verstrynge (see 10.3.3.2), Fraga resigned from the leadership of the party, leaving the Centre–Right of Spanish politics in considerable disarray yet with the opportunity of making a badly needed fresh start.

10.9 Conclusion

In any democratic country, political parties clearly play a crucial role in legitimising the system. This is no less the case in post-Franco Spain than in other democratic nations. It should be clear from the foregoing that all the major national parties are system-supportive in that they accept the values of democratic politics and indeed offer relatively moderate programmes which appeal to what currently appears to be a moderate electorate. The only exceptions here are the radical Basque parties like *Herri Batasuna*. It is significant that in recent years both the major parties have moved towards the Centre of the political spectrum, AP to occupy space vacated by the UCD and to promote a more moderate image, and the PSOE in order to confirm its conversion from a Marxist to a basically Social-Democratic party. Popular support for the system has been reflected in such things as the support for the monarchy, the massive demonstrations following the attempted *coup* of 1981 and the generally high turnout in most general, regional and local elections.

The average turnout for the 1982 general elections, for example, was just under 80 per cent. The increasing stability of the party system has also been reflected in the relationship between the major parties, particularly during the crucial transition period. Consensus operated between the four major parties of the day following the 1977 elections when they signed the

Moncloa Pacts (see 11.5.1) agreeing on a dual programme for the consolidation of democracy and the stabilisation of the ailing economy. It continued during the period of the drawing up of the Constitution – a period when the Left and the Right, with the minimum of protest, made substantial concessions in order to reach a workable compromise. A similar spirit of co-operation was evident following the events of February 1981 when the PSOE offered to join a grand coalition with the UCD, to protect democracy.

Thus, in terms of their relationship with the state and with each other, the Spanish parties would seem to have passed the test of legitimisation. However, to what extent they carry their electorates with them and how deeply rooted they now are in society may be other questions. It has to be recognised, in fact, that none of the parties, not even the PSOE, the membership of which is still below what it was in the 1930s, can claim to be a mass party with a stable electorate. Compared to their counterparts in Western Europe, the Spanish parties, in terms of membership, are still very small. Moreover, allegiances can change dramatically, as the UCD found to its cost in 1982; even the PSOE was aware after 1982 that its major challenge was to hang on to the estimated three million votes 'borrowed' from the UCD following the collapse of the Centre party. Although it is encouraging that, in general, the turnout in elections has been high, with the exception of the Basque Country and Galicia, it is significant, and mildly disquieting, that, in the period leading up to general elections, the number of undecided voters hovers around 30 per cent, and even at election time there seems to be a low level of party identification. In 1982, for example, only 54 per cent of Spaniards identified with a particular party. While the prospects for the future of the party system look relatively bright, in the interests of the long-term stability of the new democracy, the parties would be advised to look carefully at this evident Achilles heel.

11 Trade unions

11.1 Labour organisations under Franco

The trade unions, like the political parties described in the previous chapter, have re-emerged as a significant force in the rapid transformation which has occurred in Spanish society since 1975. In order to appreciate the status of the unions today, it is appropriate to discuss, albeit briefly, the situation which existed during the Franco era.

The Civil War, as in so many aspects of Spanish life, marked a turning point in trade union history. The National Confederation of Labour (*Confederación Nacional del Trabajo*/CNT), the General Union of Workers (*Unión General de Trabajadores*/UGT) and the Union of Basque Workers (*Solidaridad de Trabajadores Vascos*/ELA–STV), which had been prominent prior to the war, were declared illegal in 1937. Thereafter their leaders and members were subjected to such severe repression that the labour movement was effectively left leaderless and crushed for nearly twenty years.

The vacuum was officially filled by a system of vertical syndicates (*sindicatos verticales*) intended to bring together all producers, employers and employees within a single corporativist organisation under the auspices of the state. There were twenty-eight *sindicatos* corresponding to different branches of production organised at local, provincial and national level. It was an authoritarian system which ensured that government policy on wages was adhered to strictly. It left advisory and consultative tasks, such as training programmes, education, recreation and legal services, to be discussed by the sections intended to represent the rights of workers and employers. Strikes were expressly prohibited and were classed as crimes of sedition under Article 222 of the Penal Code of 1944.

Gradually, however, the system was modified in the light of the requirements of economic development. In 1956, in response to internal pressure, firms were permitted to pay workers above the minimum salary. As a result of external pressure, occasioned by Spain's desire to gain international respectability, collective bargaining was legalised under the Law on Collective Agreements (*Ley de Convenios Colectivos*) of 1958.

The 'economic miracle' of the 1960s was accompanied by growing confidence and solidarity among workers. Employers became increasingly anxious to negotiate with authentic representatives of labour in order to introduce new methods and to increase productivity. For a while there was tacit toleration of unofficial bodies which represented labour, such as the Workers' Commissions (*Comisiones Obreras*/CCOO), until they were declared illegal in 1967 (see 11.3.2).

Meanwhile attempts were made to refashion the existing structure in order to meet this increasing challenge. Thus the much heralded Union Law (*Ley Sindical*) of 1971 gave more representation at lower levels and more autonomy to workers and management as separate groups. A complex series of measures were introduced to legalise industrial conflicts in certain circumstances. All this was largely pseudo-reform which, in practice, did nothing to bring the system within the mainstream of Western European trade unionism.

11.2   Developments since 1975

At a very early stage, in the transition from dictatorship to democratic government there was pressure for and expectation of labour reforms. Indeed, some difficulties were created by groups anticipating change and flouting the existing legislation. However, major alteration came with a Decree Law in March 1977 which introduced the right to strike and made provision for collective bargaining.

From 28 April 1977 the new independent but still *de facto* illegal unions were eventually able to gain legality through registration. The most significant developments, however, came in the forms of: the Constitution of 1978; the Workers' Statute (*Estatuto de los Trabajadores*) of 1980; and the Organic Law of Trade Union Freedom (*Ley Orgánica de Libertad Sindical*) of 1984, each of which will now be considered.

11.2.1 The Constitution of 1978

Article 7 of the Constitution acknowledges the rights of unions and employers' organisations to defend their own legitimate interests within the provisions of the Constitution and the law, provided that they are democratically constituted and run. The right to join a union is granted to all citizens other than members of the armed forces (Article 28.1) and members of the judiciary (Article 127.1), and there is an equal right not to join a union (Article 28.1).

Article 28.2 expressly recognises the right of workers to strike in defence of their interests but reference is made to exceptions to this in the public interest which will be clarified by subsequent legislation. This point is reiterated in Article 37 which guarantees the right to collective bargaining;

the implication here is that employers may resort to a lockout (*cierre patronal*). However, this has been a particularly sensitive issue and as yet no agreement has been reached on its specific enactment.

Reference is made in Article 40 to the need to ensure a limit to the length of the working day as well as the proper provision of paid holidays. Indeed these matters are adopted in the subsequent legislation of 29 June 1983 which establishes an effective forty-hour week and a minimum of twenty-three days annual holiday.

Article 35 establishes the duty and the right of every Spanish citizen to work and to earn a living wage without discrimination between the sexes. The second section of this Article also recognises the specific issue of workers' rights by referring to their enshrinement in a special workers' statute. Once again the Constitution is laying down basic principles which require subsequent legislation. In this particular case, action followed relatively soon with the approval in March 1980 of the Workers' Statute.

11.2.2 Workers' Statute (Estatuto de los Trabajadores) 1980

This elaborates on workers' rights under three broad headings: the relationship of the individual to his work; worker representation; and collective bargaining.

11.2.2.1 Relationship of the individual to work

At issue here are the rights and duties of workers as well as details of their contracts. However, there is also reference to the concept of the minimum wage (*salario mínimo interprofesional*/SMI) to be fixed annually by the government in consultation with unions and employers bearing in mind the anticipated consumer price index (*índice de precios de consumo*/IPC). In order to safeguard workers in cases of bankruptcy or closure the Statute provided for the establishment of the Guaranteed Wage Fund (*Fondo de Garantía Salarial*) which was to provide wages for up to a maximum of four months. The *Fondo* was constituted as an autonomous administrative body under the Ministry of Labour and Social Security.

11.2.2.2 Worker representation

In firms which have less than fifty and more than ten employees, workers are represented by delegates (*delegados de personal*) elected on the basis of one delegate for up to thirty employees, and three for between thirty-one and forty-nine employees. In firms which have more than fifty employees, workers are represented by works' committees (*comités de empresa*) the size of which is in proportion to the number of employees, as shown in Figure 11.1. If elections are required candidates are presented in lists containing at least as many names as there are places to fill, with a clear indication of the union or the group of workers who have proposed the

Figure 11.1. *Representation on works' committees*

No. of employees in company	No. of members on works' committee
50–100	5
101–250	9
251–500	13
501–750	17
751–1000	21
1000 +	21 + 2 per thousand employees up to a maximum number of 75 members

candidates. Voting is then by secret ballot and the term of office for those elected is usually four years. The composition of the committees, therefore, usually reflects the relative strengths of the unions at the work place. This system has been favoured by the *Comisiones Obreras* which are not so keen to see changes which would transfer negotiating rights from the broader based works' committees to plant-based single union branches (see 11.2.3.6).

The works' committees receive regular statistical information and financial statements from management. They issue reports to the workforce on the implications of any pending restructuring, organisational changes or financial adjustments. They monitor the fulfilment of legislation concerning industrial relations, social security and health and safety. In general, therefore, their role is to negotiate on behalf of the employees concerning their day-to-day work and their job security. This may also include local wage agreements, although wage negotiations may well take place at another level.

11.2.2.3 Collective bargaining

The procedure for negotiating collective agreements (*convenios colectivos*), their format and their status is established in the Workers' Statute with subsequent modification resulting from the Organic Law of Union Freedom (see 11.2.3). Collective agreements can be negotiated at a variety of levels depending on the consent of the parties involved. When they occur at company level the works' committee is the appropriate body to represent the workers, with a maximum of twelve representatives per side. If they are negotiated at local, provincial or national level, a negotiating committee has to be formed consisting of representatives from those unions which have the status of 'most representative unions' (see 11.2.3.4). This committee can have a maximum of fifteen union representatives. Negotiations have to start within one month of a properly constituted request being presented by either side and agreement must be reached by 60 per cent of each party before it can be finalised. Once agreed, it is binding on both parties for as long as stipulated. The agreements have to be lodged with the Mediation, Arbitration and Conciliation Institute (see 11.4) and they have to be published in the *Official State Gazette* or its regional equivalent.

11.2.3 *Organic Law of Trade Union Freedom* (Ley Orgánica de Libertad Sindical/*LOLS*) 1984

This law was approved in July 1984, but due to the fact that an appeal against it was lodged with the constitutional court (see 2.5) it did not come into effect until August 1985. The law stems from Article 28.1 of the Constitution which recognises but does not spell out the basic freedoms and rights of unions. Because of the fundamental and far-reaching significance of the details of these freedoms, they require a law with the status of organic law (see 4.7.1.1). Hence this is the law which currently establishes the *modus operandi* of unions in Spain and it therefore merits some attention.

11.2.3.1 *Right to join a union*
The Law recognises the right of all workers freely to join a union and this includes those working in public administration. However, it stipulates two exceptions: members of the armed forces and members of the judiciary. Furthermore, the right to exercise trade union rights for certain groups, such as members of the police force, is governed by specific regulations.

11.2.3.2 *Legal responsibility of unions*
Unions are liable for their own acts but not those of individual members, unless they are acting in accordance with union instructions. Their 'quotas' cannot be sequestrated. There is uncertainty, however, as to the meaning of 'quotas' and whether it is confined to funds or whether it includes property in general.

11.2.3.3 *Representation*
Although all legally constituted unions enjoy the same basic freedoms, this Law recognises the special position of the 'most representative union'. The criterion to be used to decide which unions qualify for this status is that of election results rather than membership. The Law stipulates that the election process must be completed within three months, which will help to produce more precise results than were previously available. The precise period within which the elections can take place is to be determined by the conciliation agency, the IMAC. This body is also responsible for recording union election results, labour agreements and union statutes (see 11.4).

11.2.3.4 'Most representative unions'

This classification is given to those unions which have obtained 10 per cent or more of the total number of delegates or members of works' committees. Based on the 1986 results (see Figure 11.2) Workers' Commissions (*Comisiones Obreras*/CCOO) and the General Workers' Union (*Unión General de Trabajadores*/UGT) have attained this status at national level. This means that all the unions and federations which belong to these bodies also enjoy that status within their own ambit, even if they have not directly obtained 10 per cent of the delegates. To acquire this status at regional level, it is necessary to obtain a minimum of 15 per cent of the delegates, who must correspond to at least 1,500 individuals. Therefore, in addition to CCOO and the UGT, the Basque ELA–STV union qualifies for this status, while the Federation of Unions in Galicia (*Intersindical Nacional de Trabajadores Gallegos*/INTG) lost this status in 1986.

11.2.3.5 Rights of 'most representative unions'

These unions are automatically entitled to become part of a negotiating committee for collective agreements above the level of the single company and to nominate representatives to the boards of public bodies (see 6.3). These and other rights are restricted to the specific region where the status was achieved in the case of those unions which qualified on a regional basis.

11.2.3.6 Union rights within companies

Formal recognition is given to the single union, plant-based branch or section (*sección sindical*) as a representative and negotiating force within individual firms. It represents a move away from reliance on the broader based works' committee (*comité de empresa* or *consejo obrero*) favoured by the CCOO and as such it appears to favour the UGT model of organisation.

11.2.3.7 Protection of union freedom

Ample protection is built into the Law to protect unions and individual members from any form of discrimination by employers. A formal procedure for recourse to the courts is laid down starting with the labour court (*magistratura de trabajo*) and extending as far as the constitutional court (*tribunal constitucional*), with penalties in the form of fines for acts of discrimination.

11.2.3.8 Collective agreement levy

In order to help unions defray some of their costs, they can establish provision within a collective agreement for the employer to deduct a payroll levy (*canon de negociación*) from those workers who opt into the

Figure 11.2. *Trade union election results (% of representatives elected)* *

	UGT	CCOO	USO	ELV–STV	INTG	Unaffiliated	Others
1982	36.71	33.4	4.64	3.3	1.17	12.09	8.69
1986	40.9	34.8	3.9	3.2	0.9	7.5	8.8

Source: IMAC (1983), Cambio 16 (1986, provisional)

scheme. Likewise, unions can request that firms, with the agreement of the employee, deduct union fees from the payroll.

11.2.3.9 Election of workers' representatives
The procedure was laid down in the Workers' Statute and modified by subsequent legislation in 1983. However, the LOLS established a four-year period for elections instead of every two years. This brings union elections into line with parliamentary elections. However, this move was not welcomed by the CCOO who felt that it would link union fortunes too closely with those of political parties and would therefore work to their own disadvantage. Thus, while CCOO secured 35 per cent of the delegates elected in 1986, the Communist Party, with which they are associated, gained only 4.6 per cent of the votes cast in the parliamentary elections of the same year.

11.3   Major unions

The 1982 results of the elections for delegates and members of works' committees (see Figure 11.2) indicate that the only 'most representative unions' on a national basis in terms of the 1984 Organic Law are the UGT and the CCOO. The former has consolidated its position in small- and medium-sized firms, while the latter are now well represented in public sector enterprises such as *Telefónica, Renfe* and *Hunosa*.

The number of unaffiliated or unattached delegates elected in 1982 was quite significant. This was partly due to the earlier attempt by the UCD to encourage more independents to stand as workplace representatives in the hope of creating an alternative third force. However, the emphasis in the Organic Law is on union-sponsored candidates and thus, not surprisingly, the proportion of independents fell in 1986. The category 'others' consisted of a large number of delegates representing unions which may be relatively strong only in particular localities or firms. As a result of this Law, open lists (*listas abiertas*) which gave workers the opportunity to choose from a wide range of candidates, some of whom would be selected because of their personal attributes, will be replaced by closed and restricted lists (*listas cerradas y bloqueadas*). The latter will limit choice to candidates drawn from the unions in direct relation to the number of delegate posts to be filled.

11.3.1 *General Workers' Union* (Unión General de Trabajadores/ UGT)

The General Workers' Union was founded in Barcelona in 1888 and is closely, although informally, linked to the PSOE. It was strong prior to the Civil War but then was savagely repressed during the Franco era. The union has gradually emerged as the strongest numerically in the post-1975 period and it has been very prominent in negotiating national agreements on economic and social matters both with the government and the employers (see 11.5).

The UGT is organised as a union of local unions (*sindicatos locales*) which draw their members from the same branch of activity from within firms where they are organised in union sections (*secciones sindicales*). These local unions are then organised on a provincial or regional basis. Finally, the different unions representing each branch come together in federations (*federaciones*) of which there are some twenty-five, including activities such as iron and steel, agriculture, construction, chemicals, hotels and the banking sector. Although the terminology varies slightly from union to union, the basic structures are roughly the same. Workers engaged in the same activity are usually organised in a *sindicato*, while a territorial grouping of workers within the same labour organisation is known as a *unión*. Larger groupings organised either within the same industry or on a territorial basis are generally known as *federaciones* or *confederaciones*.

The highest body in the UGT is the congress (*congreso*). This usually meets every three years and elects the executive committee (*comisión ejecutiva*) as the union's governing body. Between congresses representation is maintained through the confederal committee (*comité confederal*) which consists of members of the executive committee and the general secretaries of the industrial federations and the provincial and regional unions.

In the UGT power is vested at grassroots level. Each local union (*sindicato local*) is autonomous and may call a stoppage. The UGT favours the idea of giving more negotiating power to the union section (*sección sindical*) in each firm rather than to the multi-union works' committees (*comités de empresa*). The new Organic Law on Trade Union Freedom (*Ley Orgánica de Libertad Sindical*/LOLS) opens the way further for this to take place (see 11.2.3.6).

11.3.2 *Workers' Commissions* (Comisiones Obreras/CCOO)

The workers' commissions began as a clandestine and disparate way of encouraging worker representation on the former works' councils (*jurados de empresa*) as an alternative to the official vertical union organisation (*organización sindical*). The *comisiones* grew in strength in the early 1960s and for a while appeared to be tolerated within the system. However, the authorities, alarmed by their success, started a crackdown in 1967 and many of the leaders, including Marcelino Camacho, who was later to emerge as the legally recognised general secretary, were imprisoned.

The CCOO are organised as federations (*federaciones*) of workers in roughly the same branches of industry as in the UGT. These activity-based federations are then linked together as confederations (*confederaciones*) in territorial congresses (*centrales*). The national congress (*congreso confederal*) meets every two years. The management of the union between congresses is in the hands of the confederal council (*consejo confederal*) made up of fifty representatives of the federations and fifty of the territorial confederations, together with the general secretary and members of the executive committee. The executive committee is entrusted with the application of the policies decided by the congress and the council. It appears that the CCOO are a more centralised union and expect decisions taken at the top to filter down and be followed at the lower levels. Because of their historical development, they have favoured the works' committee as the basis for negotiations and now feel threatened by moves to shift this responsibility to plant-based union branches.

They have strong links through their leading members with the Spanish Communist Party, although in origin and support they also draw upon Christian and Social Democrats. They currently see the danger of being too closely associated with a party which in the general elections of 1986 gained only 4.6 per cent of the total national vote.

11.3.3 Workers' Syndical Union (Unión Sindical Obrera/USO)

Like the CCOO this union arose from a group of workers who were opposed to the official Franco unions. Many of its founder members came from a Catholic workers' background, being members of the Catholic Youth Workers (*Juventud Obrera Católica*/JOC) or Catholic Action Workers' Brotherhood (*Hermandad Obrera de Acción Católica*/HOAC). Its strength was largely centred in the heavy industries of Northern Spain and large organisations such as Spanish Railways (*Red Nacional de Ferrocarriles Españoles*/RENFE).

The USO is organised on the basis of union sections (*secciones sindicales*) within firms, which are then brought together in eight industrial branches: iron and steel; banking; transport; food; construction; textiles; chemicals; and fuels. These are then joined in local, regional and national federations. The supreme decision-making body is the confederal congress (*congreso confederal*) which meets every two years, and then elects the confederal council (*consejo confederal*) to exercise control over the union. Day-to-day management is in the hands of the confederal secretariat (*secretariado confederal*).

11.3.4 *Confederation of Unitary Workers' Syndicates* (Confederación de Sindicatos Unitarios de Trabajadores/ *CSUT)*

This splinter group, which believes in a single-union system, was formed from the CCOO in 1976 and has strong links with the *Partido del Trabajo Español* (PTE), a far-Left political party. It is organised on the basis of industrial groups with its congress, executive committee and secretariat.

11.3.5 *Unitary Syndicate* (Sindicato Unitario/*SU)*

This was a further splinter group from the CCOO, formed in 1977. It is closely linked with another party on the extreme Left, the *Organización Revolucionaria de Trabajadores* (ORT). It is against negotiations involving the government and has therefore opposed the various social pacts which have played a significant part in regulating labour affairs since 1977 (see 11.5). Its organisation is based on union sections (*secciones sindicales*) of workers, irrespective of area of activity. It, too, has its congress, council and executive committee.

11.3.6 *National Confederation of Labour* (Confederación Nacional de Trabajo/*CNT)*

Although it was not formally established until 1911, it is rooted in nineteenth-century Anarchosyndicalism. The CNT has ignored political affiliation and rejected what is considers bourgeois democracy. It has therefore officially boycotted the elections for union representatives, although some candidates have stood in Catalonia. Its basic organisational forum is the general assembly (*asamblea general*) at which each lower division is represented in turn by representatives nominated by general assemblies.

11.3.7 *Regional unions*

The only two regional unions which have gained sufficient support to qualify for negotiating status have been the Basque union, *Euzko Langilleen Alkartasuna – Solidaridad de Trabajadores Vascos* (ELA–STV) closely allied to the Basque Nationalist Party (see 10.5.1) and the Federation of Unions in Galicia (*Intersindical Nacional de Trabajadores Gallegos*/INTG. In 1982 both unions gained more than the fifteen percentage regionally to give them a formal place on negotiating bodies under the provisions of the Trade Union Freedom Law (11.2.3). In 1986, however, INTG lost this status. The Catalan workers have likewise attempted to unite several unions in Catalonia in the hope of securing the necessary 15 per cent of votes. There the leading union is currently the *Solidaritat d'Obrers Catalans* (SOC) which had earlier ties with *comisiones obreras*.

11.3.8 Other unions

In the first flush of freedom granted by the new right to register unions in 1977, more than four hundred were said to exist at one time. However, although many have disappeared completely, there are still a number of unions at national level which are identified with a single area of activity (*sindicatos unitarios*). The most significant among these are the *Sindicato Libre de la Marina Mercante* (SLMM) for the merchant navy; the *Unión de Pagesos* (UP) and the *Federación Independiente de Sindicatos Agrarios* (FISA) for agricultural workers; the *Sindicato Libre e Independiente de los Cuerpos de la Administración de Justicia* (SLICAJ) for law officials; and the *Federación Española de Cuadros* (FEC) and *Confederación General de Cuadros* (CGC) for white-collar workers.

11.4 Mediation, Arbitration and Conciliation Institute (*Instituto de Mediación, Arbitraje y Conciliación*/IMAC)

When Franco's vertical system of unions was officially disbanded in 1976, the problem of what to do with the full-time employees who enjoyed the rank of state civil servants (*funcionarios del estado*) was resolved by transferring them to a newly created body responsible for the 'administration of social and vocational services', the so-called *Administración Institucional de Servicios Socioprofesionales* (AISS). Some of these *funcionarios* were subsequently entrusted with some of the work of the IMAC which was established in 1979 as an autonomous administrative body (see 6.3). It operated as an independent body under the auspices of the Ministry of Labour with its own director and a governing council which included union and employers' representatives as well as ministry appointees. Although it was intended to perform the role of arbitrator between unions and employers, this was not put into effect and it has been confined to providing conciliation services. These are largely aimed at individual workers weeking information on their rights prior to having recourse to the labour courts. Within each province there is at least one labour court (*magistratura de trabajo*) which handles most ordinary cases of dismissals, breaches of contract and social security problems. More serious matters and appeals are sent to the central labour tribunal (*tribunal central de trabajo*) and at the highest level to the social division of the supreme court (*sala de lo social del tribunal supremo*). In these cases, the IMAC acts as a filter by resolving approximately half the complaints it receives from individuals before they need to go to court. It is seen largely as a registry for the results of union elections, statutes, collective agreements and private agreements concerning termination of employment.

However, its existence as an independent body has been relatively short-lived. Many of its functions have been transferred to the autonomous communities and in April 1985 its remaining functions and personnel were transferred to the newly created Subdirectorate General for Mediation, Arbitration and Conciliation (*Subdirección General de Mediación, Arbitraje y Conciliación*) of the Ministry of Labour and Social Security.

11.5   Pacts with government and employers

The consensus approach adopted in the post-Franco era by political and labour groups towards major economic and political problems has undoubtedly been important in securing a relatively smooth transition from one system of government to another. As part of this process, lengthy negotiations have taken place in order to achieve major agreements on, for example, wage restraint, employment, industrial restructuring and social security. The discussions have not always been carried out between the same parties because, as yet, a permanent consultative structure is lacking. Article 131.2 of the Constitution envisages the creation of a council to assist the government in economic planning. The composition and functions of such a council are left for elaboration in subsequent legislation. The reference in the text of the Constitution to the participation of unions and employers' organisations is generally taken to mean that the aim is to establish an economic and social development council (*consejo económico-social*) as a consultative body to collaborate with the government in the process of planning and in the establishment of priorities. The fact that this has not yet been constituted may be due to the existence of other more pressing demands on legislators' time. It may also, however, have something to do with the lack of unity within the trade union movement.

Various attempts were made in the immediate post-Franco years to achieve a measure of unity and solidarity among labour organisations. A co-ordinating body for the UGT, the CCOO and the USO, the *Coordinadora de Organizaciones Sindicales* (COS) was tentatively established in 1976, when it succeeded in organising a general strike. However, it only survived a short time and it has not been resurrected since. On the other hand, the employers' organisations have been more successful in settling their differences and in creating an Employers' Confederation, the *Confederación Española de Organizaciones Empresariales* (CEOE), which is described in 12.11. Nevertheless, despite the lack of cohesion on the union side, several major pacts (*pactos*) and agreements (*acuerdos*) have been signed as described below (see also Figure 11.3).

11.5.1 Moncloa Pacts (1977)

Following the UCD general election victory in June 1977, an economic package was agreed by the major political parties. It included pay guidelines which related wage increases to the level of inflation (penalised firms

Figure 11.3 *Social pacts*

Year	Pact	*Pacto*
1977	Moncloa Pacts	*Pactos de la Moncloa*
1980	Inter-Confederation Framework Agreement	*Acuerdo Marco Interconfederal* (AMI)
1981	National Agreement on Employment	*Acuerdo Nacional sobre Empleo* (ANE)
1983	Inter-Confederation Agreement	*Acuerdo Interconfederal* (AI)
1984	Economic and Social Agreement	*Acuerdo Económico y Social* (AES)

paying above the norm) and allowed for the shedding of labour if pay increases were due to union pressure. It covered a whole gamut of other measures, including tax reform, social security, housing, employment, prices and monetary policy. Although on this occasion the employers and labour representatives were notable by their absence in the negotiations, the Pacts established a pattern which was to be followed by subsequent employer–union and tripartite negotiations involving the government.

11.5.2 Inter-Confederation Framework Agreement (1980)

This Framework Agreement was signed in January 1980 by the UGT and Spanish Employers' Confederation. As such it was not legally binding but it provided pay guidelines which were revised in 1981 in the light of price rises. The parties agreed to co-operate in reducing working hours, banning overtime and increasing productivity. The success of this agreement prompted a more ambitious tripartite agreement.

11.5.3 National Agreement on Employment (1981)

This National Agreement on Employment was signed in 1981 by the government, the CEOE and the two major unions, the UGT and the CCOO, to come into effect in 1982. It established pay norms with provision for their automatic modification in accordance with changes in the consumer price index. The unions also secured the promise of government measures to boost employment and reform social security. The government also acknowledged the need to compensate the unions for their assets (*patrimonio sindical*) which had been expropriated during the Franco era.

11.5.4 Inter-Confederation Agreement (1983)

This was a further agreement, without the participation of the government, between the employers and the two largest unions, the UGT and the

CCOO. It set pay norms with an adjustment mechanism along the lines previously established in the tripartite national agreement of 1981. It also stressed the importance of co-operation on working conditions.

11.5.5 Economic and Social Agreement (1984)

This Economic and Social Agreement was designed to apply to the two-year period 1985–6. It was a return to the tripartite system of 1981 involving government, management and workers and the first therefore to be entered into by the Socialist government of Felipe González.

This was the most far-reaching of the agreements signed to date. It included a number of commitments which the government undertook to honour, including measures concerning unemployment, health and safety at work, and training. Agreement was reached to boost job creation through the services of the National Employment Institute (*Instituto Nacional de Empleo*/INEM). This is an autonomous administrative body (see 6.3) created by a Royal Decree in 1978 which has become particularly significant in the light of Spain's high unemployment level, estimated in 1986 to be in the region of 20 per cent. In addition to being responsible for administering unemployment benefits, the INEM is empowered to negotiate public works schemes with regional governments and generally to act as a catalyst in job creation in both the public and the private sector. The Economic and Social Agreement also contained a decision to set up a special solidarity fund, the *Fondo de Solidaridad*, based on levies on employers and employees as well as direct government funding. This is administered jointly by the signatories to the agreement and is used for vocational training schemes.

The UGT and the employers' organisations, the CEOE and the CEPYME (see 12.11), entered into a legally binding contract regarding pay norms and productivity. They undertook to introduce a voluntary disputes procedure as they were dissatisfied with the services of the IMAC (see 11.4). They also agreed to phase out or incorporate into collective agreements the labour ordinances (*ordenanzas laborales*) which date from the Franco period. These are detailed regulations for specific industrial sectors governing such matters as categories of workers, overtime payments, working conditions, health and safety and dismissal procedures. Such regulations have proved difficult to remove in the past and may yet be difficult to eliminate in practice.

The growing divisions on the union side were highlighted by the refusal of the CCOO to enter into the agreement, although they subsequently sought to be involved in aspects of its implementation. One of the major stumbling blocks was the agreement between the participants to pursue a more flexible approach towards the hiring and firing of labour in line with other EEC countries. The CCOO, however, saw this move as a sell-out of the safeguards against dismissal traditionally enjoyed by Spanish workers.

11.6   Conclusion

From the results of the elections for shop-floor representatives, it emerges that the UGT and the CCOO are clearly the two major forces in union affairs at the expense of the others which have been losing ground. Both of these unions are strongly represented in the iron and steel and metal industries, but the UGT is better supported in agriculture, while the CCOO has a bigger following in the construction industry. The UGT itself claims to have over two million members with the CCOO claiming just under that figure, and the USO nearly half a million. However, these figures are less reliable than the election results. The number of paid-up members is variable and generally low compared to other EEC countries, despite the low level of contributions, which for the UGT, for example, is 0.7 per cent of the annual gross minimum wage. The lack of funds has clearly been an obstacle to mounting a thorough national network with adequate publicity and full-time officers. The return of union assets which were seized at the time of the Civil War, together with the income derived from the compulsory dues, is long awaited, but the precise destination of these is currently a source of dispute among the unions themselves and the Employers' Confederation. The large number of small firms is also a handicap to the organisation of mass movements. A general apathy also pervades workers, who can elect representatives at shop-floor level without the need for formal union membership. The success of national pacts or consensus agreements may also have removed some of the pressing urgency of earlier calls for union militancy.

Despite the lack of formal consultative machinery and the lack of cohesion in the trade union movement, it has been possible for the government, management and labour to come together and agree programmes of joint action. This degree of partnership has doubtless been encouraged by the severe economic problems faced by Spain and by an awareness of the political dangers inherent in disrupting Spain's new democracy. In general the attitude of the unions has made a positive contribution towards overcoming some of these difficulties and towards preparing the Spanish economy for harmonisation with the EEC.

12 Business and professional organisations

12.1 Legal background

Article 39 of the Constitution recognises and guarantees the rights of private enterprise in Spain. It specifies that this right is to be exercised in accordance with the overall needs of the economy and within the general framework of economic planning. The scope for private enterprise in Spain is, thus, likely to be similar to that of business in other EEC countries. However, despite references in the Constitution, this is an area where the existing legislation is still largely pre-1975. The laws governing the legal status of limited liability companies are now more than thirty years old and obviously in need of reform. These laws are the *Ley de Régimen Jurídico de las Sociedades Anónomas* of 1951, concerning the legal framework of the public limited company (*sociedad anónima*/SA) and the *Ley de Régimen Jurídico de las Sociedades de Responsibilidad Limitada* of 1953, concerning the legal framework of the private limited company (*sociedad de responsabilidad limitada*/SRL/SL).

Details of business organisation and procedure are incorporated into the Commercial Code (*Código de Comercio*) which itself dates from 1885. However, the Code is constantly updated to take account of legislative changes. One of its most important provisions is the requirement that all businesses, with the exception of the sole trader, have to register their existence in the Mercantile Register (*Registro Mercantil*) in the capital of the province in which the registered head office of the company is located. Thereafter a record of the main details is kept in the Directorate General for Registration (*Dirección General de los Registros y del Notariado*) in Madrid. The basic data which must be entered includes name, address, nature of business, date of foundation and capital. Subsequent changes in any of these particulars must be reported. Foreign companies which wish to establish branches are also required to follow this procedure and at the same time to produce a certificate from their local Spanish consul verifying that they have met the legal requirements of the country of origin. The importance of the Register lies in the fact that the filed data is assumed to be public knowledge. The corollary of this is that failure to register a particular aspect could lead to a charge of fraud. The Mercantile Register is open for inspection by the public who may obtain details of specific companies by personal enquiry. The reference number relevant to a company's entry in the Register is usually included on the company's official stationery.

12.2   Sole traders (*comerciantes*)

The one-man business is still the most numerous form of business organisation in Spain. This is regulated in the Commercial Code and, although registration in the Mercantile Register is not compulsory for sole traders, it does nevertheless have the advantage of giving legal status to their documentation. Examples of sole traders are found in many sectors, especially in regard to retail sales, food and drink, and crafts and services. They are automatically members of their local chamber of commerce from which they can derive technical and legal support (see 12.12).

12.3   Companies (*sociedades anónimas*/SA)

The 1951 Law which provides the legal basis for the SA-type of organisation stipulates that companies with capital in excess of fifty million pesetas have to adopt the SA format but no minimum size is laid down. This means that the title SA may be misleading since it covers not only the large, quoted company but also smaller family businesses. However, legislation has been pending for some time in order to remove this and other anomalies and a draft new company law envisages future SA companies with a minimum capital of three million pesetas. It should also be noted that the range of enterprises covered by the present law is also considerably widened by the inclusion of the public sector companies (see 9.2/3/4) which likewise carry the suffix SA.

The Law contains full details of the classes of shares which companies may issue, as well as details of the rights and obligations of shareholders on whom ultimate authority rests through their annual meeting (*junta*). Although such meetings are normally formalities, there are signs recently that the return of democracy has increased interest in some of the issues involved and that the economic climate has made investors more anxious to see how management performs.

Probably the main area of concern in recent years has been the financial accountability of companies, as it is widely accepted that much of the data published by Spanish companies has been of a cosmetic nature for tax purposes. Furthermore, for some time it has been thought that the present legal requirement for the shareholders to choose amongst their number two shareholder–auditors (*accionistas censores*) has been inadequate and a mere formality. The expropriation in February 1983 of the RUMASA conglomerate and the ensuing revelation of financial scandal and tax evasion highlighted the absence of an efficient system of checks and balances in Spanish business. This lack of independent scrutiny and accountability was clearly responsible for enhancing the business elite during the Franco era.

Nevertheless, despite the absence of legislation to compel independent audits, many private as well as public sector companies have been making greater voluntary use of external auditors (see also 9.7.4). This is particularly the case with larger firms who want to obtain funds from abroad or to convince potential customers of their financial worthiness. At the same time a great measure of harmonisation has been achieved regarding the presentation of financial data, which now generally follows a standardised chart of accounts contained in the General Accounting Plan (*Plan General de Contabilidad*) along the lines of the EEC IV Directive.

12.4　Companies (*sociedades de responsabilidad limitadas/ SRL/SL*)

The aim of the 1953 Law for SL companies was to provide a more flexible type of company organisation requiring less documentation and formality. In this case there is no minimum capital requirement, although the maximum is fifty million pesetas, above which a company must, of course, be constituted as an SA company as outlined in 12.3. In this type of company there are restrictions on the transfer of shares designed to keep ownership within the hands of the founder members. The formal requirements for producing financial information are minimal and there is no provision for the audit or filing of financial returns. This type of organisation can be found particularly in the service and retail sector. It can be seen, for example, at airports in the contracted-out airport cleaning and catering services. Nevertheless, many smaller firms have preferred to choose the SA form, possibly because of the prestige it affords.

12.5　Partnerships (*sociedades colectivas*)

Although partnerships are recognised in the Commercial Code and they must be recorded in the Mercantile Register in the same way as the two forms of business organisation described above, they are not widely found in Spain. There are two basic kinds: the general partnership with unlimited liability (*sociedad colectiva* or *sociedad regular colectiva*); and the limited partnership with at least one general, unlimited partner and one limited partner (*sociedad en comandita* or *sociedad comanditaria*). While, in some countries, professional people prefer to organise themselves in this way, in Spain they tend to act on their account, to form limited companies or co-operatives or to organise themselves into professional associations (see 12.10).

12.6 Co-operatives (*cooperativas*)

Much interest has been shown recently, both inside and outside Spain, in this form of organisation. The Spanish Constitution expressly refers to the encouragement of the development of co-operatives in Article 129.2. There is a special Co-operative Register (*Registro de Cooperativas*) in which co-operatives must be recorded and their statutes must be approved by the Ministry of Labour. Although the term 'co-operative' was not always in favour politically, nevertheless major resettlement schemes like the *Plan Jaén* and *Plan Badajoz*, drawn up after the Civil War, relied on the principle of sharing common marketing and distribution services as well as pooling the use of expensive equipment. In more recent years, the use of co-operatives has grown considerably and they have been actively encouraged by the Ministry of Agriculture, which has promoted legislation to facilitate financial assistance and training for those involved. This is the form of organisation which has been favoured in the promotion of land development programmes to counter the problems of the large estates (*latifundios*) on the one hand, and excessively small holdings (*minifundios*) on the other. The newly autonomous regional governments have been active in this area and, despite bureaucratic and technical difficulties, an increasing number of co-operatives are beginning to function, for example, in some of the traditionally neglected areas of Andalusia. On the other hand, the motivating force in many cases has been the realisation of the opportunities available for Spanish farmers to compete in EEC markets and elsewhere if they can be well organised, especially in regard to marketing and distribution.

The economic problems facing industry have led to rationalisation programmes prompted by the government as well as to the collapse of private firms. This has led in some instances to attempts to establish worker co-operatives in industry as workers have attempted to salvage divisions of companies which their owners have decided to sell off or close down. Alternatively, the organisational framework used in these rescue bids has been the creation of a worker-controlled company with the safeguards of limited liability (*sociedad anónima laboral*/SAL).

A lot of attention in recent years has centred on Mondragón, a town in the Basque province of Guipúzcoa. In 1956 the seeds were sown for the growth of a significant movement through the creation of ULGOR, a co-operative taking its name from the initials of its five founder members. It initially employed twenty-three people making paraffin heaters but by 1982 the industrial co-operatives there had grown to include some one hundred enterprises employing over 17,000 people. Among the individual co-operatives is the original ULGOR, a major producer of consumer durables, as well as others responsible for foundries and forges, capital goods, component industries, consumer durables and building. One of the significant strengths of the movement has been its strong financial organisation based on its own bank, the *Caja Laboral Popular*/CLP with some 700 staff distributed among ninety-three branches throughout the Basque region. In addition to carrying out normal banking business with the public, it lends money to the co-operatives and has become the commercial headquarters of the movement, responsible for technical research and planning. (See 13.6 for other financial co-operatives.) The Mondragón movement also includes its own social security organisation, a medical and hospital service, a laundry and meals service, a technical college, housing co-operatives and agricultural co-operatives.

As co-operatives are open to the admission of new members, their capital is variable and they therefore require a different organisational framework to that of the SA company. Hence use is made of a general assembly (*junta general*) as the supreme body which meets when required and takes decisions by majority votes on issues such as the initial contributions of new members and the modification of internal regulations. This elects a board of control (*consejo de vigilancia*) which in turn appoints the board of management (*junta rectora*) to look after the day-to-day running of the co-operative. Within each enterprise there is a social council (*consejo social*) which, like the works' committee in SA companies, acts as a channel of communication between management and shop-floor workers with powers in matters such as health, safety and welfare.

12.7   Joint ventures

A common feature of business organisation in recent years has been the formation of joint ventures. This has been particularly important in regard to carrying out major expansion programmes, promoting a particular service or product, acquiring and exploiting new technology and research, developing export markets and tendering for public works schemes. The government has provided a number of financial and fiscal incentives to encourage firms to act together and this is one way in which foreign technology and know-how has been acquired. Under a law of May 1982 these joint ventures may be formed either as temporary consortia of companies (*uniones temporales de empresas*) for a maximum period of ten years, or as groupings of companies (*agrupaciones de empresas*) which are contracts of co-operation between companies. The Commercial Code also has provision for companies to act jointly under a system of joint accounts (*cuentas en participación*) where one participant conducts business under his own name and liability but with the addition of capital from others.

12.8   Foreign investment

Since the early nineteenth century, foreign investment has played a significant part in the development of the Spanish economy, except during the period of autarky imposed by Franco between 1939 and 1959. Since then the massive influx of foreign capital into Spain has provided a major boost to the economy and has accelerated the process of industrialisation. At times, however, this has been largely uncontrolled and unselective with little real monitoring taking place. This situation was remedied by Decree 3021 of October 1974 which consolidated and clarified the existing legislation and by Decree 3022 of the same year which added further regulations. The measures contained in these decrees can be considered as a foreign investment code which has been supplemented by further decrees and orders in the light of changing circumstances.

Among other provisions of the 1974 legislation was the establishment of the Directorate General of Foreign Transactions (*Dirección General de Transacciones Exteriores*/DGTE). This body has assumed an important role in the control of foreign investment and foreign exchange and it has replaced the former administrative body for foreign currency control, the Spanish Institute for Foreign Currency (*Instituto Español de Moneda Extranjera*/IEME) (see also 13.2.5). It is responsible for the monitoring of acquisitions and disposals of foreign investments which have to be registered in the Investment Register (*Registro de Inversiones*). Ultimate responsibility for granting the authorisation needed for investments of over 50 per cent in specific sectors and in special circumstances rests with the council of ministers which, in turn, takes advice from the Foreign Investments Board (*Junta de Inversiones Exteriores*). All matters concerning foreign investments which are not assigned elsewhere are dealt with by the Ministry of Economy and Finance.

Normally investment of up to 50 per cent of the share capital of a Spanish company can be undertaken without prior authorisation. Investments of more than 50 per cent are automatically authorised by the *Dirección General de Transacciones Exteriores* (DGTE) where the share capital of the Spanish company does not exceed twenty-five million pesetas. In certain sectors such as mining, shipping, public utilities and banking, the percentage investment requiring authorisation is lower and there are other restrictions. In those cases where authorisation is not automatic or where it concerns one of the restricted industries, authorisation must be obtained from the council of ministers following a report from the *Junta de Inversiones Exteriores*.

In contrast to this relative freedom to gain control over Spanish companies, there are a limited number of sectors, such as defence industries and the mass media, where no foreign investment whatsoever is allowed.

12.9   Foreign branches

Spanish legislation also permits foreign companies to set up branches (*sucursales*) in Spain. This provision is regulated by the Foreign Investment

Code and authorisation in some cases must be obtained from the DGTE. There are, for example, specific restrictions concerning banks which are referred to in 13.4. Branches are required to keep the same official books as SA companies and their existence must also be recorded in the Mercantile Register.

12.10   Professional associations (*colegios profesionales*)

Unlike the working classes whose independent unions were abolished under the Franco regime, the professional and middle classes in Spain have been able to organise their own associations (*colegios*) relatively unhindered. Indeed, on occasions, these bodies stubbornly refused to co-operate with the wishes of the authorities and at times risked being disbanded. Now, however, their position is formally recognised in Article 36 of the Constitution which states that the special characteristics of the professional associations will be regulated by law and that their internal structure and operation must be democratic in nature. (Examples of these associations are provided in Figure 12.1.)

The basic legislation covering these associations is the Law of 1974 modified by that of December 1978 which stipulates that in order to exercise a particular profession it is necessary to belong to the local branch of the relevant association, eligibility for membership in the first instance being based on the appropriate academic qualification. The *colegios* are empowered to regulate their own affairs in accordance with their statutes, which have to be approved by the particular ministry to which their profession pertains. Thus, for example, the Lawyers' Association (*Colegio de Abogados*) comes under the auspices of the Ministry of Justice to which any subsequent modifications of statutes have to be submitted. While internal structures vary from association to association, each normally includes a general council (*consejo general*) and a president, who is likely to represent the association nationally and internationally. The major associations are organised on a regional basis as well as having a national headquarters.

The associations also have a legal right to be informed of any legislation which is likely to affect their profession and in this respect they will be consulted on draft legislation within their ambit. Furthermore, they keep their members up-to-date through their own courses, conferences and publications.

In general the professional associations act to protect the interests of their members, serving both as pressure groups and as advisory bodies. They safeguard professional standards and the observation of professional etiquette and anyone found failing in these respects may be struck off the register and disqualified from exercising the profession. The associations are also responsible for officially certifying documentation issued by their

Figure 12.1. *Examples of professional associations*

Title of association	Profession
Colegio Nacional de Administradores de Fincas	Estate managers
Colegio Oficial de Físicos	Physicists
Colegio Oficial de Ingenieros de Construcción	Construction engineers
Colegio de Oficiales de la Marina Mercante	Merchant navy officers
Colegio de Abogados	Lawyers
Colegio de Economistas	Economists
Colegio de Médicos	Doctors
Colegio Oficial de Arquitectos	Architects
Colegio Oficial de Agentes de Cambio y Bolsa	Stockbrokers and exchange dealers
Instituto de Censores Jurados de Cuentas de España	Auditors

members. This is one of the ways, in addition to compulsory membership subscriptions, in which they raise income, since they make a percentage charge on the certification.

With the increase in lucrative auditing work in Spain as a result of the greater demand for openness in both public and private business, conflict has arisen between two associations. On the one hand the Institute of Auditors (*Instituto de Censores Jurados de Cuentas de España*/ICJCE) has always considered that auditing which was legally required was its prerogative, while, on the other hand, the Economists' Association (*Colegio de Economistas*) has argued that its members had the authority to perform this work. Matters came to a head when, in 1982, the economists established a special register for auditors (*Registro de Economistas Auditores*/REA) which the international accounting firms in Spain were obliged to support in order to safeguard their rights to carry out audits. The question of who can and should carry out audits has not been finally resolved and it remains another area where legislative reform is long overdue despite the appearance a few years ago of draft proposals for an auditing law.

12.11 Employers' associations (*asociaciones empresariales*)

With the exception of some regional organisations, as in Catalonia, there has not been a long tradition of employers' organisations. However, Article 7 of the Constitution recognised their significance and their right to defend and promote the interests of their own members. The basic constitutional requirement made of them is that their structure and operation must be democratic and they must be properly registered (Article 22). Allusion, if not specific reference, is also made to them in Article 37 in the context of the representation of employers in the collective bargaining process, and in Article 131.2 regarding their involvement in economic planning.

In the absence of any more precise legal definition, it is perhaps not surprising that a considerable number of organisations have sprung up at different levels. Under the Franco regime employers compulsorily formed part of the syndical organisation (see 11.1) and many of the present organisations have evolved out of the sectorial links created at that time. This may well partly explain the extremely high membership figure of the Spanish Confederation of Employers' Organisations (*Confederación Española de Organizaciones Empresariales*/CEOE) which claims to have 1,300,000 members who in turn represent 80 per cent of the labour force in the private sector. At the same time, it must be borne in mind that this figure is inflated by the fact that, since some 90 per cent of enterprises employ fewer than 500 workers, there are a large number of potential members of employers' associations in Spain. This figure includes, therefore, the small- and medium-sized firms which belong to the affiliated CEPYME organisation (see below).

The CEOE was formed in 1977 in order to bring this large number of diverse organisations together in one representative body. The need for this was further highlighted by the initiation of a consensus approach to economic and labour problems in 1977 which culminated in the Moncloa Pacts (see 11.5.1) and in which the employers were not represented. Since then, however, the CEOE has grown into an effective body incorporating some 165 individual employers' organisations of which forty-nine are intersectorial and region-based and the remainder are sectorial, representing activities such as banking, iron and steel, advertising and construction, organised on a national or regional basis (see Figure 12.2).

The Spanish Confederation of Small- and Medium-Sized Firms (*Confederación Española de Pequeñas y Medianas Empresas*/CEPYME), itself a national and regional organisation, was integrated into the CEOE in 1980 but it still preserves a special status within the Employers' Confederation and appears as a separate signatory to the social and economic agreements made with the government and unions (see 11.5).

Representation of constituent associations is conducted through the principal policy-making body of the CEOE, the general assembly (*asamblea general*), which comprises 600 delegates elected by the 165 employers' organisations which form the confederation. Every three years this assembly elects the chairman and a board of management (*junta directiva*) which in turn appoints the executive committee (*comité ejecutivo*) of twenty-four members. There are also a number of specialised committees, supported by the full-time secretariat, which study and report on economic, labour and international matters of concern. It draws its financial resources largely from membership fees but, as with the political parties and the trade unions, it receives subsidies from the government in recognition of its special role within the Constitution.

Figure 12.2. *Examples of membership of Spanish Employers'*
Confederation

Ambit	Title	Sector
National	*Confederación Española de Pequeñas y Medianas Empresas* (CEPYME)	Small- and medium-sized firms
	Confederación Española de Mujeres Empresarias (CEME)	Women employers
Regional	*Confederación de Empresarios de Andalucía* (CEA)	Andalusia
	Fomento del Trabajo Nacional	Catalonia
Sectorial	*Asociación Empresarial de Agencias de Viajes* (AEDAVE)	Travel agencies
	Asociación Española de Banca (AEB)	Banks
	Asociación Empresarial de Publicidad Exterior (AEPE)	Advertising
	Asociación Nacional de Fabricantes de Automóviles (ANFAC)	Car manufacture
	Asociación de Navieros Españoles (ANAVE)	Shipbuilding
	Confederación Empresarial de Metal (CONFEMETAL)	Iron and steel
	Confederación Nacional de la Construcción (CNC)	Construction

The fundamental role of the CEOE is to act as the representative organisation for the employers, a position which it has secured at the expense of two rival national bodies – the General Confederation of Small- and Medium-Sized Firms of Spain (*Confederación General de las Pequeñas y Medianas Empresas del Estado Español*/COPYME) and the Union of Small- and Medium-Sized Firms (*Unión de la Pequeña y Mediana Empresa*/UNIPYME), both of which have failed to gain sufficient support. The CEOE does not negotiate collective agreements (*convenios colectivos*) on behalf of employers. This is left to the individual associations. It does, however, negotiate on pay norms and working conditions at a national level. This, in fact, has been one of its major achievements, as reflected in the succession of agreements negotiated since the Moncloa Pacts of 1977 (see 11.5.2/3/4). It also represents employers on official bodies in which provision is made for employer and worker participation, such as the social security institutions INSS, INSERSO and INSALUD (see 6.4.3/4/5). Moreover the CEOE provides advisory, consultative and training facilities for its members and it represents employers at an international level, for example, *vis-à-vis* the International Labour Organisation (ILO). It also established an office in Brussels where it maintained a high profile during Spain's negotiations for EEC membership.

12.12   Chambers of commerce (*cámaras de comercio*)

The chambers of commerce are legally classed as professional organisations (*organizaciones profesionales*). Such organisations are normally considered to include all those, other than unions, employers' organisations and professional associations, which have as their specific objective the defence of their members' economic interests. Provision for this type of organisation is made in Article 52 of the Constitution, which stipulates that they must be regulated by law and they must be democratic. They are also governed by the general regulations of Article 26 regarding the formation and registration of associations. Chambers of Commerce, Industry and Navigation (*Cámaras Oficiales de Comercio, Industria y Navegación*) are long-established institutions, dating (at least formally) from the nineteenth century. The defend the interests of the individuals and the firms which they represent by providing a variety of services. These generally include legal services, economic and financial advice, research and information, representation abroad, help in export promotion, documentation and trade missions. At the same time, they act as consultative bodies at local, regional and central government level on matters pertaining to industry and commerce. Therefore, they are involved in discussions on matters ranging from local issues such as markets and postal codes to the consideration of draft legislation on trade regulations and changes in taxation. Thus, for example, they were involved in discussions with the government regarding the practical implications of the introduction of value added tax (*impuesto sobre el valor añadido*/IVA) to coincide with Spain's entry into the EEC on 1 January 1986.

They are officially recognised bodies which depend for approval and modification of their statutes on the Ministry of Commerce (since 1982 incorporated into the single Ministry of Economy and Finance). Unlike their counterparts in most EEC countries, membership is not on a voluntary basis. All those engaged in the activities covered by the chamber are automatically members, either as individual traders or as firms, and their fees come in the form of tax surcharges. The Treasury informs the specific chamber of the tax position of the individual traders and the chamber then is responsible for collecting a two per cent surcharge on this amount.

Their internal organisation depends on their respective statutes, but normally they have a general meeting (*pleno*), elected on the basis of the different sectorial interests which the chamber represents, to decide policy, and an executive committee (*comité ejecutivo*) for management purposes.

In 1985 there were eighty-five chambers located in all the major cities of Spain and including co-ordinating chambers at provincial level. The specific title of each *cámara* depends on the activities which it represents and therefore *navegación* is confined to those operating in coastal areas. The National Council of Chambers of Commerce (*Consejo Superior de Cámaras*) located in Madrid, acts as a central coordinating body disseminating information to the others and representing the chambers nationally and internationally.

12.13 Conclusion

The emphasis on political change in Spain has occupied a large part of the time of legislators and hence there are several principles enshrined in the Constitution concerning the private sector which have yet to be developed. This is particularly the case in respect of company law where, in accordance with normal procedures, a draft law was circulated to interested parties in 1980 but up to the time of writing had not reached the statute book. However, undoubtedly there have been many more important demands on legislative time and this has not been considered a priority area. Nevertheless, it is becoming more urgent to bring Spanish business into line with that of EEC practice and therefore sooner or later legislation will have to be approved to harmonise Spanish company law with EEC directives.

However, the influence of democracy has already encouraged a greater openness in company and professional affairs. There is more willingness to publish information and to reveal financial details to workers, shareholders and even to the tax authorities. At the same time, some companies have attempted to diversify their ownership and to encourage workers to obtain shares. Nevertheless, the victory of the Socialist Party in the 1982 elections caused some misgivings among entrenched capitalist interests and there were some cases of capital being illegally moved out of the country. Similarly some feared that the expropriation of RUMASA in 1983 heralded a move towards sweeping nationalisation. However, these fears have proved to be unfounded and a measure of partnership has developed between the state and the private sector. Clearly the downturn in the fortunes of the Spanish economy since the 1973 oil crisis has necessitated more dependence on the state and thus greater acquiescence with its wishes.

13   Financial institutions

13.1   Background to reforms

The banking sector in particular played a very significant role within the economy during the Franco era since, in the absence of viable alternative sources of finance, banks directly and indirectly controlled large areas of industry. During most of the period the sector was characterised by a high degree of specialisation, maintained by a rigid system of rules which regulated the functions of different institutions within the system and limited the number and type of branches that could be established. However, in the early 1970s there was a growing awareness of the need to introduce reforms in order to liberalise the financial system, to stimulate savings, to combat inflation and to bring Spanish institutions more into line with those of other developed economies. Thus, from 1974 onwards, measures were introduced in order to reduce excessive specialisation. Greater flexibility was granted to set up banks and to open new branches. Some measure of freedom was given to banks to fix interest rates and new monetary instruments were permitted in order to attract funds. At the same time, there was a lowering of the obligatory investment and cash ratios which had previously tied the institutions to certain privileged clients in both the private and public sectors. Finally a major step towards harmonisation with the EEC was taken in 1978 with legislation permitting the establishment of foreign banks in Spain for the first time since the Civil War.

Furthermore, in parallel with these changes, the position of the Bank of Spain was strengthened by a series of measures designed to enable it to play a greater role in managing monetary policy and in controlling liquidity. Its supervisory role was broadened and it was empowered to protect depositors if and when banking institutions found themselves in difficulties.

The capital market, on the other hand, did not provide an effective source of finance for industry and it lagged behind its counterparts in other developed Western economies. Therefore, a special commission was established in 1977 to examine these problems and its report subsequently led to the introduction of new measures to make the market more effective. It too became more flexible in its operations and more demanding in terms of the information it required from quoted companies. At the same time, new types of securities began to appear on the market in conjunction with other reforms within the financial system. This too was accompanied by the introduction of financial intermediaries which were new to the Spanish system.

Responsibility for overseeing all financial institutions rests with the Ministry of Economy and Finance (*Ministerio de Economía y Hacienda*). This is a vast and complex ministry consisting of what were formerly the separate Ministries of Finance (*Hacienda*), Economy (*Economía*) and Commerce (*Comercio*). It therefore embraces all aspects of the economy from fiscal and monetary policy to economic planning and domestic and overseas trade. Its general role of co-ordination and inspection is, of course, particularly important (see 9.7.2) and to this end it is subdivided into a large number of departments which look after specific responsibilities. The long-established Ministry of Finance (*Hacienda*) also maintained provincial offices (*delegaciones provinciales*) as part of the system of delegated administration (see 6.5) but some of the functions of these offices are now gradually being devolved to the autonomous communities.

While overall control over financial institutions is in the hands of the Ministry of Economy and Finance, day-to-day control and regulation is vested in a number of different bodies: the Bank of Spain (*Banco de España*), the Official Credit Institute (*Instituto de Credito Oficial*/ICO), the Directorate General for the Treasury and Financial Policy (*Dirección General del Tesoro y Política Financiera*) and the Directorate General for Insurance (*Dirección General de Seguros*). The principal financial institutions which are described in this chapter are listed in Figure 13.1.

13.2   Bank of Spain (*Banco de España*)

The Bank of Spain is the nation's central bank and as such it needs to be distinguished from the commercial bank which bears the name *Banco Central*. It owes its origin to an eighteenth-century bank, the *Banco de San Carlos*. However, it was given the name *Banco de España* in 1856 and from that time onwards it assumed the role of central bank, although it remained nominally in private hands until it was nationalised in 1962. It is now, therefore, a public sector institution responsible to the government, through the Ministry of Economy and Finance, for the day-to-day working of the monetary system and the overall supervision of the institutions which constitute the banking system (see Figure 13.2). Its role is very much the same as that of central banks in other countries.

Figure 13.1 *Structure of financial institutions*

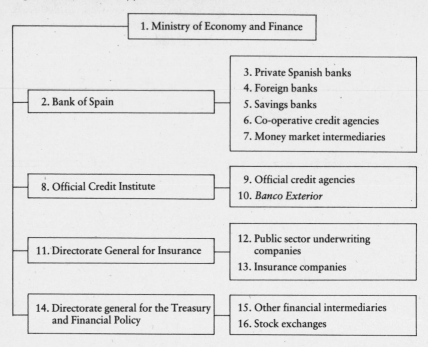

13.2.1 Bank of sole issue

It is the sole issuing bank of legal tender. This is done in accordance with the limits established by the government of the day. Currently it is engaged in withdrawing paper notes of smaller denominations and replacing them with coins.

13.2.2 Government's bank

It handles the government's income and expenditure and it services the national debt, arranging government borrowing and making the appropriate interest payments. It also provides loans for the large and economically significant number of public sector institutions which have been referred to throughout this volume.

13.2.3 Banker's bank

It looks after the compulsory reserves which banks and other financial institutions are obliged to deposit with it and it is their lender of last resort. It is responsible for the official bank clearing system (*cámara de compensación*).

Figure 13.2. *Relative size of banking institutions (31 December 1983)*

	No. of institutions	No. of offices	% of total deposits	% of total loans
Bank of Spain	1	53	0.2	15.1
Banks	135	16,062	61.0	51.8
Savings banks	80	11,787	34.7	23.0
Official credit institutions	4	23	0.0	8.0
Co-operative credit agencies	151	3,197	4.1	2.1
Total	371	31,122	100.0	100.0

Source: Bank of Spain

13.2.4 Centralised data source

It receives reports from all financial institutions on loans exceeding a certain amount (currently four million pesetas). As part of an early warning system of crisis points within the economy it gathers information on loans which have become subject to bankruptcy proceedings or where there is an exceptional concentration of risks. Since 1983 it has also begun to receive and analyse balance-sheet data from non-financial companies.

13.2.5 Exchange control

This responsibility is divided between the Bank of Spain and the Directorate General for Foreign Transactions (*Dirección General de Transacciones Exteriores*/DGTE). This division of functions was formalised in 1973 with the sharing out of the functions of the then defunct Spanish Institute for Foreign Currency (*Instituto Español de Moneda Extranjera*/IEME) (see also 12.8). The Bank of Spain is responsible for managing the nation's foreign currency reserves. It also supervises overseas borrowing by the public sector.

13.2.6 Monetary policy

The Bank of Spain carries out monetary policy in accordance with government directives, using its discretion to exercise control over the money supply through compulsory cash reserves, interest rates and the use of financial instruments in the open market.

13.2.7 Control and inspection

Control has been progressively increased as the system has become more sophisticated and the Bank of Spain has established limits to the risks which various types of banking institutions are authorised to bear (see 13.2.4). It issues circulars advising banks on the interrelationship which it wishes them to secure between items on their balance sheets and profit and loss accounts. It has established a strict procedure for financial reporting by banks and it has increased its inspection generally of the other financial institutions. Since 1978 it has had power to appoint temporary boards of management to assume responsibility for a bank's operations.

In 1977 the Bank of Spain was instrumental in setting up the Deposit Guarantee Fund (*Fondo de Garantía de Depósitos*) to cope with bank failures and to give depositors some protection at a time when increasing strains were appearing within the financial system. The Fund consists of compulsory deposits from the banks together with an equal contribution from the Bank of Spain. Since 1980 the *Fondo* has been strengthened and it has assumed the functions of the bank 'hospital' (*Corporación Bancaria*).

The Fund is now run by its own board of management consisting of four representatives from the Bank of Spain and four from the banks themselves. It is also empowered temporarily to take over a bank considered to be in difficulties. There are similar funds for the savings and co-operative banks (see 13.6).

The importance and effectiveness of the Bank of Spain's role was highlighted by its intervention in the banking crisis of 1978–83. A number of factors, ranging from the consequences of the economic crisis to defective banking practices and weak management, led to over fifty banks finding themselves in a state of crisis during this period. Twenty-six of these were assisted by the Deposit Guarantee Fund, while another four were taken over by other banks and one was dissolved. The problem was compounded by the RUMASA affair when the government expropriated the holdings of this conglomerate, which included some twenty banks. The Deposit Guarantee Fund administered the RUMASA group banks pending their somewhat controversial disposal by the *Dirección General del Patrimonio del Estado* (see 9.3 and 13.4).

13.3   Private Spanish banks

13.3.1   Classification

Traditionally there have been a number of separate classifications used when referring to private sector Spanish banks (see Figure 13.3). However, in practice, the distinction, which used to refer to their permitted sphere of activity, as between national, regional and local, has disappeared. Similarly, the distinction between industrial banks and non-industrial or commercial banks has come to mean less, as both are now engaged in sectors which were once by law the prerogative of the other. Nevertheless, some degree of specialisation does remain and the industrial banks concentrate more on corporate finance. Furthermore the distinction still has some bearing with regard to the technical details of adjustments which

Figure 13.3. *Classification of private Spanish banks (1985)*

By area		By function	
National	37	Commercial	74
Regional	13	Industrial	24
Local	48		
Total	98	Total	98

Source: Consejo Superior Bancario

may be required by the Bank of Spain in their respective cash and investment ratios (see 13.3.5). The traditional classification of national, regional and local banks is still preserved by the National Banking Council (*Consejo Superior Bancario*). This is a long-established advisory and consultative body which serves as a meeting point for representatives of public and private sector banks and which is responsible for issuing regular statistical information on the situation of the banks themselves.

13.3.2 Services

While there remains some distinction between the commercial banks, which concentrate on ordinary banking business with the public, and the industrial banks, which lend to industry, these differences are becoming less and less important. Spanish banks in general offer a similar range of services to their UK counterparts. Their opening hours are generally from 9.00 a.m. to 2.00 p.m. on weekdays and from 9.30 a.m. until 1.30 p.m. on Saturdays. Cash dispensers known as 'automatic' or 'permanent cashiers' (*cajero automático* or *cajero permanente*) are very common and are generally shared on a network basis by several banks. In addition to current accounts (*cuentas corrientes* or *cuentas a la vista*), there are ordinary savings or deposit accounts (*cuentas de ahorros*), fixed-term savings accounts (*imposición a plazo*) and, more recently, special savings accounts which combine current accounts and high interest rate savings' facilities. The discounting of trade bills or bills of exchange (*letras de cambio*) is also very common, as this is still a major way of doing business in Spain.

13.3.3 Concentration

Although the number of banks appears to be very high, there is in fact a high degree of concentration. The seven largest commercial banks are: *Banco Central*; *Banco Español de Crédito (Banesto)*; *Banco Hispano Americano*; *Banco de Bilbao*; *Banco de Vizcaya*; *Banco de Santander*, and *Banco Popular Español*. Between them these account for approximately 80 per cent of total banking resources. At the same time there are strong links between the commercial and industrial banks with, for example,

Banco Hispano Americano owning the *Banco Urquijo* and the *Banco Central* owning the *Banco de Fomento*. However, despite appearances, the Spanish banks are relatively small in world terms and the largest Spanish bank, the *Banco Central*, was only ninetieth in world rankings by assets in 1984.

13.3.4 Banking crisis

The crisis of 1978–83 affected fifty-one of the 110 Spanish banks which existed in 1977. It was caused by a number of factors which included the restrictive monetary policy being pursued by the authorities in the light of the prevailing economic difficulties, the oil crises and the wage push inflation of the pre-social pact days (see 11.5). The situation of these banks was exacerbated by the increased competition to obtain business and the downward spiral of fortune resulting from their close ties with industry. At the same time, the authorities were endeavouring to secure more authentic declarations of assets and liabilities, while the Bank of Spain itself was insisting on the closer scrutiny of accounts. The net result was the revelation in several instances of poor financial management and of a substantial number of banks in an official state of crisis. It was in these circumstances that the *Fondo de Garantía de Depósitos* came into its own, as indicated in 13.2.7.

13.3.5 Cash and investment ratios

Although there had been moves during the late 1970s to reduce the amount that banks had been obliged to lend to certain privileged borrowers, such as public sector enterprises, the trend was reversed at the beginning of the 1980s. There were two main reasons for this: on the one hand, in view of the banking crisis, it was considered important to encourage banks to maintain acceptable levels of liquidity; on the other hand, public expenditure, in such areas as housing, education and social security, was escalating, due particularly to the new demands of a more democratic Spain. Hence the authorities turned to the banks for more of their funds and the various ratios (*coeficientes*) were raised. For example, higher investment ratios meant that 13.5 per cent of total deposits had to be invested in government stock, 5 per cent had to be lent to the public or private sector for the purchase of capital goods, and 3 per cent had to be directed to finance exports. To this should be added the cash ratio of 18 per cent of deposits which had to be retained with the Bank of Spain. On the other hand, the savings banks (see 13.5), which were becoming more competitive with the ordinary banks, did not have such high obligatory ratios. However, in November 1985 it appeared that there might be a return to the liberalising trend of the earlier part of the post-Franco period.

The Bank of Spain announced that it would be reducing the level of obligatory investments and that this would take place gradually over five years so as not to distort the market. Furthermore, there would be a gradual move towards ensuring greater uniformity with regard to the various financial institutions in order not to distort competition.

13.4 Foreign banks

The Royal Decree of 24 June 1978, which established regulations allowing foreign banks to set up in Spain, marked a significant, although still cautious, step towards reducing the control over the Spanish economy exercised by the domestic banking system. Previously only the four foreign banks established before the Civil War, namely the Banco Nacional di Lavoro of Italy, Crédit Lyonnais and the Société Générale of France and the Bank of London and South America had the right to operate normally. Other foreign banks were restricted to representative offices and were not permitted to engaged in normal banking activities.

The new legislation, however, imposed significant restrictions on the foreign banks and appeared designed, at least in the short term, to protect the interests of the existing financial oligarchy. Thus, there are limits to the funds these banks can raise, they may not open more than three offices, including their head office and their securities portfolio must consist exclusively of public sector stock.

Nevertheless, by November 1985 there were thirty-seven foreign banks engaged in branch-making in Spain which, despite the restrictions placed upon them, had managed to secure a significant 14 per cent of total banking business. As they cannot take deposits from customers, they have to obtain their resources on the inter-bank market and consequently, a much more sophisticated inter-bank market has developed than existed previously. Their main area of activity is in the field of corporate finance and they use their resources and their know-how to provide specialised services, such as foreign exchange dealing, export finance and leasing facilities. They have introduced new financial instruments, such as commercial paper (*pagarés de empresa*), and also new institutions, such as vehicle finance companies.

Other foreign banks have chosen to go in for retail banking by taking over ailing Spanish banks. Although foreign investment in Spanish firms may require authorisation (see 12.8), the banking and RUMASA crises provided an ideal opportunity for foreign investors. The Arab Banking Corporation secured the most viable RUMASA bank, the *Banco Atlántico*, and in April 1981 Barclays, which had progressed from representative office to branch-banking following the 1978 legislation, purchased the *Banco de Valladolid* from the Deposit Guarantee Fund. A year later the name was changed to *Barclays Sociedad Anónima Española* (SAE), i.e.

Spanish Public Limited Liability Company, to distinguish it from the branch known as *Barclays PLC Sucursal en España*. These banks are subject to the same legislation as other SA companies, together with whatever additional requirements may be demanded of them by the Bank of Spain. However, they have a deposit base from which they can raise funds to lend, especially to multi-nationals, foreign-owned companies and public sector companies. These banks can be expected not only to increase competition within the system, but also to bring about further modernisation and technological advance. The authorities, however, became concerned that some thirty-seven foreign branch-based banks and some five new foreign-owned retail banks could be making too many inroads into the system. A stop was put to further entries in November 1985 but this is seen as a temporary measure. In any case, after a seven-year transitional period, all the present restrictions will be removed for banks from EEC countries.

13.5   Savings banks (*cajas de ahorros*)

As can be seen from Figure 13.2, in 1983 there were eighty savings banks with 11,787 offices responsible for securing 34.7 per cent of total deposits and providing 23 per cent of all bank credit. They are therefore significant financial institutions which are becoming increasingly competitive as the authorities attempt to broaden their role and generally put them on an operating par with the high street banks. Traditionally they were seen as sources of finance for specific sectors such as the INI, the public sector, housing and small-sized firms and, although they currently have higher obligatory investment ratios than the commercial banks, these are being altered in order to allow them greater flexibility.

Originally they were tied to the province from which they drew their finance and their names tend to indicate their highly localised nature: *Caja de Ahorros de Murcia, Caja de Ahorros Provincial de Toledo, Caja de Ahorros Popular de Valladolid*. They have been obliged to place a certain percentage of their investments in the province or region from which they obtained their funds and, although they are in the process of obtaining greater freedom, this tendency is likely to continue. Attempts have been made, in fact, to establish statutory links with the savings banks and their local area through a new law in 1985 which aimed at securing a minimum proportion of local representatives on the governing bodies of the savings banks. However, this has been challenged as being unconstitutional in that it appears to concentrate power in the hands of municipal authorities to the detriment of other local and regional authorities. Likewise, while they were restricted previously to branches within their own province, greater freedom has now been granted in this respect.

The savings banks are non-profit making institutions and they do not have shareholders, as SA companies do. Surplus funds arising from their

Figure 13.4. *Example of confederation of savings banks in Galicia*

Name	Level
Confederación Española de Cajas de Ahorros (CECA)	National confederation
Federación de Cajas de Ahorros de Galicia	Provincial federation
Caja de Ahorros de Galicia – La Coruña Caja de Ahorros Provincial de Orense Caja de Ahorros Provincial de Pontevedra Caja de Ahorros y Montepío Municipal de Vigo	Local savings banks in the four provinces of Galicia

operations go into reserves and into their social welfare fund (*obra benéfico-social*). These funds can be used to finance local welfare projects, cultural activities and research grants and so on, provided that the proposal of the Welfare Committee (*Comisión de Obras Sociales*) is approved by the general council (*asamblea general*) and duly authorised by the Ministry of Economy and Finance. The general council consists of representatives of savers and local interests. It in turn nominates the board of management (*consejo de administración*) and appoints the director general who has to be technically qualified and approved by the Ministry of Economy and Finance.

The savings banks, at local level, belong to regional federations, such as, for example, the *Federación de Cajas de Ahorros de Galicia*. Subsequently, at national level, co-ordination and representation is through the National Confederation of Savings Banks (*Confederación Española de Cajas de Ahorros*/CECA) in Madrid (see Figure 13.4). This body provides advisory and statistical services, research and representation on behalf of the constituent savings banks, as well as acting as a clearing house for the twenty-eight savings banks which have offices in Madrid.

13.5.1 *Post Office Savings Bank* (Caja Postal de Ahorros)

This is similar to the savings banks described above but it is not a member of the National Confederation of Savings Banks and it depends on the Ministry of Transport, Tourism and Communications. It has the backing of the state and through post offices (*oficinas de correos*) it takes in deposits, manages current accounts and grants loans. It is subject to the same investment ratios as the other savings banks but, unlike them, it does not have a social role and any surplus funds are transferred to reserves and to *Hacienda*.

13.6   Co-operative credit agencies (*entidades de crédito cooperativo*)

As can be seen from Figure 13.2, there were 151 of these institutions in 1983 and their total share of the financial market was relatively small.

They are basically of two types: rural savings banks (*cajas rurales*) or agricultural co-operatives; and general co-operatives (*cooperativas de carácter general*). The rural savings banks are, in general, extremely small and localised yet they provide almost a third of the total bank credit for agriculture. However, this concentration has made them vulnerable to risk because of the particular vicissitudes of the agricultural sector. In 1984 nineteen of them had recourse to the Co-operative Deposit Guarantee Fund (*Fondo de Garantía de Depósitos de Cooperativas*). In order to reduce their risks, seventy-four of them formed an association (*grupo asociado*) and signed a formal agreement with the Agricultural Credit Bank (*Banco de Crédito Agrícola*/BCA) which provides a bridge for them with the official credit institutions and gives them the benefit of priority access to credit facilities. The arrangement also helps to decentralise the BCA.

On the other hand the general co-operatives operate in sectors such as construction, housing, commerce or the professions. The workers' co-operative bank (*Caja Laboral Popular*) at Mondragón provides a particularly important example (see 12.6).

These institutions, while they can accept deposits from members and non-members, because of their co-operative nature may only lend to the members themselves. Like the other financial institutions described in this chapter, the co-operative credit agencies have been subject to reform in recent years and an attempt has been made to make them more flexible and broader based. Firmer rules and conditions were set down in a Royal Decree of November 1978 concerning their establishment, supervision and integration into the overall monetary system and they, too, are subject to compulsory investment ratios.

13.7   Money market intermediaries (*sociedades mediadoras en el mercado de dinero*/SMMD)

These new institutions are closely related to the role of the banking institutions described above. They were introduced in 1981 on an experimental basis to give greater liquidity to the Spanish financial system as, until this time, there was not a true secondary market for treasury bills, certificates of deposits and bills of exchange. The growth of the inter-bank market, following the entry of the foreign banks into Spain, indicated the important role that these intermediaries could play. They take and place deposits from and with banks, savings banks and co-operative credit agencies, and they buy and sell short-term financial instruments such as treasury bills, certificates of deposit and bills of exchange.

The SMMD are constituted as SA companies and they are strictly regulated by the Bank of Spain. They are intended to be independent of the banking institutions and for this reason no bank is allowed to hold more than 10 per cent of the capital of one of these companies.

13.8   Official Credit Institute (*Instituto Oficial de Crédito*/ICO)

This is an autonomous administrative body (see 6.3) under the jurisdiction of the Ministry of Economy and Finance. It receives an allocation of funds in the annual state budget which in 1983 amounted to some 63 per cent of its budget, the rest being obtained by the issue of bonds, syndicated loans and borrowing from abroad. The ICO then provides funds for the use of the specialised agencies which it is responsible for controlling and co-ordinating, i.e. the official credit agencies and the *Banco Exterior*, both of which are described below (13.9 and 13.10).

13.9   Official credit agencies (*entidades oficiales de crédito*/EOC)

These agencies are responsible for channelling state lending into priority sectors of the economy. They are constituted as SA companies and their shares are owned by the state. They provide loans within their particular remit in accordance with government guidelines as follows:

(i)   *Agricultural Credit Bank* (Banco de Crédito Agrícola) for agriculture, directly and indirectly and through the *Cajas Rurales* (see 13.6);

(ii)   *Mortgage Bank of Spain* (Banco Hipotecario de España) for housing. In 1982 it absorbed the Construction Credit Bank (*Banco de Crédito a la Construcción*);

(iii)   *Local Authorities' Credit Bank* (Banco de Crédito Local) for local authority projects; and

(iv)   *Industrial Credit Bank* (Banco de Crédito Industrial) for new firms and growth industries. This bank supervises the operations of an autonomous Fisheries' Credit Institution (*Crédito Social Pesquero*) which promotes funds for the purchase, improvement and repair of fishing vessels, and it has also taken over loans to the shipbuilding industry previously carried out by the *Banco de Crédito a la Construcción*.

13.10   Overseas Trade Bank (*Banco Exterior de España*)

Although the *Banco Exterior*, or Overseas Trade Bank, receives some credit and guidelines from the ICO, it is not a totally state-controlled institution. It is, in fact, a mixed institution with some 60 per cent of its capital being owned by the state while the rest belongs to private shareholders, who include bank employees. In addition to its export-related activities it also carries out normal banking business and it is subject to the same regulations as the commercial banks. In general, therefore, this bank comes under the jurisdiction of the Bank of Spain as far as monetary policy is concerned, although administratively it belongs to the DGPE (see 9.3).

13.11   Directorate General for Insurance (*Dirección General de Seguros*)

This directorate general is the department within the Ministry of Economy and Finance which is responsible for the control and co-ordination of the insurance sector. All private insurance companies have to be officially registered with the department and they must submit their annual financial statements for scrutiny in order to ensure that proper regard is paid to their investment ratios and reserve levels. In general, then, this department acts as a watchdog over the activities of insurance companies and their fulfilment of current legislation.

13.12   Public sector underwriting companies

Where the risks involved are particularly high, the state provides special underwriting facilities. This is done mainly through two autonomous bodies: the Insurance Compensation Consortium (*Consorcio de Compensación de Seguros*); and the State Agricultural Insurance Company (*Empresa Nacional de Seguros Agrarios*/ENESA).

13.12.1 *Insurance Compensation Consortium (*Consorcio de Compensación de Seguros*)*

This is an autonomous commercial body with its own legal identity dating back to 1953 and reformed in 1981. It was given responsibility for three other insurance underwriting bodies: the Insurance Guarantee Fund (*Fondo Nacional de Garantía de Riesgos de la Circulación*), the Road Vehicle Third Party Insurance Fund (*Comisaría del Seguro Obligatorio de Viajero*) and the Central Insurance Fund (*Caja Central de Seguros*). It covers the civil responsibility of all sectors of public administration in the event of accidents or losses concerning both their own personnel and members of the public. Insurance cover for natural disasters such as forest fires and floods form an important area of its work, particularly in the light of the extent of the damage in Catalonia and the Basque Country in recent years as a result of these phenomena. In the case of vehicle insurance, it provides for those cases where accidents have been caused by unknown persons or where the insurance company involved has collapsed. On the other hand, its responsibility for underwriting exporting finance has been largely taken over by the Spanish Export Insurance Company (*Compañía Española de Seguros a la Exportación*/CESCE), a company in which there is a mixture of public and private investment but in which the state holds a majority of shares through the DGPE (see 9.3).

13.12.2 *State Agricultural Insurance Company (*Empresa Nacional de Seguros Agrarios/*ENESA)*

This too is an autonomous commercial body which, because of its responsibility for agricultural insurance, is nominally under the jurisdiction of the Ministry of Agriculture and Fisheries. Its board of management, however, is made up of an equal number of representatives from the Ministry of Agriculture and Fisheries, the Ministry of Economy and Finance and representatives of the farming sector. The high risks involved in this important sector of the economy have long posed a problem which private insurance has not been able to resolve fully. ENESA therefore co-ordinates and underwrites insurance in the sector and prepares an annual plan for consideration by the Directorate General for Insurance. It also draws up formal agreements with private insurers especially associated for the purpose in the Consortium of Insurance Entities (*Agrupación de Entidades Aseguradoras*).

13.13 Insurance companies (*empresas aseguradoras/compañías de seguros*)

The insurance sector at present plays a relatively small part in the Spanish economy in comparison with its importance in other economies. On the other hand, however, with more than 600 companies engaged in insurance, it incorporates far more companies than is normally the case in other countries. This means that most of the member companies of the National Insurance Association (*Unión Española de Entidades Aseguradoras, Reaseguradoras y de Capitalización*/UNESPA) are small, and localised, with the exception of a limited number of national concerns such as *La Unión y el Fénix Español, Plus Ultra* and *La Estrella*. A further significant entity within the sector is the mutual benefit society responsible for providing cover for the employees of over two hundred companies in the INI and the INH state holding groups, that is the *Mutualidad de Seguros del Instituto Nacional de Industria* (MUSINI). In 1984 a new Law (*Ley de Ordenación de Seguro Privado*) was passed in order to rationalise the private insurance sector and, while it is still too early to judge its effects, already a large number of companies have voluntarily ceased to exist, many have merged and nearly 200 have been found to be in need of reform.

Insurance is generally considered to be a reflection of cultural attitudes and traditions, as well as a function of *per capita* income. In Spain, for a variety of reasons, there has not been a great volume of business. This has particularly been the case in the life assurance sector where less than 10 per cent of the population are thought to be covered by voluntary schemes. In this particular case there has been heavy reliance on the state's social security provision which has given the highest state cover in Western Europe with pensions at up to 90 per cent of wages on retirement. However, it has now become very clear that the state can no longer sustain such a generously high level and hence reform is pending in order to stimulate private pension schemes. While large SA companies already organise their own schemes, the legislation pending is to boost broader based pension funds (*fondos de pensiones*) which it is hoped will become important financial intermediaries in their own right and major institutional investors, as in other EEC countries. This legislation will also pave the way for harmonisation with the EEC since the terms of entry include immediate freedom of access to Spain for insurance companies.

13.14 Directorate General for the Treasury and Financial Policy (*Dirección General del Tesoro y Política Financiera*)

This department of the Ministry of Economy and Finance is responsible for keeping a register and record of all the financial intermediaries listed below (13.15.1–6) which come under its auspices. It also exercises a general supervisory role on behalf of the Ministry and tries to ensure that the regulations are kept up to date in the light of any changing circumstances. The Directorate also carried out inspection and acts as a filter for financial records.

13.15 Other financial intermediaries (*intermediarios financieros*)

As most of these are still relatively new and not as yet very significant, they are merely indicated for future reference if and when their future becomes more established.

13.15.1 Finance companies (entidades de financiación)

These are hire-purchase finance companies which provide finance for the sale and purchase of all classes of goods. They were first regulated in 1978 and they have to be registered with the Directorate General for the Treasury and Financial Policy. They have to be constituted as SA companies and their minimum capital depends on whether they are operating at local, regional or national level. They can deal in trade bills, used for buying and selling goods, they can issue their own bonds and they can borrow from other institutions. They are not, however, allowed to invest in companies engaged in the same sphere of activity.

An older form of finance company concerned with the sale of capital goods on hire purchase, the *Entidad de Financiación de Ventas a Plazos de*

Bienes de Equipo still exists and is attempting to adapt itself to the new regulations.

13.15.2 Leasing companies (entidades de arrendamiento financiero or entidades de leasing)

These are relatively new and their regulation is not complete. They are involved in leasing capital equipment.

13.15.3 Investment companies (sociedades de inversión mobiliaria)

These are involved in investment in securities. There are strict rules in regard to the reserves which they are required to hold.

13.15.4 Investment funds (fondos de inversión mobiliaria)

These are securities' portfolios administered by a management committee.

13.5.5 Mutual guarantee companies (sociedades de garantía recíproca)

They were established by a Royal Decree in 1978 to facilitate access to finance for small- and medium-sized companies.

13.15.6 Mortgage credit companies (sociedades de crédito hipotecario)

They are concerned with granting credit for the construction industry and they are a new part of the attempt to create a wider mortgage market.

13.16 Stock exchanges (*bolsas de comercio*)

Stock exchanges in Spain come under the jurisdiction of the Ministry of Economy and Finance and are the particular responsibility of the Directorate General for the Treasury and Financial Policy. They have their own co-ordinating council, the *Consejo Superior de Bolsas*, which represents their interests in discussions with the Ministry and other bodies but which does not have the supervisory role of the stock exchange commissions which are found in many other countries.

While the trend in most other countries has been towards the concentration of stock market activity into one central exchange, this has not been the case in Spain. The growth of regional autonomy has perhaps made such a move inopportune and indeed it has even resulted in the formal recognition of the exchange in Valencia (1980), in addition to the established exchanges in Madrid (1831), Bilbao (1890) and Barcelona (1915). However, market forces are not always in accord with political considerations and there has been an increasing concentration of business in the Madrid Exchange which in 1984 recorded almost 75 per cent of business in contrast to Valencia which could barely muster 1 per cent; Barcelona drew approximately 20 per cent and Bilbao 5 per cent.

Until relatively recently there was not a great volume of transactions on the exchanges. Many companies in Spain are, of course, small in size and often strongly controlled by family interests and unwilling therefore to go public. At the same time, there has been a marked reluctance by companies to disclose the necessary amount of information which would encourage investors and the veracity of many of the published financial statements has been questionable. Many companies have not considered it necessary to look further than the banking sector as a source of finance. The corollary of this, however, has been the insistence of the banks on board-room influence if not control.

The authorities in the post-Franco period, aware of these deficiencies and the need to produce a more open system, capable of generating the resources needed for economic growth, established a commission to explore means of stimulating activity on the stock market. The report of the *Comisión para el Estudio del Mercado de Valores* in 1978 has led to a significant number of technical reforms which have gradually begun to take effect. There are now much more stringent requirements regarding the information which quoted companies are required to produce. New methods of dealing have been introduced and a streamlining of procedures has been undertaken.

At the same time, new financial instruments have begun to appear and there has been far greater variety of investment opportunities, with the foreign banks playing a significant role (see 13.4). However, the principal growth area in recent years has been in short-term government stock – which is perhaps not surprising in view of the fact that public debt in 1985 stood at some 5 per cent of gross domestic product. At the same time the buoyancy in trading in this area, largely through treasury bills (*pagarés del tesoro*), has provided a fillip to the market in general. Among the other most frequently traded securities are public sector companies and public utilities, especially electricals. There has also been increased interest in private sector securities where the banks continue to be market leaders. With all of this, more companies have turned to the issue of new shares in order to increase their capital and to expand.

The increase of interest in the stock market has led to the Madrid Stock Exchange extending its opening hours so that currently the hours for trading are Mondays to Fridays, 10.00 a.m. until 1.30 p.m. The Exchange is open to the public who can even walk on the trading floor and hear the cries of the dealers at close hand. However, the only people who are authorised to trade are the stock exchange brokers (*agentes de cambio y bolsa*) and their representatives (*apoderados*). Where there are not official exchanges, transactions may be carried out by other authorised dealers (*corredores de comercio*). Both the *agentes* and the *corredores* have to be appropriately qualified and must be members of their respective professional associations (see 12.10).

The stability of the political system after earlier periods of doubt and the successful negotiations for Spanish entry into the EEC have clearly helped to encourage foreign investors who are free to invest in the stock exchange provided that this does not result in the acquisition of more than 50 per cent of a company's stock, in which case special authorisation is required (see 12.8).

13.17 Conclusion

In general, Spanish financial institutions have made considerable progress since 1975. They have become more mechanised, more streamlined and more outward-looking. Spanish banks now play a fuller part in the interbank market and the Eurobond market and they now regularly partner other Western European banks in syndicated loans. Clearly, the impact of the foreign banks on the financial system as a whole has been very significant. However, it has not been possible to update immediately a system which has lain dormant for many years and further measures, such as the modernisation of the insurance sector and the introduction of legislation concerning pension funds, are now being implemented as part of the ongoing process of evolution which will take some time to come to full fruition.

However, since 1983, there has been a slowing down of, if not a halt to, the process of liberalising reforms. Against the background of economic difficulties and greater budget deficits, the government has increased its degree of intervention within the system. This has led to a reversal of the trend to reduce obligatory investments in public sector funds and instead it has led to a greater use of investment ratios to direct the flow of bank funds towards certain sectors in line with government policy. However, these are seen as temporary measures designed to respond to the particular needs of the moment. Likewise, the decision of the authorities towards the end of 1985 to limit the entry of further foreign banks will be reviewed in the light of changing economic circumstances as well as in response to EEC requirements. The need to continue the liberalising process within the financial system is clearly recognised, but it has, however, coincided with circumstances which have required more, rather than less, government intervention, which, in turn, must reduce the flexibility and competitiveness of Spain's financial institutions.

The stock market is a useful measure of the broader fortunes of a nation. In the case of Spain, the increase in stock exchange activity is not only an indication of improved market facilities but it is, perhaps more importantly, a reflection of the economic and political progress which Spain itself has made since 1975.

14   General conclusions

Obviously the political and economic institutions of Spain are by no means static. In fact they are undergoing continuous evolution and reform in the light of new and changing circumstances.

The Constitution of 1978 provided a natural break with the past and a starting point for the creation of a new democracy. However, this only established the principles which should characterise the new state; it merely pointed in the direction in which institutions in particular needed to move. Its successful realisation requires not only the political will of legislators but also the patience and understanding of citizens eager for quick results.

A great deal has been achieved and many new laws impinging upon institutions have been approved. Again, however, some degree of caution is required. First of all, these laws in turn generally only establish principles and guidelines. In many cases detailed regulations are still needed to bring these laws into full effect. Thereafter, care needs to be taken to distinguish between the theory and the practice of government. High ideals still require changes in attitudes and mentalities in order for them to work effectively. It is not sufficient to change the title, or even the structure, of an institution if those behind the façade insist on clinging to old customs; moreover, appointments made as the result of political patronage, of whatever shade, do not ensure technical expertise or stability.

Two significant influences emerge which are making an enormous impact on all the institutions which have been considered. One is the growing reality of regional autonomy and the speed at which the transfer of power is taking place. This is creating a shift in emphasis away from central bodies to new regional institutions which are still untried and untested. The other influence is Spain's entry into the European Community. Students of Spanish and contemporary Spain, who have themselves waited a long time for this to become a reality, will be aware of how the waiting period has been used to prepare for eventual entry. Much, however, remains to be done to achieve full and lasting harmonisation. Indeed, an already strained legislature with a backlog of reforms to complete will be under renewed pressure to comply with the additional burdens imposed by further EEC directives.

Regardless of the speed at which future modifications do take place, what has occurred to date is remarkable in itself. The ability to change Spain's political and economic institutions, particularly against such a difficult economic background, shows considerable political acumen, courage and maturity. It also reveals a firm commitment to democracy which deserves to succeed.

Appendix 1
Chronological résumé of
Spanish history since 1939

Dictatorship of General Franco (1939–75)

1939–45	Second World War; Spain 'neutral'
1947	Succession Law; monarchy restored
1953 August	*Concordat* signed with Vatican
September	Military and economic agreements signed with USA
1955	Spain admitted to United Nations
1956	Spain admitted to International Labour Organisation (ILO)
1957	Appointment of more liberal cabinet
1958	Spain admitted to International Monetary Fund (IMF) and International Bank of Reconstruction and Development (IBRD)
1959	Stabilisation Plan
1961	Spain admitted to Organisation for Economic Co-operation and Development (OECD, formerly OEEC)
1962	Spain requests associate membership of EEC
1964	First of three Development Plans
1967	Organic Law of the State
1969	Juan Carlos named heir to Franco
1970	Preferential Trade Agreement with EEC
1973 June	Luis Carrero Blanco appointed prime minister
December	Carrero Blanco assassinated by ETA
1974	Carlos Arias Navarro appointed prime minister
1975	Death of General Franco (20 November)

Spain since 1975

1975	November	Juan Carlos crowned King of Spain
	December	Arias Navarro re-appointed prime minister
1976		Adolfo Suárez González appointed prime minister
1977	June	First democratic elections; victory for UCD; Suárez elected prime minister
	July	Spain requests full membership of EEC
	October	Moncloa Pacts
	October	Spain admitted to Council of Europe
1978		New Constitution approved
1979	March	Second democratic elections; victory for UCD; Suárez re-elected prime minister
	October	Basque and Catalan statutes of autonomy approved
1981	January	Resignation of Adolfo Suárez
	February	Attempted *coup* via seizure of *Cortes*; Leopoldo Calvo Sotelo elected prime minister
1982	May	Spain admitted to NATO
	October	Third democratic elections; victory for PSOE; Felipe González Márquez elected prime minister
1985	February	Re-opening of frontier with Gibraltar
	June	Treaty of Accession to EEC signed in Madrid
1986	January	Spain admitted to EEC
	March	Referendum confirms Spanish membership of NATO
	June	Fourth democratic elections; Victory for PSOE; Felipe González re-elected prime minister

Appendix 2
National, regional and local elections since 1977

June 1977	General elections (won by UCD)
March 1979	General elections (won by UCD)
April 1979	Local elections (won by UCD)
March 1980	Regional elections in Basque Country (won by PNV)
March 1980	Regional elections in Catalonia (won by CiU)
October 1981	Regional elections in Galicia (won by AP)
May 1982	Regional elections in Andalusia (won by PSOE)
October 1982	General elections (won by PSOE)
May 1983	Local and regional elections (dominated by PSOE)
February 1984	Regional elections in Basque Country (won by PNV)
April 1984	Regional elections in Catalonia (won by CiU)
November 1985	Regional elections in Galicia (won by AP)
June 1986	General elections (won by PSOE)
June 1986	Regional elections in Andalusia (won by PSOE)
November 1986	Regional elections in Basque Country (won by PSOE)

Select bibliography

1   Introduction: political and economic background

Abel, C. and Torrents, N. (eds.) 1984, *Spain: Conditional Democracy*, Croom Helm

Brenan, G. 1943, *The Spanish Labyrinth*, Cambridge University Press

Carr, R. 1982, *Spain. 1808–1975*, Clarendon Press

Carr, R. and Fusi, J. P. 1979, *España: de la dictadura a la democracia*, Planeta

Gilmour, D. 1985, *The Transformation of Spain*, Quartet

González, M. J. 1979, *La economía política del franquismo (1940–70)*, Tecnos

Graham, R. 1984, *Spain: Change of a Nation*, Michael Joseph

Harrison, J. 1985, *The Spanish Economy in the Twentieth Century*, Croom Helm

Harvey, C. 1981, *The Río Tinto Company 1873–1954*, Alison Hodge

Hills, G. 1970, *Spain*, Ernest Benn

Hooper, J. 1986, *The Spaniards. A Portrait of the New Spain*, Viking

Lieberman, J. 1982, *The Contemporary Spanish Economy: An Historical Perspective*, Allen and Unwin

Martínez Serrano, J. A. *et al.* 1982, *Economía española: 1960–80*, Ediciones H. Blume

Preston, P. (ed.) 1976, *Spain in Crisis*, Harvester Press

Preston, P. 1986, *The Triumph of Democracy in Spain*, Methuen

Share, D. 1986, *The Making of Spanish Democracy*, Praeger

Wright, A. 1976, *The Spanish Economy 1959–76*, Macmillan

2   The Constitution of 1978

Alzaga, O. 1978. *Comentario sistemático a la Constitución Española de 1978*, Foro

Aparicio, M. 1983, *Introducción al sistema político y constitucional español* (2nd edn), Ariel

Attard, E. 1983, *La Constitución por dentro*, Vergara

Esteban, J. de, 1981, *Las Constituciones de España*, Taurus

Esteban, J. de and López Guerra, L. 1982, *El régimen constitucional español*, vol. 1, Labor

Peces-Barba, G. 1981, *La Constitución Española de 1978*, Torres

Sánchez Agesta, L. 1980, *Sistema político de la Constitución Española de 1978*, Editorial Nacional

Sánchez Goyanes, E. 1979, *Constitución española comentada*, Paraninfo
Tamames, R. 1980, *Introducción a la constitución española*, Alianza

3   The monarchy

Areilza, J. M. de, 1977, *Diario de un ministro de la Monarquía*, Planeta
Bayona, J. M. 1976, *Juan Carlos I*, Editorial Bruguera
Borbón y Borbón, J. C. de, 1973, *Por España y con los españoles*, Doncel
Cernuda, P. *et al.* 1981, *Todo un Rey* (4th edn), Editorial E.Y.E.
López Rodó, L. 1977, *La larga marcha hacia la Monarquía*, Noguer
Lucas Verdú, P. (ed.) 1983, *La Corona y la Monarquía Parlamentaria en la Constitución de 1978*, Universidad Complutense
Pérez Mateos, J. A. 1981, *El rey que vino del exilio*, Planeta

4   Parliament

Aragón Reyes, M. 1980, *Legislación política española*, Centro de Estudios Constitucionales
Esteban, J. de and López Guerra, L. 1980, *El régimen constitucional español*, vol. II, Labor
Gil Robles, J. M. and Pérez Serrano, N. 1977, *Diccionario de términos electorales y parlamentarios*, Taurus
Maravall, J. M. 1982, *The Transition to Democracy in Spain*, Croom Helm
Punset Blanco, R. 1983, *Las Cortes Generales. Estudios de derecho constitucional español*, Centro de Estudios Constitucionales
Santaolla López, F. 1984, *Derecho parlamentario español*, Editorial Nacional

5   Central government

Amodia, J. 1977, *Franco's Political Legacy*, Allen Lane
Martín Villa, R. 1984, *Al servicio del Estado*, Planeta
Medhurst, K. 1973, *Government in Spain*, Pergamon Press
Melía, J. 1981, *Así cayó Adolfo Suárez*, Planeta
Osorio, A. 1980, *Trayectoria política de un ministro de la Corona*, Planeta
Reviriego Márquez, R. 1982, *Felipe González, un estilo ético*, Planeta

6   Public administration

Beltrán, M. 1985, *Los funcionarios ante la reforma de la Administración*, Centro de Investigación Sociológico
Entrena Cuesta, R. 1985, *Curso de derecho administrativo*, vols. 1 and 2 (8th edn), Tecnos
Gala Vallejo, C. 1980, *Gestión institucional de la Seguridad Social*, Ministerio de Sanidad y Seguridad Social
García de Enterría, E. (ed.) 1984, *España: un presente para el futuro*, vol. II, Instituto de Estudios Económicos

7   Regional government

Acosta, R. *et al.* 1984, *La España de las autonomías*, vols. I and II, Espasa-Calpe
Alvarez Conde, E. 1980, *Las Comunidades Autónomas*, Editorial Nacional
Beneyto, J. 1980, *Las autonomías. El poder regional en España*, Siglo XXI
Clavero Arévalo, M. 1980, *Forjar Andalucía*, Argantonio
Gispert, C. and Prats, J. M. 1978, *España, un estado plurinacional*, Ediciones
    H. Blume
López Rodó, L. 1980, *Las autonomías, encrucijada de España*, Aguilar
Rokkan, S. and Unwin, D. W. (eds.) 1982, *The Politics of Territorial Identity*
    (selected chapters), Sage Publications

8   Local government

Centro de Estudios Municipales 1980, *Provincia y Diputaciones Provinciales en
    el Estado de las Autonomías*, CEM
García-Escudero Márquez, P. 1985, *Estudio sistemático de la Ley 7/1985 de 2 de
    abril, reguladora de las Bases de Régimen Local*, Editorial Praxis
Martín Rebollo, L. 1984, La Administración local. In E. García de Enterría (ed.)
    España: un presente para el futuro, vol. II, Instituto de Estudios Económicos

9   Public enterprises

Alvarez Blanco, R. 1982, *El sector público en España: clasificación, fuentes y
    cuentas, Banco de España*
Carballo, R. *et al.* 1980, *Crecimiento económico y crisis estructural en España
    (1959–80)*, Akal
Fernández, Ordóñez, F. 1980, *La España necesaria* (3rd edn), Taurus
Schwartz, P. and González, M. J. 1976, *Una historia del INI (1941–76)*, Tecnos

10   Political parties

Bell, D. (ed.) 1983, *Democratic Politics in Spain*, chapters 1, 2 and 3, Frances
    Pinter
Carrillo, S. 1977, *Eurocommunism and the State*, Lawrence and Wishart
Claudín, F. *et al.* (eds.) 1980, *¿Crisis de los partidos políticos?*, Dédalo Ediciones
Esteban, J. de and López Guerra, L. 1982, *Los partidos políticos en la España
    actual*, Planeta
Figuero, J. 1981, *UCD: la empresa que creó Adolfo Suárez*, Grijalbo
Kohle, B. 1982, *Political Forces in Spain, Greece and Portugal*, Part I, Butterworth
    Scientific
Linz, J. J. 1980, The New Spanish Party System. In R. Rose (ed.), *Electoral Partici-
    pation: a Comparative Analysis*, Sage Publications
Morodo, R. 1979, *Los partidos políticos en España*, Labor

232   *Select bibliography*

11   Trade unions

Albentosa Puche, L. 1983, *El paro en España*, Instituto de Estudios Económicos
Almendros Morcillo, F. *et al.* 1978, *El sindicato de clase en España (1939–77)*,
     Península
Guinea, J. L. 1978, *Los movimientos obreros y sindicales en España 1833 a 1978*,
     Ibérico Europeo de Ediciones
International Labour Organisation (ILO) 1985, *The Trade Union Situation and
     Industrial Relations in Spain*, ILO
Ministerio de Economía y Comercio 1982, *El mercado de trabajo*, Secretaría
     General Técnica
Setién, J. 1982, *El movimiento obrero y el sindicalismo de clase en España*,
     Ediciones de la Torre

12   Business and professional organisations

Alvarez Puga, E. 1974, *MATESA: más allá del escándalo*, Dopesa
Auger, S. 1974, *La empresa española como problema político*, Plaza y Janes
Díaz González, E. 1983, *RUMASA*, Planeta
Henk, T. and Logan, C. 1982, *Mondragón: an Economic Analysis*, Allen and
     Unwin
Marzal, A. 1977, *España hoy; la empresa como problema*, Cuadernos para el
     Diálogo

13   Financial institutions

Gil, G. 1984, *Spanish Financial System*, Banco de España
López Roa, A. 1981, *Sistema financiero español*, Nueva Generación Editores
Revell, J. 1984, *Changes in Spanish Banking*, Institute of European Finance
Tamames, R. 1977, *La oligarquía financiera en España* (2nd edn), Planeta
Torrero Mañas, A. 1982, *Tendencias del sistema financiero español*, Ediciones
     H. Blume

Index of institutions

Entidad de Financiación de Ventas a Plazos de Bienes de Equipo, 220
Entidad local menor, 132–3
Entidades de arrendamiento financiero, 220–1
Entidades de crédito cooperativo, 215
Entidades de financiación, 220
Entidades de leasing, *see* Entidades de arrendamiento financiero
EOC (Entidades oficiales de crédito), 148, 217
ERC (Esquerra Republicana Catalana), 9, 151, 169, 171, 175
Ertzantza, 114
ETA (Euskadi Ta Askatasuna), 169

Fábrica Nacional de Moneda y Timbre, 138
FCI (Fondo de Compensación Inter-territorial), 51, 52, 106, 116, 118
FEC (Federación Española de Cuadros), 184
Federación de Alianza Popular, 166
Federación de Cajas de Ahorro de Galicia, 215
Federation of Municipalities and Provinces, *see* FEMP
Federation of Unions in Galicia, *see* INTG
FEMP (Federación Española de Municipios y Provincias), 128
Finance companies, *see* Entidades de financiación
Financial institutions, 206–23
Financial intermediaries, *see* Intermediarios financieros
FISA (Federación Independiente de Sindicatos Agrarios), 189
Fiscal general del estado, 73, 149
FN (Fuerza Nueva), 9
Fomento del Trabajo Nacional, 203
FONAS (Fondo Nacional de Asistencia Social), 91
Fondo de Garantía de Depósitos, 210, 212
Fondo de Garantía de Depósitos de Cooperativas, 215
Fondo de Garantía Salarial, 87, 181
Fondo Nacional de Garantía de Riesgos de la Circulación, 218
Fondo de Solidaridad, 192
Fondos de inversión mobiliaria, 221
Fondos de pensiones, 219
Foreign Affairs Committee, *see* Comisión de Asuntos Exteriores
Foreign banks, 213–14
FORRPA (Fondo de Ordenación y Regulación de Producciones y Precios Agrarios), 138
FP (Federación Progresista), 167
Friendly societies, *see* Mutuas patronales

Gabinete del ministro, 84
Gabinete del presidente del gobierno, 67
Galerías Preciados, 145
Galician Coalition, *see* CG
Galician Left, *see* EG
General Confederation of Small and Medium-Sized Firms, *see* COPYME
General Council of the Judiciary, *see* Consejo General del Poder Judicial
General secretary (ministries), *see* Secretario general (ministerios)
Generalitat (Generalidad), 98, 99
General Workers' Union, *see* UGT
Gobernador civil, 95–6, 128
Gobierno civil, 94–6
Gobierno de Canarias, 99
Gobierno de la Comunidad de las Islas Baleares, 99
Gobierno Valenciano, 99
Gobierno Vasco, 99
Government delegate, *see* Delegado del gobierno
Grupo de Cataluña, 44, 45
Grupo CDS, 44, 45
Grupo mixto, 43, 44, 45
Grupo patrimonio, *see* DGPE
Grupo popular, 44–5
Grupo socialista, 44–5
Grupos parlamentarios, 43–4

Hacienda, *see* Ministerio de Economía y Hacienda
HB (Herri Batasuna), 169–70, 175, 177
Head of government, *see* Presidente del gobierno
Head of the Royal Household, *see* Jefe de la casa real
Head of the Security Service, *see* Jefe de seguridad
Head of state, *see* Jefe del estado *and* Monarchy
Health service institutions, 91–2
High Court of Justice (regional), *see* Tribunal Supremo de Justicia (regional)
Hijos de J. Barreros, 140
Hilaturas Gossypium, SA, 143, 145
Hispanoil, 146, 147
HOAC (Hermandad Obrera de Acción Católica), 187
HUNOSA (Empresa Nacional Hulleras del Norte), 141
HYTASA (Hilaturas y Tejidos Andaluces), 143

Iberia, Líneas Aéreas de España, 141
ICJCE (Instituto de Censores Jurados de Cuentas de España), 201
ICO (Instituto de Crédito Oficial), 138, 148, 216–17

Standing committee (Parliament), *see*
Diputación permanente (Cortes)
Standing committee (regional assembly), *see*
Diputación permanente (asamblea
regional)
State Agricultural Insurance Company, *see*
ENESA
State Lawyers' Offices, *see* Abogacías del
estado
State Security Committee, *see* Comisión de
Seguridad del Estado
Stock exchanges, *see* Bolsas de comercio
SU (Sindicato Unitario), 188
Subdirección General de Mediación,
Arbitraje y Conciliación, 189
Subdirectores generales, 83
Subsecretario de estado, 80, 81, 82

Tabacalera, 142, 143, 144
Teatros Nacionales, 138
Technical General Secretary, *see* Secretario
general técnico
Telefónica, *see* CTNE
Teniente de alcalde, 124
Tesorería General de la Seguridad Social,
89, 92
Trade unions, 179–83
TRAGASA (Empresa de Transformación
Agraria), 143
Tribunal Central de Trabajo, 189
Tribunal Constitucional, 19–21, 40, 51,
54, 75, 140, 184
Tribunal de Cuentas, 49, 60, 93, 116, 134,
149–50
Tribunal Supremo de Justicia (regional),
111–12

UCD (Unión de Centro Democrático), 5, 6,
52, 65, 68, 98, 120, 153, 163, 164, 174,
175, 176, 177, 178, 190
UGT (Unión General de Trabajadores),
157, 179, 184, 185, 186, 190, 191, 192,
193
UL (Unión Liberal), 167
ULGOR, 197
Under-secretary of state, *see* Subsecretario
de estado
UNED (Universidad Nacional de Educación
a Distancia), 87
UNEPSA (Unión Española de Entidades
Aseguradoras, Reaseguradoras y de
Capitalización), 219
Unión Democrática de Catalunya, 169
Union of the Democratic Centre, *see* UCD
Unión de Juventudes de Comunistas de
España, 161
Union of the Navarrese People, *see* UPN
Union of Small and Medium-Sized Firms,
see UNIPYME
Uniones temporales de empresas, 198
UNIPYME (Unión de la Pequeña y Mediana
Empresa), 203
Unitary Syndicate, *see* SU
UP (Unión de Pagesos), 189
UPN (Unión del Pueblo Navarro), 172
Upper House, *see* Senado
USO (Unión Sindical Obrera), 185, 187,
190, 193
Universities, 86
UV (Unión Valenciana), 172

Valencian Union, *see* UV
Viajes Marsans, 140, 141
Vicepresidente del gobierno, 67–8, 71, 74

Workers' Commissions, *see* CCOO
Workers' Revolutionary Organisation, *see*
ORT
Workers' Syndical Union, *see* USO

Xunta de Galicia, *see* Junta de Galicia